BREATHE

BREATHE

A Memoir of Motherhood, Grief, and Family Conflict

KELLY KITTEL

SHE WRITES PRESS

Published: 2014
Printed in the United States of America
ISBN: 978-1-938314-78-0
Library of Congress Control Number: 2013957197

For information, address:
She Writes Press
1563 Solano Ave #546
Berkeley, CA 94707

This memoir is my attempt to write the story of my sons as best I can and is the result of many years of researching a wide variety of documents—including newspaper clippings, deposition transcripts, courtroom videotapes, and birth, death, and medical records—from the five-year span in which the story unfolded. I tried to the best of my ability to recall and retell events and conversations as truthfully as possible; in order to weave a creative nonfiction story, however, it was necessary to recreate (perhaps imperfectly) some dialogue. It was not my intention to harm anyone in the telling of this story, and I apologize up front if I have.

This book is dedicated to my first loves—reading and writing—and to Mimi, who taught me how to read; to Mom and Dad, who left me happily alone in my playpen while I practiced; to my children, Hannah, Christiana, Micah, Noah, Jonah, Isaiah, and Bella, to whom I spent countless hours reading aloud; and to my husband, Andrew, who still lets me read myself to sleep. And to my sons, who taught me how to write their story.

Monday's child is fair of face,
Tuesday's child is full of grace,
Wednesday's child is full of woe,
Thursday's child has far to go,
Friday's child is loving and giving,
Saturday's child works hard for his living,
And the child that is born on the Sabbath day
Is bonny and blithe, and good and gay.

Prologue
The Book of Kelly

I AM PART FISH. I grew up on an island where I spent most of my summers submerged in water, which perhaps explains why I became a fish biologist. I've spent the better part of my career swimming and studying fish in one way or another. Water is the symbol of the womb, since we all begin life swimming around in our mothers' bellies. From water springs life, as from the biblical flood of Noah, we emerged. Fish are a symbol of fertility, and I've been pregnant thirteen times.

Recently, I learned about microchimerism, which is the presence of cells in one person's bloodstream that originated from a different person and are therefore genetically distinct from the other cells swimming around them. In humans, the most common form of this is called fetomaternal microchimerism. This occurs when cells from a fetus pass through the placenta and establish cell families within the mother. As far as we know, these fetal cells remain and multiply for several decades, perhaps even forever. This means that swimming around in my body could be cells from thirteen different babies. I am the embodiment of my children, most of whom are otherwise dead. And as I'm carrying them, they, too, are carrying me. This also means that when my children died, a part of me died, too. I knew this. I felt this. I just didn't know exactly why. And now I do.

I was born with a book clutched in my fat little fist, and I always knew that someday, I would write one. This is not the story I dreamed I'd tell. But this is the story that life placed in my hands. I've spent a long time worrying and massaging it, shaping and molding the theme and structure of this story. I've examined the weave of my life—unraveling the many threads, following the ones that are connected, and tying up loose ends. One thing I discovered in my journey is the circularity of what I'd always been taught were linear opposites—without joy, we cannot truly know sorrow; without pain, there's no pleasure; without birth, no death. This book contains all of these things.

They say you should write what you know, which perhaps explains why, when I first sat down to write this story, I wrote five pages about salmon. I don't know why; it's just what came swimming out of my fingertips. Perhaps I did so because I thought fish stories were more believable, because I was afraid that if I wrote this story, nobody would believe me. It took me seven years to weave this narrative—the tale my small sons taught me to write, even though one of them never even took his first breath. Between the covers of this book is the only place all of the children I've birthed will ever exist simultaneously in this world, besides their cells within me. Writing it has allowed me to spend these years watching them play together on the pages, for which I am grateful. Some days I would look up from my keyboard and half expect to see one or another of them toddling across the floor, arms outstretched, toward my waiting embrace.

This is the story of a girl who always dreamed of having a large, loving family, and it's the story of the struggles she survived as a woman to realize that dream. It's also the universal tale of the forces that can tear a family apart. A memoir about grief and family conflict might not be the book you feel like reading; Lord knows it's not the story I felt like living. We are given many gifts in this life, and when some of them are delivered, we want to grab a Sharpie, scribble *Return to Sender* and scream, "This is not meant for me!" What I've learned is that we must embrace them all, whether we ordered them or not, clutching them tightly in our fists and rubbing their rough edges with our shredded fingers until they are worn smooth.

Telling the story of my sons is the last thing I can do for them besides carry their cells to my grave. My story isn't always pleasant, though it has many joyful moments. And it may not always be believable, because truth is stranger than fiction. But if you need a kindred spirit to help you untangle the weave of your own undeniable grief or family drama, know that I wrote this for you.

The Book of Noah

Chapter One

"BREATHE, KELLY, breathe, breathe, breathe," Dr. Chopra said through the blue hospital garb that covered her entire body like a burka. All I could see of her face were her round brown eyes ringed by a halo of coffee-colored skin beneath her safety goggles. "Don't push, just breathe," she added in a slight Indian accent from between my legs as she prepared my perineum—or whatever it was she was doing down there where, as my mother would say, "the sun don't shine." The nurse wheeled a full-length mirror over, adjusting it for my viewing pleasure.

"Ohhhh," I said, tears blurring my view of the reflected reward for all my hard labor: the crown of my baby's head surrounded by what used to be a small opening into my womb, now stretched like Silly Putty to allow the miracle of birth to happen. I panted and practiced my feather breathing, trying to ignore the primal screams of "Push!" emanating from every cell in my body.

"Come on, honey, you're doing great." My husband, Andy, encouraged me through tears of his own while stroking my arm and breathing along with me and chanting, "Feather breathing, feather breathing, whoo, whoo, whoo." Even though this was our fourth time in the delivery room, we were awestruck by the miracle of birth, and somehow, after carrying this child around inside of me for nine months, I felt amazed and a little surprised to see a real, live baby coming out of me. I couldn't keep my eyes off that glistening head of hair between my legs, and I panted along with my husband like a dog in heat—"whoo, whoo, whoo"—waiting for what seemed an eternity for the doctor to give me permission to push.

"Okay," Dr. C said while Andy and I continued watching the magic mirror, "now push, easy and steady."

I complied, straining a bit to accomplish the seemingly impossible; yet I was distracted from the yawning pain by the reflection of my baby's head emerging in a spectrum of patriotic colors.

"Okay, stop pushing," Dr. C said. I inhaled sharply and squeezed Andy's large hand instead as we watched the doctor clear the nose and part the lips of our baby with a blue rubber syringe. Tears once again blurred my vision as she turned its blue face sideways. Its cheeks were streaked with red blood and white vernix and its eyes were squeezed shut. "Okay, push gently," she said. I did. Out slipped a whole body attached to this baby's head in a flood of life.

"It's a boy!" she pronounced, and sure enough, all those swollen boy parts presented themselves as she wrestled with our slippery son who then gasped his first breaths, cried heartily, and turned from blue to pink before our very eyes.

"A brother for Micah," Andy said as my eager arms reached for our baby.

Dr. C gave him a quick wipe-down, then passed my warm, buttery son through my legs to fill my empty arms. I pulled him close, pressing him against my chest and wrapping myself around him so completely I could almost feel him back inside of me. "Ohhhh," I exhaled, naming the unbroken vowel I drew with my arms around my son. I pressed him against the rhythm of my heart and craned my neck to kiss his soft fontanel. His skin against my own was perfect womb temperature—familiar, like wearing myself inside out. Caressing his cheek with my index finger, I smoothed in the vernix—nature's body butter—that filled his folded and wrinkly spaces, protecting his skin from the water he'd been swimming in for the past nine months. His weight on my chest felt substantial, and I wore him proudly like a medal won for the marathon I'd just endured. A flood of endorphins replaced the screaming in my cells.

Closing my eyes, I collapsed against the glory of exhaustion and accomplishment, content and needing nothing more than this.

After the frenzy of action I had nothing to do but lie quietly and whisper soft welcomes to my son. I inhaled our commingled breath and would have happily extended this sweet moment on beyond forever—unable then to imagine that someday only one of us would be breathing.

"Watch out," Andy said, and I snapped out of my reverie, opening my eyes just as he cut the fat umbilical cord—still pulsing with each beat of my heart—that had connected my son's bloodstream to mine. Blood sprayed across the hospital room as the life-giving bond I'd shared with my son was severed with a pair of scissors. A few drops landed on the mauve, flowered wallpaper. The year was 1996, and this designer color could be found in living rooms all across America, including my own. *Mauuuuve.* The color sounded like so many pretentious East Coast accents I'd heard growing up. I wondered if anybody would notice that sprinkle of blood and wipe it off, or if my son and I would be forever memorialized by the slightly distorted pattern.

"Now, just one more push," the doctor said, and I barely felt the placenta emerge, enamored as I was by my son. With this third and final stage of labor concluded, we enjoyed our new, untethered freedom. I pulled my baby a little closer, nuzzling his earthy baby smell and inhaling the natural scent of myself by which we knew each other. The nurse bustled over and tucked a hospital-scented blanket around us. Safe and snug, our skin melted together.

Andy leaned over to hug us both, and we admired our new son together. "Great job, honey," he said with a sigh. "I love you so much." I untied my hospital gown and introduced our son's bow-shaped lips to my nipple, which he accepted with a slight frown.

"Two boys, two girls," I said. Either gender would have been fine with me. I'd had only one ultrasound, done by our friend, Peter, while on vacation in Jamaica, but I'd asked him not to tell us the baby's sex. I liked being surprised. "Otherwise all you have to look forward to is labor," I explained whenever people asked that particular top-ten question. Plus, my only real concern was that the baby was healthy.

"Come here, Hannah, come and meet your new brother," I said to our oldest child, who was still watching the doctor and had just witnessed her first birth through her thick, red-framed glasses. Her eyes had widened along with my cervix while her brother was squeezed into the world that she, herself, had inhabited for only seven years. We'd decided she was old enough to witness this miracle she so eagerly awaited, and she'd graduated from the hospital's Siblings at Birth class in preparation.

She stepped to our side and stroked his drying hair. "He has red hair, Mom," she said. I noticed that her fingers appeared to have lengthened in comparison to her brother's, which now clutched my index finger; he would be the new point against which she and her siblings would be measured. Her touch had a tenderness that belied her youth. She'd stayed home when Micah and Christiana had entered into the world. Seeing the maturity she now demonstrated confirmed our instincts and opened a window through which I glimpsed the woman that she would become.

"I just need to make a few stitches," Dr. C said.

"Okay," I said, trying not to think about needles and thread. Even after four births, I felt a little embarrassed talking to a doctor who sat between my legs. Fortunately, I was still numb from the epidural and had my baby to concentrate on while she sewed me up. I distracted myself by gazing into the squinting eyes of my son, who was nursing easily now, and we stared at each other, our souls connecting through our pupils.

"Look, Mom," Hannah said, watching her brother, "he has blue eyes like you."

"I think you're right, honey," I said. "Hopefully they'll stay that color."

I'd always imagined that my babies would be born with blond hair and blue eyes like me, and I'd been surprised each time I'd caught my introductory glimpse of the first three in the mirror. As the opening to my womb stretched and the crowning achievement was imminent, their dark-haired heads had glistened between my legs. Those first three babies had all emerged to stare at me with brown-eyed gazes instead of blue. Four times appeared to be the charm for my expectations. As they'd grown, their brown hair had disappeared and turned blond, though I never could find a trace of the hair they'd shed anywhere. I searched in vain for blue, but their eyes adored me in shades of green and brown.

Regardless of his coloring, I was filled with love for this new boy as completely as I'd been with the others who came before him, and I began yet another love affair, pasting his face onto my heart as though it were a locket. It amazed me that with each birth, my heart expanded instantly to accommodate so much love, as if it had switched sizes with my heretofore extended belly.

"Sorry to interrupt," the nurse said, "but I just need him for a minute." I extracted my nipple from my baby's mouth, startling him from his repose, and reluctantly handed him over. Then I adjusted my pillow behind me and lay back with my right arm crossed behind my head, propping it up so I could watch the nurse in a position I found comfortable. She laid our son on the scale, where his arms flailed about in a classic startle reflex, unaccustomed to so much cold space around him after the confines of my heated womb and warm embrace. Andy took his first photo as she inked his feet for his first footprints, and we all laughed at their black bottoms sticking up in the air above the edge of the scale as we tried to guess what the numbers would reveal.

"Eight pounds, one-half ounces, and he's twenty inches long," the nurse declared—a good size for arriving two weeks early.

"No wonder," the doctor remarked from between my legs, where she sewed the final stitches in the seam he'd split with his eight-pound exit.

"Here you go, Dad," the nurse said. She handed Andy his package, swaddled tightly in flannel, with a flair I could never manage to imitate, no matter how many babies I birthed. "Congratulations."

"So there you are, little man," Andy said, cradling his new son, who looked so small in Andy's long arms. His large green eyes twinkled, but he cautioned, "Now the work begins. It's a good life if you don't weaken, right, honey?" He looked up at me with a dimpled grin.

I laughed, remembering the many things our British landlord used to say when we were Peace Corps Volunteers in Jamaica. Andy placed the baby into the waiting arms of Hannah, who sat patiently in the visitor's chair against the wall next to my bed, ready to receive her new brother. The room lights dimmed in the wee hours of the morning, and the activity level subsided around us while I watched my oldest and my youngest discover each other. Hannah folded herself around her new brother with a protective embrace. Her long blond hair enshrouded their faces, his white hospital blanket completing her red-and-blue-striped shirt.

May 18 had just begun, and the hands on the clock had shown 1:40 on this Saturday morning when our son was delivered into our lives. I silently recited the nursery rhyme that had scrolled around the top of the blackboard I'd written on when I was Hannah's age until I reached the line for this day, most of which still lay before us. "Saturday's child works hard for a living," I said. I certainly looked forward to watching this child grow into a man who enjoyed working, like the one now leaning over two of his children. But just then, all I wanted to do was wrap my brand new boy in my arms and keep him a baby forever.

Chapter Two

A FEW HOURS LATER, I awoke from the deep sleep of the exhausted to a sun-filled mother-baby recovery room and the face of my new son, hungry and waiting to nurse. Struggling to get back in the swing of things, I adjusted the bed and my pillow, our hospital clothing, and our combined limbs while he squawked at me to hurry up. Maneuvering his squirming body into position opened the floodgates of memory, and I remembered the football hold. I tucked his lower arm out of the way and tickled his cheek so he'd turn his head toward me; then I tickled him again underneath his chin so his mouth would yawn open and jammed as much of my nipple into his mouth as possible to prevent blisters. His desperate lips clamped down with surprising strength, and his first intent gulps brought the labor pains of earlier that morning screaming back in full force as my uterus contracted in response to his sucking—nature's way of tightening things up.

"Yikes." I gasped through clenched teeth, throwing my head back onto the pillow and gazing in the direction of heaven. I panted like a Lamaze expert until the gripping pain in my uterus dissipated, which allowed me to switch my focus to the burgeoning rawness in the tender skin of my nipple. I'd forgotten this part in the three years since Micah's birth, but now I sure remembered. *Like riding a bike*, I thought as I climbed back on, skinned knees and all.

As we adjusted to our first day of life together, Andy opened the door and entered our room, his dimpled grin leading the way, and his green eyes twinkling with that look that was largely responsible for the condition I found myself in. Again.

"Hi, honey," he said, walking over to the bed to kiss me and our son. Then he noticed the tears spilling from between my eyelashes. "Hey, what's the matter?"

"Nothing." I laughed, puffing a little feather breath for good measure. "I just forgot how much this hurts."

"Hey, you take it easy on your mom," he warned our son, who squinted up at him but kept right on sucking. Andy grinned again and my heart responded in kind, remembering this look from twelve years ago when I'd first encountered it while playing a game of Hearts at the dining room table of my Jamaican host family. Glancing up from my cards, I locked onto his green eyes and noted him grinning with more than friendly intent. My stomach flip-flopped and my breath stuck in my throat as I swallowed a surprised "Oh," snapping my gaze back to the cards in my hand. Although it would be months before I admitted it, that was the moment our romance began. Andy smiled with his whole face, and that look still had the same effect on me now as he admired our son and me proudly. I wondered if this would be our last child or not.

"Here's your coffee, just the way you like it," he said, proffering a warm cup of liquid salvation from Starbucks. I puffed my cooling breath like a flute player into the oval hole in the white lid and took the first careful sip of my usual: a decaf grande, 2 percent, extra-hot, light whip, two-pump mocha. The smooth vanilla whipped cream hit my tongue first, followed by the rich chocolate and coffee combination—heavenly. I considered myself low-maintenance, but my coffee argued otherwise. You can learn a lot about a person by the coffee they drink. I drank decaf because I was usually pregnant or nursing and didn't want the caffeine to affect the baby. I drank a grande because a tall was too small and a venti was way too big for me. I drank 2 percent for the same reason—whole milk had too much fat, skim not enough. I liked it extra-hot because otherwise, I had to drink it too quickly before it got cold. I liked light whip because although the whipped cream was delicious, the baristas usually added way too much of it. And the same for the two pumps of chocolate—half the usual amount, not too sweet, just right.

"Where are the kids?" I asked Andy.

"Home. Hannah's sleeping, and the other two are watching cartoons," he said. Micah, three, and Christiana, four, had woken from their early-morning dreams to digest the happy news of their brother along with their Cheerios. "They wanted to come, but I told them I'd bring them all later," he added, squeezing into bed next to us. "Cally's watching them."

"I'm really glad you didn't bring them all with you," I said. I looked forward to our other kids meeting their new brother, but I was also certain that one or more of my nieces would have insisted on coming along, and I just wasn't ready for the onslaught of cousins yet, remembering it well from my last two births. Hannah was born in San Francisco, and we'd been alone there. But for the other two, Andy's sister, Cody, and her four girls had filled my recovery room with chaos, fighting over who would hold the baby first. Cally was fifteen now, the second oldest of Cody's daughters, and she, especially, pushed everyone around until she got her own way. As much as I loved being part of Andy's big family, sometimes I really needed some privacy. "I think I'll stay here tonight," I told him. Because I'd given birth in the wee hours of the morning, I still had my one insurance-allotted night to use.

"Okay," he said, "you probably need your rest." I knew he'd also be relieved to leave my caregiving in the hands of the nurses for another night anyway. He was a loving husband but not the best nurse—that was for sure.

"You, too," I said, as he hadn't had much sleep either.

"You're so beautiful," he said, kissing me. He said this often, but I was never overly focused on my looks, even though I was a Monday's child—fair of face. *Cute*, they'd called me as a girl, but I'd never connected myself to *pretty*, growing up as I had on an island in Rhode Island filled with ravishing dark-haired, bronze-skinned beauties. As a preteen, I'd devoured *American Girl* magazine, searching for the clues to a winning personality and flawless skin. But I'd always felt a bit pale in comparison. And having an older brother who nicknamed me "Beak" for my Mayflower nose didn't help. I admired the pro-file of Andy's nose and high cheekbones and hoped our kids would inherit his cute ski slope instead of my beak.

The three of us snuggled in together and drank our respective milky breakfasts, perfectly content, needing nothing more in that moment—a feeling I have not known now for a long time. There was nothing to want, nothing to wish for, and certainly nothing to regret. We were both healthy thirty-four-year-olds with good jobs and now four lovely children. Life was good. We adored our new son, and the cares of the world fell away.

All too soon the nurse bustled in and interrupted us. "Let me check your bottom," she said, so I handed Andy his son, dutifully rolling onto my side and holding my breath while he moved over to the chair. This must be a professional term they all learn in nursing school, because her true interest lay in the region just above bottom. My mother would call the area of her examination my "ying-yang," as in, "You are not wearing that skirt. It is clear up to your ying-yang!" I rolled onto my back, and before I could protest, she kneaded my uterus firmly for a double whammy. I grunted in response to the pain and tried not to cry out, breathing, "Whoo, whoo, whoo."

"There you go," she said while I panted, speechless. "I know it hurts, but we need that uterus to shrink right back down. Now, it's time for his first bath. Dad, do you want to help me?" This must also be something nurses are taught—the propensity to call all new moms and dads by exactly those terms, lest we forget our new roles. I wondered, if we were famous, would they still address us this way? We lived in Salem, the state capital, and the governor lived in the next neighborhood over from us. Would she say to him, "Okay, Dad, I mean, Governor, would you like to help me give your son his first bath?"

She rewrapped our bundle of joy, and she and Andy wheeled him out of the room while I eased myself out of bed to take my own first shower, testing my legs like I, too, was a newborn. Gravity pressed a throbbing discomfort in my "ying-yang" as I hobbled along in their wake. I'd have happily traded my fashionable mauve-print wallpaper for a private shower, but I enjoyed peeking into all the other mother-baby rooms and seeing the hum of newborn activity as I passed by. I felt honored to be counted among them, these new moms, all busy like me with the joy and business of our bouncing new babies. I loved babies, and I loved this place—their place, our place—the mother-baby floor. Balloons, flowers, and cards decorated every happy room, some of which were bursting with extra-proud family members. Surrounded by so much newness, so much promise, I wondered what lay in store for all these new little beings. I felt right at home here, a veteran with four nicks in my maxi pad belt.

Happy to find that nobody else was in the shower room, I selected one of the stalls along the wall, closing the dressing room curtain behind me. I cautiously disrobed; my body was sore all over as if I'd come from the boxing ring instead of the delivery room. Stepping into the shower, I gave thanks for the hand-held nozzle hanging there, since my "ying-yang" was currently a full-fledged crime scene, yellow-taped and off-limits to touch. Washing my hair felt wonderful, as if it had been months instead of only one day since I'd last used shampoo. I gingerly scrubbed at the Betadine bruises and leftover tape marks with a washcloth, attempting to reach the small of my back, where the remnants of the epidural remained. I erased most of the tackier souvenirs from the night's activities, and when there was nothing more to do, I reluctantly turned off the warm water and carefully towel dried.

Pulling aside the dressing room curtain, I made sure I was still alone, then stood on my tiptoes to see myself in the small mirror above the sink on the wall across from me. But I couldn't really get much of a view. One thing was certain: my belly had deflated from the day before, but it was definitely not what you'd call flat. I massaged it as if I'd never touched it before, thinking that only yesterday I'd been kick-ball-changing at Jazzercise. *Tomorrow, sit-ups*, I thought. Unlike beauty, fitness was something I worked at. I hitched up my belt and strapped on a clean maxi pad, ancient technology and something now used only for childbirth. Then I put on two clean Johnnies—one forward, one backward—and waddled back down the hall to my breakfast and the "New Baby" stack of paperwork, feeling like I'd been dipped in the river and born again.

I'd devoured two plastic bowls of Raisin Bran and two bananas with the ravenous appetite of a nursing mom and I was halfway through filling out the stack of forms when Andy and the nurse returned, wheeling before them a clean, sleeping baby boy in his Plexiglas cart.

"We need to decide on a name," I said to Andy while he parked the baby and snuggled in next to me. "It's the first line item on every one of these forms." I loved words, and naming my babies was one of my favorite parts of having them. "Obviously, Emma is out."

But before I could give voice to the boys' names we'd considered, Andy said, "Well, while we were bathing him, he looked at me with a wisdom that seemed greater than his age. With his reddish hair and that look, I knew—he's a Noah."

And so he was.

I eyeballed my sleeping baby and said "Noah" out loud a few times, feeling it in my throat like a breath of fresh air. I'd always liked the story from Genesis about Noah and the Ark—all those animals rocking side by side in a boat made from gopher wood. I've lived near one ocean or another all of my life, and I spent the summers of my childhood floating over Atlantic waves on my back with my ears underwater, all sounds erased except my own thoughts. I'd watch the herring gulls circling beneath the clouds overhead and listen to the sounds of the ancient flood that had drowned the rest of the earth's creatures. How lucky I felt to be held so easily by that salty element.

"Okay. Let's call him Noah. Noah Patrick." I said, adding Andy's middle name.

"Noah Patrick Moore," we recited, expanding the name to include my own maiden name, a practice we began when Micah was born. And so it was that Noah Patrick Moore Kittel was named conclusively after God's chosen one, reminding us of God's promise to preserve life. And although the rain had fallen steadily for forty days and forty nights that spring, on that day, the sun finally shone on Oregon—just like in the scriptures—while our newly expanded family floated along in our ark, two by two, singing, "Rise and shine and give God your glory."

The tidal demands of the day lapped impatiently at the door, and Andy went home to take the girls to a school relay race. He returned with Micah, who, like Hannah, appeared to have grown overnight in comparison to Noah, his hands and feet magnified by his brother's tiny appendages. I was so happy to see him—it felt as if I'd been away for ages instead of hours. Before I'd left for the hospital the night before, Andy had taken a photo of the kids and me with my protruding belly, but Micah had wanted no part of it, frowning for the camera. I worried that he would be unhappy about being kicked out of his spot as the youngest, but he was all smiles. He kissed his brother's hands and feet and cheeks and was completely enamored by him.

Micah spent most of that day in bed with me and Noah, fascinated by every aspect of his new brother. And by the bed controls. "Why is he doing that, Mommy? Can I move the bed up? What's he doing now? Do you want to lay down?" He questioned me constantly with the typical curiosity of a three-year-old boy who loved anything that had a motor or made noise. Micah would even vacuum for me because it included those qualifying traits. Once he discovered the TV remote next to my hospital bed, he was kept busy for a while.

While Micah settled on *Rugrats*, I tucked Noah into his transparent crib next to us where we could watch him sleep, and I called my mom. "It's a boy!" I announced, my voice traveling three thousand miles in a flash to her eagerly waiting ear. I could picture her sitting at our kitchen table underneath the wall hanging of a Rhode Island Red rooster with *Moore* embroidered along the top; it had silently crowed over our family dinners for as long as I could remember.

"Well heavens to Betsy, I've been dying to hear," she said. "Now you have four, just like me, funny, except I had boy, girl, boy, girl, and you have two and two, of course. So, what did you name him?" Always her first question.

"Noah. Noah Patrick Moore Kittel," I said, waiting for it.

"I love it," she said to my surprise. When Hannah was born, I had chosen Isaac for her name if she'd been a boy, thinking this would please my mother because one of our ancestors on the Mayflower was Isaac Allerton. We'd heard so much about Isaac growing up, I'd half expected him to show up for Thanksgiving dinner some day. "Isaac!" she exclaimed when I told her. "But he was a scoundrel." Somehow that salient detail had been lost in translation. After that, I avoided discussing baby names with anyone until they were written in ink on the "New Baby" forms I'd just finished filling out for Noah.

"Hmm, the quilt I made might be a little bit girly for him," she mused aloud. "It's got some pink in it, but it also has green . . . it's adorable, with mice, which is kind of boyish, and I made a pillow to match . . . but you'll see it soon . . . oh, I can't wait to hold him!" I answered all her questions about the birth, including assuaging her doubts about Hannah being scarred for life from having been there to witness it, and then she asked, "So, what does he look like?"

"He has reddish hair, and I think his eyes will be blue."

"Really? Red hair? Well, bless his heart. Mimi always wanted a red-headed boy, and I hope his eyes will stay blue, sometimes they change, you know." Mimi was her mom and my beloved grandmother, gone now for over a decade. Mom asked, "Does he have all his fingers and toes? Mimi always counted to make sure they were all there. She also made sure the eyes weren't too close together," she laughed, adding, "they aren't, are they?" My mom's family hailed from Maine, where the incest rate was rather high.

"No, his eyes are just perfect, and his ears don't stick out either," I said, preempting the question I knew she'd ask next. "I think Mimi would approve. I wish she could meet him." I said the last bit to myself, missing Mimi as always. "So, how was your big party?" I asked, changing the subject. While I'd labored the night before, my mother was being feted at her retirement party; she had left her job as school secretary, or, as my dad put it, "the pulse of the school." My dad had just retired from his career as an electrical engineer, and they were preparing to sell their house in Rhode Island and live the New England snowbird dream: six months in sunny Florida and six months in Maine.

"Oh, it was nice, very, very nice," she said. Then she sighed. "But

Uncle Don had to get up and tell everyone stories about when we were growing up and how my nickname was 'Bones.' He told everyone that I was so skinny the dog tried to bury me in the backyard."

"That's kind of funny, Mom."

"Ayuh," she said, always reverting to her Maine vernacular when the topic arose, like talking about her only brother, "but he was three sheets to the wind, and I was so embarrassed in front of the superintendant and everyone."

"Well, when he retires you can tell all the firemen about his nickname, too."

"Bumps," she laughed. "Ayuh, I will. I'll tell them all about how he fell down and bumped his head all the time. I don't get mad, I get even."

We talked awhile longer, and she said, "Oh, I wish I was there; give Noah a great big hug and kiss from Grandma. I'm taking my sweatshirt to get his name put on it right now." We said our goodbyes. She'd wanted to be there for each of my children's births but had always just missed them one way or another.

I hung up and pictured her navy blue sweatshirt with "Grandma's Crew" embroidered on the front, beneath which the monogram store kept adding gold anchors with the names of her grandchildren as they came along. Noah's anchor would be the seventh, the bulk of the decorations being my children.

A few friends stopped by to meet Noah, and by the time Andy returned with Hannah and Christiana, my room had a healthy collection of flowers and balloons to cheer it up. Christiana was the last to greet her new sibling, and she climbed into the bed and held him for so long—smiling and laughing at him with her usual sunshiny attitude—that Hannah grew impatient, saying, "It's my turn." Christiana was the embodiment of Sunday's child—"bonny and blithe and good and gay." They both fussed and cooed over Noah, calling him "my baby" and taking over my bed like he really was theirs.

"Let me take a picture," I suggested, now that my arms were suddenly empty. They all tumbled onto Andy in the visitor's chair, squirming around to make sure they could each touch a part of Noah. Hannah and Christiana squeezed in on either side of Andy, with Micah in the middle with his brother. I looked through my viewfinder at my kids, two matched sets each three years apart. Four happy faces and one wondering baby smiled back at me. *This will make it easy for hand-me-downs*, I thought. Because that was the type of thing that preoccupied me as a mom in those days.

Chapter Three

THE NEXT MORNING, I laid Noah on the white blankets of the hospital bed to dress him for the first time. His arms and legs were all scrunched up in the fetal position, and I pried them gently apart one at a time, unfolding each limb and slipping them into his too-big going-home outfit before they could spring back into place. I stopped to admire him in the onesie I'd chosen for its neutral color. It had looked so tiny in the store, but now he was swimming in soft, white velour, a one-piece with two doves and three hearts embroidered on the yoke. I brushed my thumb over the textured hearts and thought, *Two doves for Noah and one heart for each of his siblings.* He looked like an angel, and I wrapped him as tightly as I could in a thermal blanket, also white. "Noah," I leaned over and whispered in his ear, still getting used to the feel of this new name on my tongue, "Are you ready to go and see your new home?"

When Andy and the kids came bustling in, I strapped Noah's squishy, womb-shaped body into his car seat and rang for the nurse.

"Can I get our placenta?" I asked when she arrived pulling a wheelchair through the door behind her. She tried not to look shocked, but I'd already requested that they save the placenta for us to take home. A tradition we'd upheld for each of our children was to plant a birth tree, nourishing it with each baby's placenta. Hannah had a dogwood tree in California, and Christiana and Micah had twin redwoods planted on the coast of Oregon at their Uncle Buster's house. Now we'd have to figure out what to plant for Noah and where to put it.

"Let me check on that," she said and left, returning after a bit with a covered white plastic container like you might find filled with a quart of ice cream.

"I got it, Mom," said Micah, bounding across the room toward her, always eager to help.

"No, thanks," Andy said. He stepped in to take it from the nurse and then continued on out the door to get the car.

"Thanks, anyway, honey," I said to Micah, cringing at the thought of him tripping and spilling the contents on the floor. The nurse wheeled me down the hall, into the elevator, and out of the hospital to our waiting blue minivan. I didn't like being coddled and felt a little silly in my chariot, but with the kids around me carrying balloons and flowers, I assumed the role of the proud matriarch in our impromptu parade.

"I'm sitting next to Noah," Hannah declared in no uncertain terms, jumping into the middle bench seat next to the new car seat and establishing her birthright as soon as Andy unlocked the doors. "Hey, we want to sit by Noah," Christiana said. Micah nodded his agreement.

"Hannah is the oldest," Andy said, "so she can sit next to Noah. You'll all have to take turns from now on." *One more thing for me to keep track of*, I thought, wondering if I should add this to our busy wall calendar.

Christiana and Micah gave in, tumbling into the third row, where they helped each other buckle into their own car seats.

"I see Noah," Christiana said, realizing that they could see their baby anyway since he was facing backward in his own car seat.

"I see Nowee, too," Micah said, already nicknaming him as he did with everyone.

On that sunny Sunday in May, flowers bloomed in all the yards we passed while we took our first trip in our new family configuration. Driving up the hills of our neighborhood in south Salem, I admired the white blossoms of the star magnolia trees, which were bursting into bloom, exploding on the end of each naked branch like fists springing open with splayed white fingers. Springtime in Oregon means a Technicolor treat with carnelian rhododendrons and bubblegum pink camellias and fancy, flowering fruit trees draped protectively over yellow daffodils and red tulips and purple hyacinths, all blooming under the sweet-scented spell of Daphne odora, snips of which women wear in miniature glass vases pinned to their pastel sweaters. Nature provides this opulent coat of many colors as just reward to every Oregonian, replacing the scratchy wools of monochromatic winter, whose color is gray and whose flavor is dreary and whose caustic perfume is wet pavement and mud. Spring: the perfect season to rejoice and bring forth our own new life. We added the sweet baby smell of Noah to the bouquet surrounding him. His cheeks were tender like tulip petals, and he would unfold with the fiddlehead ferns.

Our driveway was at the end of a short private drive, and beyond us was a large, hillside cemetery that overlooked the Willamette River, as did our house. Having grown up following my mother around cemeteries, I liked to walk along the paved roads that wound their way around the gravestones, where no traffic threatened.

"They make the best neighbors—nice and quiet!" we said.

"Let me take your picture in front of the rhody," Andy said when I got out of the minivan in front of our home. I scrunched Noah out from under the straps of his car seat and held him up like a *Lion King* cub. The sun warmed his cheek, and a breath of air whispered his name while all the elements of nature conspired to introduce themselves gently.

Andy managed to get only one photo with just Noah and me for the baby book before the other kids, unable to restrain themselves any longer, tumbled into us, laughing and happy, squealing, "Let me hold him, no, let me, hey, look No-ah, let's show Noah his house." As I entered through our red front door with Noah held securely in my arms and the kids falling in all around us, Noah's simple baby joy transformed the house and recharged the air more effectively than any of the feng shui I'd attempted. "Come on, Mom." The children pulled me forward, anxious to get their hands on him.

I eased myself carefully into my rocking chair, where I would be spending a lot of time nursing and holding my new boy, gazing out the large windows that overlooked the valley and river below from our hillside. I laid my son on my lap and cradled the back of his tiny head. We gazed at each other, blue eyes to blue eyes. "Welcome home, Noah," I said quietly. Then I sang to my new son the lullaby I had composed for Hannah and continued to sing to each child that joined us, extending it to include each new arrival. "Mommy loves you, Mommy loves you. Mommy loves Noah, and Daddy does, too, and Hannah does, too, and Christiana does, too, and Micah does, too. Everybody loves you."

By the time Noah was born, we'd been renting our modest ranch house from Andy's sister, Cody, and her husband, Chris Martin, for two years. The Martins had purchased the house several years before we'd moved in so that Cody could get rid of a bunch of trees that grew in the yard around it. Their own sprawling ranch house was located diagonally across the street on the hillside above us, where Cody liked to keep tabs on the neighborhood from her kitchen and living room windows, and those trees had been obstructing her view down the hill. After the trees were eliminated, she'd decided to keep the house for a rental, and when we sold our house in Portland, she begged us to rent this one from her while we decided where we wanted to buy next. "You'll be doing me a favor," she'd said, setting the rent at a reasonable rate with the understanding that we would pay for all the maintenance, keep up the yard, and generally improve the place.

These neighbors were not so quiet, and soon Cody came bustling through the door with all four of her daughters in tow: Cally and Cassi, flanked by their older and younger sisters, Charissa and Chane—a whole lot of C's. Chane, the youngest, was a few years older than Hannah, and the C's were all about two years apart.

"Your family picks up where mine leaves off," Cody often said. "We're like one big, happy family." She referred to all seven, now eight, of them as "my kids." I sighed, knowing our peaceful family moment was over.

"Let me hold my baby," she now commanded to the chagrin of her girls, who were already fighting over their turn to hold their new cousin. I wondered if I should install one of those "Take a Number" dispensers like they had at our grocery's deli counter. Cody was a formidable force and not easy to dissuade from any course she chose.

I never liked people holding my newborn babies, but I reluctantly handed Noah over to her. She took a seat in the other rocking chair next to me, a matched set that she'd loaned to us, as she had no use for them. They weren't mauve, but they were comfortable.

"So, what did you name him?" Cody asked.

"Noah."

"Noah. Noah Moore," she said, adding my maiden name. "No More," she concluded, snorting heartily at her play on words. I was not amused. I knew it to be her badly disguised pronouncement that four children were enough—no more than she herself had.

Andy's sisters had decided we had enough kids, and they expressed their opinions more and more frequently. Our fertility and family planning had become a casual topic of conversation, and it annoyed me that they considered even the most personal aspects of our lives to be their business. Andy was the youngest of eight. I was the second of four and was accustomed to being the oldest sister. But I had gained three of them when I married Andy, suddenly inheriting seven advice-giving older siblings, plus my in-laws.

Cody was the fourth child and the youngest of Andy's three sisters, but she acted more like the oldest, reigning over the others with her opinions and lifestyle. Eleven years older than us, she and Chris had the social and financial security that Andy and I aspired to. Chris had his own dental practice, and their social circle was filled with Salem's professional elite—doctors, dentists, and lawyers—and they often included us in their gatherings. Initially, I admired her greatly and enjoyed her company, content to follow around in her wake. Boisterous and nervy, Cody had a blatant disregard for rules, which she never thought applied to her. I am also independent and adventurous, but she was usually way ahead of me as she moved about her day on high speed. I could barely keep up.

"Awww, he has red hair like me," she said, holding our son out at arm's length from her red designer sweat suit, which her manicured nails matched. "Hey there, I'm your Auntie Cody," she informed his frowning little face as the sunlight streamed in through the window behind us and sent a blinding prism of light ricocheting off her large diamond earrings and into Noah's squinting eyes.

Noah's cousins all had their turns to hold him and then they finally went outside to play and Cody, too, left us in peace. I could hear Andy mowing the lawn, something I usually did but would not do in my present condition. *Maybe next week*, I thought as I sat and rocked my new baby, enjoying the calm after the storm and thinking about the addition of this fourth baby into our family. I was growing weary of renting our house from Cody. In the beginning we'd blended our families nicely, eating many communal dinners together. Plus, having three teenaged nieces as willing baby-sitters across the street was a lifesaver for a mother of three—now four—little kids. I was so tired from the labor and delivery that I couldn't think about a move just then, but I knew we needed to make some changes soon.

I held on to the perfect miniature hand of my new son, checking on his tiny fingernails like Mimi would have, and thought, *Now I have one hundred nails to clip.* Christiana came back inside and squeezed into the rocking chair with us. I reached my free left arm around to include my sunny four-year-old girl in my embrace, tucking her brother's feet into her lap.

"Mommy, I wanted to come see Noah be born," she said, sniffing a little and gently stroking her brother's perfect little toes.

"I'm sorry, honey, I didn't know," I said, squeezing her a little tighter. Like Micah, she seemed to have matured overnight, and I wondered why I hadn't thought she was also ready to witness her brother's birth. We rocked and admired Noah together, a scene that would be repeated often with Noah and his three siblings in various combinations. I felt really bad that Christiana had missed out on Noah's birth. I honestly didn't know if she would have another chance and didn't dare offer her a "next time" as a balm to her wound.

With his cousins across the street and the neighborhood full of their friends, Noah soon became the magnet that attracted the teenaged boredom clinging to them all. I looked forward to Hannah's return home from school each day, but I began to dread the after-school rush of the others. Noah had so many young visitors, all clamoring to hold him. My nieces felt free to walk in and out of our house like it was their own, and Cody did the same, never respecting our privacy. We were relaxed about it for the most part, but it grated on me more and more as time went by, and I wished we'd known about "establishing boundaries" when we first moved in.

"Please stop bringing your friends over," I finally asked Cally after I was home for a few days. I felt so tired all the time and just wanted some rest. She stomped off unhappily. "Like shoveling shit against the tide," my mother would say.

I looked forward to nap time and that day was no exception. Micah and Christiana picked out two books each, though even on a good day I could barely get through all four books without putting myself to sleep. Noah was asleep already, so I put him in his cradle next to my bed, collapsing onto the mattress, where Christiana and Micah snuggled in on either side of me with their blankies, sucking on their favorite fingers in preparation—Micah his thumb and Christiana both her pointer and middle fingers. Sure enough, I barely got through the last page of *Go, Dog, Go* before we were all sound asleep, but soon I was awakened by my nieces screaming and jumping on their trampoline outside my bedroom window.

We had a paved sport court at the corner of our front yard, which was a safe, off-street surface for the kids to ride their bikes or play with their trucks and balls. It was also a nice flat spot for a trampoline, and Cody had decided some months back that she needed to put hers there because her own yard was too sloped. Before I knew it, the big blue trampoline was on our lawn, half on and half off the sport court. Cally was chubby, and Cody had bought the trampoline as yet another attempt to get her to lose weight. I tried to issue a protest, but Cody had insisted, saying, "Cally needs the exercise."

"One, two, three, four, I declare a butt war, ready, go." I heard Cally chanting, and I realized she was back and probably not leaving anytime soon.

I lay there trying to ignore the noise, but my thoughts flipped back to the week before when Micah had fallen off the trampoline, luckily landing on the grass instead of the pavement, while Cally and

Cassi were having a butt war with him on board. When he came into the house crying, I reminded him not to jump with them and walked outside to tell them—again. They weighed two or three times as much as my kids, and when their posteriors hit the canvas, my kids flew up in the air.

"Girls, I told you not to jump when my kids are on with you," I said. They kept right on taking turns launching each other into the air by landing on their butts with their legs crisscrossed underneath them, counting each bounce and ignoring me.

"Oh, it's fine, we watch them," Cally said in between landings.

"Really? Then how did Micah fall off?" I said, frustrated once again by her back talk. I turned around and strode back into the house, so tired of feeling like I was in a battle with her for control over my own kids. I agreed Cally needed to lose weight, but not with my kids as collateral damage.

Now, unable to fall back asleep, I extricated myself from between my sleeping children and tiptoed into the girls' bedroom across the hall. Looking out the window, I saw Cally and Cassi jumping with abandon once again. I was so tired. Opening the window a bit, I called out quietly, trying not to wake my kids, "Hey! Can you guys please be quiet or come back later?"

"No," Cally yelled, "you're just the renters."

And they continued jumping.

My name, Kelly, means "warrior" in Gaelic and the Irish blood in me wanted to march right on out there, leap up onto that trampoline and slap her right across the face. But my Mayflower ancestors took me by the hand and led me back to bed, where I wedged myself in between my sleeping children and tried to rest. Which now I certainly could not. I wasn't sure what bothered me the most, their blatant disrespect toward me or the fact that they didn't leave. I thought about how I would never have dreamed of talking to my own aunts or uncles like that at any time in my life, even now. The trampoline was driving me crazy, and I didn't want it in my yard any longer.

I lay there listening to my nieces counting their jumps, screaming and laughing, and thought about calling Cody at the office, but I decided I'd talk to her about it later, knowing it wouldn't be easy.

I was still in bed when Cody came down later that day after work. "Hey," she said, "why are you in bed?"

"I don't know. I'm just so tired all the time," I said. "I feel like I've been run over by a truck. Plus, the girls woke me up jumping on the trampoline."

"Well, you do feel a bit warm," she said, feeling my forehead. "Let me make some phone calls." She left to find the portable phone, totally ignoring the trampoline thing, and returned to say, "Bob said he can see you in the office tomorrow morning at nine." Bob was our neighbor and one of her doctor friends.

I mustered some energy, screwed up my courage, and said, "Cody, can you please move that trampoline back to your own yard? The girls jump in the afternoons and wake us all up at nap time, and I'm just so tired." I was just about to tell her what Cally had said to me, but she interrupted.

"No," she said, "you'll have to live with it. I'll tell them not to jump after school." And she left.

The next day, Dr. Bob listened to my lungs and diagnosed me with walking pneumonia. Cody called the next afternoon and asked, "Well, what did the doctor say?"

"He said I have pneumonia," I said.

"Well, no wonder you're so tired." She snorted. "See? It's not the trampoline after all." And she hung up.

I put the phone down, shaking with sickness and frustration. I knew that even if she told the girls not to jump after school, they wouldn't listen for long. I got out my blood pressure machine and sat down at the kitchen counter, taking a few deep breaths and closing my eyes for a minute to calm down. Then I strapped on the cuff, hit the On button, and waited for the digital numbers to stop blinking for the final result. I'd been monitoring my blood pressure off and on during my pregnancy, and the doctor had induced labor two weeks early with Noah because it had started to elevate. The numbers froze on 160/100, which was quite high. No wonder. I thought about my conversation with Andy the night before about the trampoline incident. He wasn't home as much as I was, but he totally understood my frustration, especially with our nieces and their rotten attitudes.

"I just can't believe Cally said that to me," I said. "They treat us like we're their cousins or something, certainly not like we're their aunt and uncle."

"I know," he said. "I would never have talked to my aunts and uncles like that either. But it's probably a reflection of what she hears at home—that part about us being the renters. Maybe I'll talk to my sister about it."

"Seriously? You think your sister says stuff like that about us at home? I wish you would talk to her, then." I hoped he would have better luck than I had.

Chapter Four

I TOOK FOUR MONTHS leave from my job after Noah's birth. I had planned to fly back east with the four kids to introduce Noah to his East Coast family and to take a break from my West Coast family for a while. "East meets West," my mother called Andy and me, since I hail from the Rhode Island coast and he from the Oregon coast. The trip from the left coast to the right was like returning to my natal stream, and I'd made the pilgrimage every summer since we married, usually staying for three or four weeks. Because I'm a fish biologist, my family joked that this was my spawning season, since most of my eggs were fertilized while I swam in the gravels of these waters, my babies emerging like alevin, or baby salmon, in the subsequent springs.

One week before Christmas the previous year, Andy was downsized from his job; after trying three positions in the telecommunications sector, he decided to realize his dream of self-employment. He purchased a portable sawmill and was happily custom-cutting wood for people who wanted to use their own trees to build a house or who wanted special fiddleback maple or pillowed walnut to make furniture or instruments. He met interesting people and was outside all day and active. He loved it and came home each evening smiling and covered in sawdust from doing "real" work, with our border collie, Huck, wagging his stubby black-and-white tail in the back of Andy's gray pickup truck. Micah was so proud of his dad for working with a noisy motor and getting dirty. Every day, when the pickup pulled in the driveway, he ran out to inspect it and Andy. Though his schedule was flexible, Andy typically couldn't travel for as long as we did, but he would join us for part of the time, making one of the flights with us. We always spent equal time at the Atlantic Ocean in Rhode Island and Pocasset Lake in Maine, and this year he planned to join us once we were at the lake.

Over the years, I'd spent many a plane ride walking a fresh-legged toddler up and down the aisle, stopping to greet each and every passenger while praying for the next three hours to be over soon. I'd managed the three kids by myself for the past few years, filling one row of seats, with Micah on my lap, and toting the usual mix of sippy cups, treats, board books, crayons, diapers, toys, wipes, and extra clothes. By the time Noah arrived, I'd learned that sometimes it was easier to fly without Andy. Strangers would offer to help a mom on her own, but if her husband was there, they'd assume she was all set, even if he was sitting across the aisle reading his paper. This year, with four kids in tow and no Andy, I knew I needed help, real help, so I called on my younger sister, Erin, who worked as a nanny in Rhode Island and therefore had some flexibility. (When she'd gotten married the summer before, I'd been her maid of honor, and she'd threatened me, "Don't you dare get pregnant for my wedding"—a valid concern, as I'd spent the bulk of my own married life with a baby on board. I hadn't, but Noah was conceived right afterward.) Erin said, "Sure, I'll come out for a visit and fly back with you." And she did. I dressed the girls in matching flowered dresses, and between Erin and myself, we managed to have a smooth trip, arriving in Boston to the humidity of August.

My parents were at the airport to pick us up, and the kids fell all over them, hugging and kissing them. We drove the hour south to Rhode Island, where Noah met his East Coast aunts and uncles and three cousins for the first time, and it was then that I realized my kids automatically pronounced their East Coast "aunts" like they're spelled and their West Coast "ants" like the insects. And this was also true for the way my own nieces and nephews addressed me. My parents were always happy to see us, and we spent a couple of weeks with them in Rhode Island while the kids turned browner and blonder with each day by the ocean.

"Come on, Mom!" The kids ran up to my beach chair one sunny after-noon and tugged at my arm. "Bring Noah in the water." I strapped on his sun hat and followed them across the warm, fine-grained sand. But Noah didn't like the ocean that summer—too cold or rough, per-haps—and when I tried to dip his feet in, he tucked his fat legs up underneath him. A cool breeze blew off the water, washing the smell of seaweed and clam cakes over us while the gulls screamed over-head. I held Noah and walked back and forth in the shallow waters, dragging and kicking my feet for extra resistance while watching the other kids play in the waves. "Noah, Noah," I sang, kissing his salty neck as he looked back over my shoulder and remembering how I'd thought of my younger self floating in these waters when we'd named him.

"Don't go past your waist," I called to Micah, who always wanted to follow the girls in deeper.

"No-wee," they called to Noah before diving into the waves. I turned him around to face them and he studied them all, preparing himself for the aqueous culture of his family.

Each morning, after hanging the day's laundry on the line, I filled a kiddie pool with the hose in my parents' backyard. By the time we returned from the beach, the sun had transformed it into a bathtub for the kids to play in. They splashed and shampooed one another's hair, rinsing off the sand and salt before dinner.

"Time to shuck the corn," my mom called from the back porch one evening.

"I'll help you, Dwamma," Micah answered with his own particular pronunciation of "Gramma." He climbed out of the pool and went up the stairs, ready to devour the fresh silk from each ear he peeled, an unusual treat all three kids had learned to enjoy from Andy, who also often peeled an ear of fresh corn and ate the whole thing raw.

My mom is a farmer's best friend, the original Community Supported Agriculture pinup gal. She's a fresh vegetable fanatic, and August is her high holy month, fresh picked corn her communion.

Fresh corn. Every night. We learned at her side, and would never commit the heresy of buying corn from a grocery store.

"Who knows when that was picked?" she'd sneer, wheeling her cart right on by. "It's probably from Florida."

Growing up, we were all taught how to pick out the freshest ears. "Make sure the silk is still moist," she warned us. We were rarely allowed to pick out an ear all by ourselves without her approval. She was known to sneak a quick peek at each ear when the farmer wasn't looking, pulling the husks down just a bit to make sure the kernels were not too big or too small, and we learned from her that a dozen equals thirteen, in case there were pesky borers lurking under the husks that would need to be cut out.

"Cattle corn," she declared the big-kerneled losers, shunting them aside.

As children, we knew every fresh vegetable stand within a thirty-mile radius of our house. "You need to eat a green and a yellow vegetable every night," she counseled us as we moaned over the less-favored accompaniments to our standard meat-and-potatoes dinners. The day we got out of school was reserved for picking strawberries in Rhode Island to make jam; and the last days of fall for picking boxes of apples in Maine that perfumed our cold, winter garage with their sweet, earthy scent. Then we made the sad switch back to Stop & Shop and waited for winter to blow its final cold breath.

"Did I mention I'm joining the DAR?" Mom asked me after she and Micah had shucked the corn, which was now steaming on the stove. I sat at the kitchen table under the Rhode Island Red, nursing Noah.

"No, what do you have to do?" I asked.

"Well, basically I can submit the same lineage paperwork I used for the Mayflower Society," she said.

"Your mother is more interested in her dead relatives than the ones who are still living," my dad said as he stepped in from the hallway. He opened the fridge and extracted a cold Bud, the only beer he drank. He popped the top with a *click-swoosh* flourish so familiar to me and assumed his usual kitchen position, leaning back against the kitchen sink to take the first swig. I remembered how grown-up I'd felt as a girl on the rare occasion the *click-swoosh* was followed by Dad offering me the first cold sip of his beer. And though I didn't really like the taste, I loved the moment, and accepted every time. While Mom traces her lineage back to the Mayflower, Dad is a purebred Irishman whose family didn't trace their history much past the last pub.

"Well, some of the dead ones are nicer than the living," Mom said, turning from the stove to shake her corn tongs at him.

I watched them spar and thought about my nieces and the trampoline incident. For me—half English, half Irish—my blood cells would carry out their ancient battles all my life. From Mom and Mimi, we learned to try to get along with everyone and never say anything unpleasant. From Dad, we learned to seethe silently. Either way, there was a whole lot of clamming up in our household.

My dad was born in New London, Connecticut, in the same hospital I would emerge from to later utter my first word—*donut*, not a very auspicious verbal debut. When my mom was in the winter of her senior year of high school in the small mill town of Winthrop, Maine, where she and her brother, Bumps, had lived their whole lives, Grandpa accepted a job at Electric Boat and moved his family to the Nutmeg State. "I never got over it," Mom said, and I wondered if that included meeting Dad. Mom had been a small-town success story—the top chair in the International Order of the Rainbow for Girls, Eastern Star division, with a steady boyfriend, Ray.

"Dinner's almost ready," Mom said, shooing Dad aside to drain the corn.

"I'll be right back," I said, heading down the hall of our raised ranch to my girlhood bedroom, which hadn't changed since I'd left. I changed Noah's diaper on my pink quilted bedspread that matched my sister's and laid him down in his porta-crib in between our white twin beds. I popped his pacifier, which we called a binky, into his mouth while singing, "Mommy loves you." Erin and I had matching dressers, but our beds differed in that mine had a bookcase headboard. I've always loved books, and my mother liked to tell how as soon as I could sit up in my playpen, I was content to sit for hours and read and didn't like anyone to bother me. Books are still some of my best friends, and sometimes I wished I still had a playpen to escape to.

On the way back to the kitchen, I stopped in my parents' room to grab towels for the kids, glimpsing in my peripheral vision the gold-framed double photo of my parents, a permanent feature on my dad's dresser. I spent my childhood studying these two high school photos of my attractive parents—Bill and Carol, Carol and Bill—forever linked side-by-side by tiny gold hinges. Mom's stylishly bobbed brown hair frames her hazel eyes—eyes my two brothers inherited—and her arms are gracefully folded and resting in front of her in a pose I'd never seen her recreate as she went about her daily household chores. Dad sports a blond crew cut and the smiling blue eyes my sister and I see the world with. I'd memorized every detail of their color-enhanced sepia selves, fascinated by these younger versions of the people I knew as Mom and Dad. And I wondered how Ray would have looked framed in gold instead.

I headed back down the hall to make sure my kids were ready for dinner and thought about how my childhood bedroom would soon be full of sleeping Kittels. The girls would share Erin's old twin bed and Micah would sleep on the floor, with Noah alternately in his porta-crib and in my bed with me to nurse. Even though the room my brothers, Brian and Mark, had shared was available—and still contained their old bunk beds—none of my kids liked to sleep alone, so they all squeezed in with me. I didn't mind.

Our family of four was relatively small when I was growing up. Most of my friends were Irish, Portuguese, or Italian, and all were Catholic, with seven or eight kids per family being the norm. I always wanted to be part of a big family and aspired to have one someday. I dreamed of losing myself in my friends' busy, sprawling houses. So when I found out Andy was the baby of eight, it was like a dream come true.

We played a lot of board games growing up, and the Game of Life was one of my favorites. I considered myself a big winner when my little plastic car was filled to overflowing with tiny pink and blue stick babies that had rounded ends for heads. I didn't care how much money I acquired. I cherished my plastic brood and was especially thrilled if I had twins, squeezing them all into our convertible and propping them up in the middle spaces when the six proper holes were full. An oversized house and a plastic car overflowing with round-headed pink and blue babies while I navigated my way through the Game of Life—that was my dream. And I was well on my way to fulfilling it.

After our weeks spent playing in the Atlantic, we headed on up to our lake, Pocasset, in Maine, where we settled into our lake routine, which included daily walks to the sandy beach, where the three older kids learned to swim in the calm, clear waters. I made sure all my kids mastered their swimming skills at a young age, since we were always near some kind of water from coast to coast. I waded in the shallow green water, dipping Noah's feet in; unlike the ocean, this he liked. We watched tiny fish slowly swim up to and around our legs, yet any sudden movement sent them darting away beyond our reach. When Noah yawned, I nursed him discreetly under a beach towel before laying him down to nap, tucked under the mosquito net. There he would dream for hours on the beach in the shade of a large white pine—the official tree of the Pine Tree State—that has stood watch over the sands and multicolored Adirondack chairs for longer than I can remember.

My family has been summering on Pocasset for generations, and I've spent some number of weeks there every summer of my life. I know the sweet taste, silky feel, and fresh smell of Pocasset like I was born and reared in it and would have to find it someday using only my senses. I know every rock and cove and the entire teddy bear–shaped shoreline by heart. It lives in my memories and runs through my veins. It feels like my lake, our lake, which is why I call it so.

"Mom, can we take the boat to the General Store?" Christiana asked one day when I'd just put Noah down for a nap. Every day, one or another of my kids asked to take this trip across the lake to the small town of Wayne.

"Go ahead. I'll watch Noah," my mom said. He was too small to be buckled into a bulky life jacket, and boat rides were no fun for him, so I was happy to leave him.

"Yay," the kids yelled. They buckled into their orange life jackets and stepped into my dad's aluminum boat, which we kept docked at the beach.

"Can I help drive?" Micah asked once I'd pulled the motor to start. I placed a cushion on the hot metal seat next to me and let him sit there to help me hold and steer the outboard motor handle behind us. We pulled away from the dock on our daily pilgrimage across the lake, which took about ten or fifteen minutes.

"I'll watch for rocks," the girls said in unison from the front of the boat as we entered the shallow stream that flowed under the bridge and into the millpond. I slowed the boat to almost an idle, and we ducked to avoid hitting our heads on the underside of the low, short span of concrete bridge. Here, the main road passed over us; the underside of the bridge had some very impressive spiders with webby lairs, which always made us crouch even lower.

Once safely through the spiders, we docked at the raft on the grassy lot behind the general store, just before the dam, where the lake waters sweep over the falls. Wayne is a quintessential New England village, consisting of a general store and a post office. It lies between two lakes, our Pocasset and Androscoggin, and it comes complete with an often-photographed lone white church spire, which points stoically up through the crowns of oak and maple trees, right straight to heaven. The kids took off their life vests and climbed out of the boat, stepping off the dock and onto the grass.

"Watch out for cars," I said as they skipped up to the store just ahead of me. The familiar bell rang against the door as we entered, stepping across the worn, wooden floorboards that were laid by an ancestor who'd started the store more than one hundred years earlier. I handed each of the kids a tiny brown paper bag, which they filled with penny candy.

"You can each spend a dollar," I told them, and they carefully made their selections. I bought them each an ice cream cone, and we returned to sit on the dock with the boat gently nudging against it. I gazed at the distorted reflection of the house where my maternal great-grandmother, Minnie, was born.

"That house over there is where your great-great-grandmother was born," I told the kids.

Minnie was a writer whose life's work consisted of tracing and recording our genealogy back to the deck of the Mayflower. Minnie's father ran the Pocasset House, a beautiful rambling white summer inn on our lake, and it was her nephew who'd opened the General Store. I liked to imagine what my ancestors' lives had been like, sitting on this same shore. How tall were the trees then? Was there a dock? Did they sit on it like we were doing, eating ice cream and dangling their feet in the cool water while sunfish tickled their toes?

"Mom, can we go swimming?" Hannah asked when her ice cream was all gone.

"Sure," I said, "but put your life vest back on, Micah." While I watched my kids jump off the huge, underwater rocks along the shore and splash around me in the water, I thought about my mother's family. Minnie had married a doctor, and they lived in Lewiston, but she summered in Wayne every year. In 1901, Minnie recorded the birth of her only child in her genealogy book: Catherine Amelia, my Mimi.

I'd spent my early years in Mystic, Connecticut, living in a house next door to Mimi and Grandpa. But when I was in the third grade, we moved to Rhode Island. Grandpa had just died, so Mimi moved with us. She was my savior until the day she died, when I was in college. If Mom and Dad said no, I could always turn to Mimi. She was the kindest and politest person I've ever known with never a bad word for anyone. A tiny sprite of a gal with bright blue eyes, she weighed less than a hundred pounds soaking wet.

Mimi was my role model. She went to finishing school in Pennsylvania and college in Boston and had a teaching career before finally marrying in her thirties. She was a woman ahead of her time and was much easier for me to relate to than my own mom, who didn't work outside of the house until we were all raised. Mimi's father ran his medical practice out of their home, and Mimi never liked doctors as a result, avoiding them all her life, which I then thought strange. I always thought of doctors as being helpful. What did Mimi know about doctors that I didn't? I always wondered.

"Do everything you want to do in life before you get married." Mimi counseled me wisely, and though I wore white after Labor Day, a no-no in Mimi's book, I took the bulk of her advice as gospel and followed suit, passing her wisdom on to my own children. Mimi made us memorize the Golden Rule: "Do unto others as you would have others do unto you." Then she added her own caveat: "There are all kinds of people in this world, Kelly, and you have to learn to get along with all of them."

"Can't you just avoid the ones you don't like?" I always asked in response.

I sat on the dock now with my kids splashing me, thinking about my neighbors out west and how difficult it was, indeed, to add contingencies to golden rules. And I thought about Mimi. She'd regaled me with tales of her summers here in Wayne spent trailing her fingers through the water under white parasols while young men canoed her around the lake. These same men would escort her to summer dances and her blue eyes twinkled as she recalled, "I'd get dropped off by one beau at the front door, then head out the back with another." I always liked that part.

Our lake has borne witness to each of our generations as we've grown, laughing our way through carefree summers, like my own kids were now doing. She has held us all in her watery embrace and supported us in canoes and kayaks, allowing us to fish her depths and skim across her on water skis and wakeboards. Her trees and rocks were my companions while I'd played in the pine needles lining her shores, using mushrooms as furniture for my Little Kiddle dolls—long before I had my own little Kittels to play with.

"Let's go, Mom." My living dolls interrupted my reverie as they climbed, dripping wet, into the boat.

We reversed our trip back across the millpond, ducking beneath the spiders, and headed out onto the open waters of the lake, with our beach destination still a dot on the distant shore. I let go of the motor handle now that we had plenty of space around us and let Micah steer solo. He sat up straighter with his new responsibility. I reached over the edge of the boat and trailed my fingers in the waters like Mimi once did, wondering if any of the same water molecules ran between our respective fingers these sixty years apart. As the beach grew closer, the kids squirmed with excitement, and I understood their impatience to get back to playing with their friends. When I was their age, I never wanted to leave the lake for anything. Mom and Mimi knew so many people that every trip away, even if only to get groceries, resulted in one of them having to make a "dooryard call" to someone they were reminded of suddenly and hadn't seen in years. "We won't even go in," Mimi would say. They'd reminisce for what seemed like hours on the front porch or lawn while my brother Brian and I groaned with impatience. We envisioned our friends waterskiing around the lake while we sat imprisoned in our station wagon and even the milk grew sweaty and bored.

On Friday, Andy flew east from Portland to Portland, where I picked him up, spotting his smiling face sticking up above the crowd. We'd chosen that Sunday of Labor Day weekend for Noah's baptism when my whole family converged at the cabin for the annual end-of-summer festivities. Noah looked cherubic in the antique white christening gown that all of our children had worn for this occasion. The fragile cotton dress had belonged to Grandpa when he was a baby.

"My grandmother always wanted a girl, so she dressed my father like one," Mom said. It was a practice that, apparently, was not uncommon in those days.

We scrubbed the sand from our toes, brushed our hair, put on clean clothes, and headed en masse to the town sentinel, keeping watch over its flock. The church bells rang out their welcome and the service ensued.

"Let us all welcome Noah into God's kingdom," the pastor said, carrying Noah down the church aisle to be adored.

It had been almost eight years since Andy and I stood on the deep-red-velvet-draped altar before us, promising our east-meets-west selves to each other till death do us part. Andy cried tears of joy (I presume), but I remained stoic for both of us because I didn't like to cry.

Now I watched, dry-eyed, with my family tucked in all around me, while the congregation welcomed our fourth child. Noah was quiet and serene for the entire service, like he was truly paying attention. When the service concluded and the church bells rang again, the seventeen of us crowded on the altar for a family photo with Noah in the center, an angel in white surrounded by a loving family wearing a multitude of cheerful summer colors.

I don't know if I ever read the essay on the back of the church bulletin that day before filing it away in Noah's baby book. Entitled "Crisis Faith," I found it in there a year later when I studied it with renewed interest. It said, "Anyone who has ever experienced a catastrophic event in life knows the pain and sorrow it brings. The sudden and unexpected death of a loved one . . . often leaves a person emotionally devastated and crushed. It is during these crisis times that our faith in Christ is often challenged and tested."

If I did skim this essay on that joy-filled day, when my son was nestled in my arms wearing the gown of his ancestors, I'm sure I dismissed it out of hand, perhaps fanning myself with it casually to stay cool, but certainly never imagining the meaning those words would hold for me later. Andy and I had lived through eight years of honoring our "I Do's" with few glitches—certainly nothing major to test them. No "Crisis Faith."

We stayed at the lake through the first week of September and enjoyed the tranquility of the beach in the wake of all the holiday activity. Day after day we wallowed in the joy of our four happy children, splashing and playing together while the sun marched across the sky, its rays growing longer across the lake until it reached back with a final warm caress before sinking behind the hills. When the beach burst into a feeding frenzy of dragonflies devouring mosquitoes, we relinquished it to the buzzing, leaving a trail of ten sandy footprints in varying sizes as we retreated to the screens of our cabin. Darkness filled the woods, and we read books and played card games until we all climbed into bed, where I nursed Noah and sang "Mommy loves you" to my chicks. The loons took up the chorus, filling our heads and infusing our dreams with their melancholy cries.

Chapter Five

W E FLEW HOME to Oregon feeling refreshed by the break, forcing our feet back into shoes and ourselves into the routine of fall.
Hannah entered second grade, and the time had come for me to
return to work, so I negotiated a part-time schedule, three days a
week, that allowed me to keep nursing Noah easily. I worked while
nursing all of my babies and was somewhat of an expert at pumping
milk, but Noah was still more efficient than a machine at draining all
the milk ducts, which branched inside my breasts like tree roots, and
I was anxious to be reunited with him on the days when I worked. I
managed salmon restoration projects along the Columbia River for
BPA—Bonneville Power Administration—a federal electric power
marketing agency in Portland. I didn't mind the hour commute
north from Salem because it gave me time to drink my Starbucks
mocha, listen to National Public Radio, and switch my mind from
machine-washable mom to professionally-dry-clean-only career
woman.

I worked in a male-dominated engineering culture, and keeping
the lines of segregation between my two worlds seemed necessary. I
felt like a superhero in need of a phone booth to maintain my two
personas, as well as my wardrobes, to ensure my success in each. I'd
finally achieved what I considered a great balance—working two
days from home and one day in the office, with two weekdays off
to be with the kids. But even with this perfect schedule, I still had
working mother's guilt: when I was at work, I felt like I should be

with my kids, and when I was with my kids, I felt I should be at work. I scheduled all my meetings for the one weekday I was in Portland, when I lunched on trendy salads with my coworkers and caught up on all the office gossip. I dropped the three younger kids at an in-home day care in Salem on all the days I worked. Andy's milling job was unpredictable and sometimes took him far away, but when I worked from home, I was nearby if anybody needed anything. For the most part, we were all happy with our routines.

On my machine-washable mom days, I got Hannah off to school and the other three dressed so I could go to a local Jazzercise class— my favorite form of exercise in those days. I enjoyed Jazzercise because it combined an intense but fun cardio workout with full-body floor exercises, and the routines changed each month so there was always a new challenge. Plus, the kids were happy playing with their friends in the day care. I love to dance and often played music in our living room, dancing with my kids, and my nieces, too, when they were over. We all laughed and had fun together, which made it all the more disconcerting when my nieces turned on me. Having run track in high school and competed in cross-country skiing in college, keeping fit was important to me, and I needed that one hour to myself to get flowing the endorphins that would carry me through the rest of the day with a smile.

When class had ended on the day before Noah was born, Becki had remarked, "Look at you, Kelly, you're all belly. When is that baby due again?" Just then, Christiana and Micah had raced across the polished wooden floor to be the first to hug my legs. "You know what I love about your kids, Kelly?" Becki added. "They always stay by your side."

I loved that, too. I was happy to catch my kids as they ran into me and content to be theirs for the rest of the day. By the time we left Jazzercise, I needed my Starbucks fix, and we were all hungry for a free hot slice of bread dripping with butter from Great Harvest next door. After this second breakfast, the kids and I usually ventured into Fred Meyer for groceries. I loved pushing the grocery cart over-flowing with my pink and blue kids around the store, even though sometimes there was no room for the groceries. They entertained me with their running commentary on the products we passed, and sometimes they'd spot something from a TV commercial and tell me, "Mom, you should buy that, it washes out stains."

Other days I took them to the library, another frequent stop. One morning, we left the library with our pile of nap-time treasures, the three of us pushing Noah's stroller across the parking lot to our mini-van. As I was busy unlocking the door, I overheard Christiana say to Micah, "Now we have to be careful Noah isn't runned over by a car."

"Yeah," Micah said, "because then we'd have none more baby!" Ignorantly, I chuckled to myself at their choice of words.

Noah was growing fast. He was never without arms to hold him, or a nose rubbing against his skin to smell him, or fingers to tickle him, or lips to kiss him all over. We stared at each other often, and I loved to see my blue eyes reflected back at me in his quizzical little face; sometimes I would hold him up to a mirror in private and put our faces together. I wrote his story in his Noah's Ark baby book, determined not to fall prey to the common wisdom that by the fourth child you take no photos and keep no records. I propped him up between throw pillows on my bed to take a photo every month, documenting his growth and recording every development. *He dictates our lives, and we love him completely. We are fascinated by his hunger. We are charmed by his every gurgle. We reflect his every smile. We taught him to giggle, or maybe he taught us. We respond to his every desire. We are enchanted by Noah.* I thumbed through the blank pages and dreamed of filling them with lists of his friends and presents received at birthday parties, picturing Noah blowing out all those candles.

One Saturday in September when Noah was four months old, I dragged myself out of bed and off to an early-morning Jazzercise class while Andy and the kids were still waking up. When I returned home, I was surprised to find Cassi babysitting. Cassi was just starting her teenage years, and I felt a little sorry for her. She was the third C, a little left behind and usually upstaged by her sister's dramas. She had none of the pressure to be perfect that hampered her oldest sister, Charissa, and I had watched her suffer under the tortures of the second oldest, Cally, who could be quite mean and who ruled over Cassi's childhood without mercy.

"Where is Uncle Andy?" I asked.

"My mom took him to Kaiser for an appointment," she said.

Alarm bells went off in my head, and my stomach clenched. Andy hadn't mentioned any appointment, but if he needed a ride I knew what it must be for. I rushed Noah through a nursing, thinking about the baby shower Cody had thrown after Noah was born at which Andy's sister, Phoebe, had given us a "welcome baby" card inscribed, "Time for Andy to get the Big V." Phoebe was one of Andy's three sisters, and I hadn't appreciated her comment one bit. Clearly she agreed with Cody. Four was enough.

I put Noah down for his nap, calling down the stairs to where Cassi was watching cartoons with the kids. "Can you please stay with the kids until I get back?"

"Sure," she said.

Off I sped, driving to the medical clinic as fast as my Supermom Minivan could take me, the cheerful words of Cody singing, "Noah Moore," ringing in my ears, knowing she'd driven Andy for the "Big V" with a big smile on her face.

"I'm thinking about getting a vasectomy," Andy had informed me not so long before.

"Let's just wait a little bit," I'd replied offhandedly, thinking he would forget about it like he usually did. Now I realized that I'd been wrong about that.

When I arrived at the clinic, I ran in and down the stairs, where I saw him sitting alone in the waiting room. I exhaled my relief and rushed over.

He looked up, surprised to see me standing there.

"Andy, please don't do this." I gushed with relief and anxiety, not even bothering to ask what he was doing.

"What are you . . . " he started to say, but he knew why I had come.

"Honey, can we please talk about this?" I asked.

"Well," he said, looking over at the nurse who had just noticed me, "I guess so."

"Please, just cancel this appointment until we've talked," I pleaded.

He got up and walked over to the nurse. "Um, something has come up, and I need to cancel my appointment for today."

She looked at me standing there in my sweaty Jazzercise leotard and seemed to size up the situation as if she'd seen it before. "Oh, okay," she said, "would you like to reschedule today or another time?"

"Another time," Andy said.

We climbed the stairs in silence and headed out the door, hurrying across the parking lot as rain began to fall. I jumped in the driver's side and he the passenger's as he dialed his cell phone. I heard him say, "I won't need a ride home," so I knew he was talking to Cody, though I couldn't hear her response. I didn't ask, but I wondered what she'd said. Andy turned to me and waded into the difficult conversation, speaking loudly as the rain drummed on the car roof above us.

"Kelly, we have a perfect family—two girls, two boys," he began. "I just don't think we can handle any more children."

"I know, I know," I said. It was increasingly obvious that we were very fertile, and the odds were pretty high that I would soon have my Game of Life plastic car overflowing with babies if we didn't get serious about birth control. Every time I'd had a baby and gone to the doctor for my follow-up visit, they'd asked what form of birth control I planned to use, and every time I'd asked, "Is there anything new?" None of the available options worked well for us for a variety of reasons. Plus, I loved being pregnant, and Andy loved practicing. I watched the tracks of the raindrops running down the windshield, diverging and merging, while we discussed the paths our lives might take together.

"I know we have a perfect family," I said, "but I just feel like it's too soon."

"Too soon for what?"

"For you to do something permanent," I said.

"Kelly, I love you very much. But neither one of us are big planners, and I know we've never really decided on a number. I just think four children are plenty."

I sighed. "Okay, okay," I said. I wanted a big family, and I didn't consider four to be big. "But Noah is still so little and I don't know why—I just feel like it's too soon. Can't you just wait a few more months before we do anything permanent?"

"I guess so," he said. We sat there in that parking lot for another hour and talked. Like most parents of youngsters, it was rare to have quiet moments alone together, unless we were sleeping. So we took advantage of it.

"Plus, I'm really tired of your family discussing our birth control as if it's any of their business," I said.

"What do you mean?" he asked.

"Noah Moore," I said, imitating Cody.

"Oh, yeah," he agreed, "that is annoying."

"Or how about Phoebe's card, 'Time for Andy to get the Big V'? That was so inappropriate. Like it's any of their business! I don't tell them what to do, as if I could."

"My sisters have never met anyone's business they didn't consider their own."

"Well, I'm really tired of them talking about our personal life as if it is," I said.

"I know. I agree. It's because I'm the baby of the family, and they've always told me what to do. I'm used to it. Not that I've always liked it or anything. They just can't stop thinking of me as their baby. That's one of the reasons I joined the Peace Corps—to get away from that."

"Well, I'm not the baby of my family," I said, "and I love your family and I do appreciate all that they do for us, but I'm definitely not used to it. We have to draw the line somewhere, and I think our family planning is definitely none of their business."

Andy and I wholeheartedly agreed with the adage "Family is the most important thing in life." His family kept close ties with one another and were a great support system for us. When we were first married, they'd offered us furniture and other house-hold goods they no longer needed, and Cody had even loaned us the money to buy our first house. Chris generously provided dental care for the entire clan, whether we had insurance or not. And though they were three thousand miles away, my own family, including my ancestors, was still very much a part of our lives.

Finally we drove home, and I counted on Andy's tendency to procrastinate. I didn't know how many kids I wanted, but I loved babies and wasn't feeling finished just yet. Still, I couldn't have imagined then that I'd have eight more pregnancies before he ultimately got that "Big V."

We arrived home to find Andy's dad, whose given name was Martin but who everyone called Bud, in the basement watching TV, and Andy went down to join him. After a bit, I went downstairs, too, and was just coming out of the bathroom into the TV room when Cody came down the stairs carrying a bag of frozen corn. "Here, put this ice pack on, Andy," she said, walking over to where he sat on the couch watching TV. Cody was trained as a nurse and was ready to step in and play that role. I could see that Andy was unsure of what to do as she handed him the bag with the Green Giant smiling up at him. He looked over at me.

Tell them, I said with my eyes, opening them wide at him.

"I didn't have it done," he said.

"What?" Cody said.

"I didn't have the surgery," he said.

She looked at me then looked back at Andy and shook her head with disgust. "Oh, I see," she said. "Well, I'm outta here, then." She turned and stomped up the stairs and went home, not even bothering to take her corn. Andy and his dad continued watching some sports game on TV as if nothing had happened. I was a little shocked by Cody's attitude and shook my head to myself but also said nothing.

"Here, let me take that," I said to Andy, who then tossed me the cold corn. I climbed the basement stairs and deposited the Jolly Green Giant in my freezer, knowing I was committing the heresy of having frozen vegetables on hand while there were still fresh ones on the vine. Looking out my kitchen window, I could see Cody marching up to her house. It had stopped raining, and the sun was trying to shine through the clouds. I watched Cody's back as she turned into her driveway and stopped to talk to her girls, who were all busy washing her green Tahoe, something they did often, which was strange to me. Chris always drove some kind of fancy two-seater sports car that he changed often, and I could see this year's model parked curbside, clean and drying. When we were growing up, I never washed a car nor had I seen anyone else in my family do so. "Dirt protects the paint," my dad said, and I'm not really sure if he truly believed that or if it was just an excuse. Cody disappeared into her garage, and I figured she'd marched right on over to the phone to call Phoebe. They'd have a good chin-wag about what a shame it was that we were breeding like rabbits, or whatever it was they thought about us, but I didn't really care. I turned away from the window, singing, "In the valley of the jolly, ho, ho, ho, Green Giant."

"Marrying into Andy's family is like being adopted by a tribe," I'd often said in conversations. And I loved it. At first. It fit right into my big-family dream. Mike lived in California, but Suzie, Phoebe, Cody, Steve, Buster, Joe, and now Andy all lived within an hour or two of each other and of their parents' house in the coastal town of Waldport. Like every successful Peace Corps volunteer, I eagerly demonstrated my "-ility's": adaptability, flexibility, and the ability to assimilate. I copied their family recipes and learned to bake bread and to pick and preserve all kinds of fruits and vegetables at the apron-covered sides of Andy's mother, Marcella, and my sisters-in-law.

I imagined Cody talking now with Phoebe and remembered the two of them standing at the lectern at our wedding in Maine reading a poem they had written: "Andy went off to the Peace Corps in Jamaica and met Kelly—a good choice, we think!" Well, maybe now they were changing their minds about what a "good choice" I was, but nevertheless I was happy that Andy and I had acted independently of them and their opinions for a change. I decided I'd say nothing more about it.

The next day there was a family birthday celebration at Cody's house and, as usual, the kids ran up the street ahead of us to see their cousins. Andy waited while I finished nursing Noah. "I wonder if the word is out about the Big V," I said, holding my son's hand. Noah drank his lunch, and we stared into each other's matching blue eyes lovingly.

"Oh, I'm sure it is," Andy said. And he was right.

I changed Noah's diaper, and the three of us walked up across the street together. Like many suburban wives with too much time and money on their hands, Cody was a compulsive remodeler and had added on to her formerly simple ranch house so many times that her ambition could be traced in the geometric shapes that marched up the hillside, gradually filling in her property like a Tetris game. Her sprawling house could easily accommodate the noise from our loud and boisterous family full of opinionated and outgoing people. The first person we saw as we walked through the door was Andy's brother Joe, who said with a big grin, "Hey Andy, I hear you're still all in one piece."

"Yep, I've got all my parts, just like God made me," Andy said. Andy's brothers-in-law were more introverted than the Kittels and eventually retreated to a quiet room at family gatherings, but otherwise the house was filled with lots of talking, laughter, yelling, and children and animals running around playing or rolling around in baby walkers. There was always an assortment of in-laws and cousins and friends, and the fun gatherings were frequent. Noah was the nineteenth grandchild to Bud and Marcella, who already had two or three great grandchildren by then. With that many people, we always had a birthday or a holiday to celebrate.

We hugged and kissed everyone in greeting. When I got to Phoebe, she said, "Hey, do you want to walk?"

"I'll watch Noah," Marcella said, taking her newest grandchild from me. "You little doll baby," she said to him, kissing his neck and carrying him into the living room to sit down.

"Yep," I said to Phoebe. I'd worn my sneakers, knowing we would go for a walk.

"Let's go," Phoebe called to Cody and a few other women who were working away in the kitchen.

"Okay, dinner will be ready in an hour," Cody announced to the masses, who had plenty of beer, wine, and appetizers to hold them over until we returned. At every family gathering the women would take a long walk, usually before dinner but sometimes after, our mouths keeping pace with our legs while we discussed everything and everybody. We were very good at talking about other people, dispensing advice freely and solving other people's problems with the ease and clarity only outsiders can offer. With so many family members and friends among us, we had plenty of fodder for discussion.

Cody was always on high speed, and Phoebe was a high school PE teacher; they set a brisk pace with their arms and tongues swinging, just a beat or two shy of speed walking. Suzie, the eldest, was overweight and a smoker, the only one who never joined in on these forays, even though she thrived on gossip. Andy's brother said her brain had suffered oxygen deprivation when she almost drowned in a creek as a child, and I believed him, as she didn't always make sense. She thought it was funny to wake me up by phoning either late at night or early in the morning, and she habitually exaggerated everything, including the truth, which drove me crazy, so I was happy that she didn't come along with us. I liked to exercise before eating a big meal, and I truly enjoyed the camaraderie of our women's walks, feeling better with each step as the endorphins flowed.

We made tracks down the hill toward the river, and I half listened to the conversation about an incident at Phoebe's high school while thinking about my own family back east. I come from a family in which nobody discusses anything, and Mimi's finishing school silence ensured that we maintained proper decorum. My parents are introverted, and our family gatherings were quieter, more formal affairs. "Don't you dare say a word," my mother warned me often if I caught wind of some juicy family gossip. Growing up, I'd chafed at being unable to express my thoughts and emotions, but any attempts to buck the trend had resulted in a "never mind" or a "that's just the way it is."

So my tongue had happily tasted the freedom of my new tribe, wagging right along to the beat; I was proud of myself for adopting this new culture and blending in so seamlessly. I'd felt snug and secure in this big, loving family, doing my part to increase our tribe by producing even more family members and feeding them their German heritage with the likes of "Finneman" rolls, cinnamon rolls named after Marcella's maiden name, and *pflamen kuchen*.

The controversy surrounding our family planning choices was the first inkling I had that perhaps I was not so content in the belly of this beast, and I prayed my sisters-in-law wouldn't bring it up. But, of course, Cody made some joke about the Big V, disguising her disgust with a snort of laughter. And when the topic of conversation turned to me, I wasn't so eagerly entertained. "Hmm?" I said, feigning deafness and walking a bit slower, dragging my heels and retracting my tongue back into my shell like a clam. I was determined not to talk about it anymore, and fortunately we were nearing Cody's house, where the kids were outside playing and provided a welcome diversion.

As the others headed into the house, I stopped to check on my kids and could see that Hannah was upset. "Come here, honey," I said, seeing her teary eyes magnified by her glasses. I hugged her and we walked away from the other kids as I asked, "What's the matter?"

"Cally's being mean to me." She sniffed.

"What did she do?" I asked.

"She said I couldn't swing, that Christiana could because she belongs here, but I don't."

I moved her glasses and wiped her tears away, then hugged her tight. It wasn't the first time I'd heard this. Cally had always favored Christiana, calling her, "my" girl, like her mother did. Andy and Cody looked alike, and it was true that Christiana looked more like Andy and her aunt and cousins than Hannah did, but I didn't see why that was such a big deal, especially since Cody referred to all four of our kids as "hers" anyway.

"Oh, honey, don't listen to her," I said to my kind-hearted child. "Come on, let's go in the house and see if dinner's almost ready."

Chapter Six

IN OCTOBER, Noah turned five months old. One afternoon, I bundled him up in his stroller, intent on cleaning up our garden and harvesting all the vegetables in preparation for the first frost. The crisp air woke up my skin, and the smell of dirt filled my nostrils. We always grew a big garden, and I enjoyed seeing the kids grazing on cherry tomatoes or crunching on beans they picked and ate raw. I parked Noah nearby between the garden and the clothesline, where he was entertained by the motion of the falling leaves, the swaying tree branches, and the many different sizes of clothing that danced in the wind. In spite of being raised on opposite shores, one thing Andy and I had in common was that when we were small, our mothers used to tie us to the clothesline. Wrestling wire baskets from the remnants of their clinging tomato tenants, I replayed my grandpa's home movies in my head in which our dog, Freckles, ran around the yard unfettered and free while I, strapped securely in my leather harness, had only the run of the clothesline.

"Kelly always wanted to travel," my mom told everyone when I joined the Peace Corps. "When she was little, if I didn't tie her up, she'd run away." *No wonder*, I thought, trying to recall which came first—the harness or the desire to escape?

Andy's Mom said the same thing about him, except she didn't have a fancy harness and had simply used a rope to tie him up. "But that Andy had no hips, and he'd take off his clothes and slip out of that rope, and the next thing I knew he'd be gone. One time the neighbor found him walking down the middle of Highway 34." She'd laugh, her high cheekbones accentuated by her dimples that Andy had inherited.

While I worked, Hannah, Christiana, and Micah played in the yard, stopping now and then to help pull a few corn stalks or to lean into Noah's stroller and tickle his cheeks. When Hannah was born my mom gave me my old harness, but I was horrified to think of using it on any of my kids, and now I wondered what I'd even done with it. As I pulled up the tomato vines, I thought about the liveliness my kids brought to any task, and I enjoyed watching and listening to them while I worked. Micah kept us entertained with his unique pronunciation of words. I could hear him now, yelling, "Zshana," his name for Christiana, unless he was exasperated and then she became, "Kwisty! Zshana!" The two of them were only fifteen months apart and were a dynamic duo. Together they could make cookies from scratch or cake from a box, diplomatically dividing the labor and the licking of the bowl and spoons.

Noah was more active now, trying to finesse the fine art of rolling over—he had only to discover how to get that one arm out from underneath his body and he'd have it down. He'd lie on his sheepskin rug in the middle of the living room and work on mastering this new skill over and over. He laughed at us and imitated our language in his baby babble. I chuckled to myself, thinking about how big he was getting, when I heard a voice calling, "Kelly, Kelly."

I straightened up, the dead vines still clutched in my hand, and glanced across the yard and the trampoline to up the hill where Cody stood in her driveway, calling me, cordless phone in hand. "Do you want to do tomatoes tomorrow?"

"Sure," I called back.

She stuck the phone back to her ear for a minute before saying, "Okay, Phoebe's coming down at nine. Be ready." And then she turned to go back inside her house.

Yes, ma'am, I said to myself. Every fall the women of the family canned tomatoes, and this year was no different, or so I thought.

The next morning I bundled the kids into my van and drove up the street to Cody's, where she and Phoebe were loading large plastic tubs into Cody's Tahoe. The two sisters had matching short haircuts and both drove SUVs that could hold equal parts kids and work projects, with a towing ball for good measure, just in case they needed to haul a tractor or something. They were both of that ilk, more likely to be found at Home Depot than Nordstrom.

"Ready?" they asked.

"Yep, let's go," I answered, following behind.

We caravanned out to the U-pick fields on the outskirts of town and commenced picking the biggest, reddest round tomatoes we could find along with smaller, oblong Roma tomatoes and peppers and onions for making salsa, filling what were normally my laundry tubs. The kids ran up and down the rows "helping." Once every tub was filled to overflowing, we returned to Cody's large, sunny kitchen, which accommodated all of us with two sinks, a professional-size stove, and an island fit for a cooking show. I half expected to see Emeril pop out and shout, "Bam!"

We all dug in and worked for hours, washing, blanching, peeling, chopping, and boiling tomatoes. Our tongues kept time with our hands—which gradually turned as red as the tomatoes. Clouds of steam escaped from the big black canners, and boiling-hot jars filled every towel-covered surface of Cody's kitchen, their lids popping with a metallic chime when they cooled and sealed shut.

I happily assimilated this new tribal custom while we worked communally to fill our pantries for winter. In addition to tomatoes and salsa, I also canned the peaches and pears that Andy and I picked with the kids when they ripened around us, adding the golden colors of summer to my pantry shelves, which lined the wall in the basement laundry room. My kids were expert cherry tree climbers, wrapping their tanned limbs around the peeling, bark-covered branches like hairless sloths as they grazed, laughing and spitting pits at each other while competing with the birds for the sweetest fruit. I froze plums and the many kinds of berries that grew around us and learned to make tribal freezer jam instead of cooking it the way my mom had taught me. It pleased me to descend my basement stairs in the middle of winter, pulling on the string to illuminate the overhead light, then pausing to admire my well-stocked shelves before selecting one of the sun-filled mason jars awaiting their turn from behind my dirty laundry. Choosing carefully from among the candidates all neatly in a row according to type, I'd select a sparkling container of red tomatoes for chili or golden Royal Ann cherries for dessert, feeling like a fresh arrival off the Oregon Trail.

This year while we canned I stopped intermittently to nurse Noah, and he napped in his car seat while the tomato bins were emptied and the counters were filled. The other kids ran in and out, playing all day as we worked. At the end of the day, we left the jars to cool on Cody's counters, as usual, not caring if we ever saw another tomato.

But by the next day I was over my tomato overload and decided to make pasta sauce for dinner with the freshly canned tomatoes— thinking I'd get it going in the afternoon and let it simmer. Noah was hungry and ready to nurse and take his nap.

"Hannah," I called out the door, where the kids were playing in the front yard. "Will you go up to Aunt Cody's and get me a jar of tomatoes? Wait, let me call first to make sure they're home." I looked out my kitchen window but could see no car in their driveway, and the garage door was closed. Holding Noah on my hip, I dialed their number and turned my head so he couldn't grab the phone as he swiped for it.

"Hello?" I said to one of my nieces, unable to detect who it was at first with Noah fussing in my ear. "Hey, I'm sending Hannah up to get a jar of tomatoes."

"You can't have one," the voice I now recognized as Cally's replied.

"What?" I said, thinking I'd heard her wrong.

"Mom said you can't have any tomatoes."

"What?" I said, shocked.

"Mom said you can't have any."

"Why?" I asked, thinking they couldn't still be too hot or anything.

"She said you didn't do enough of the work."

I was stunned speechless, scarcely believing my ears, but she hung up before I could catch my breath.

"What did you want, Mom?" Hannah asked from the doorway.

"Oh, never mind, you can keep playing, thanks anyway," I said, happy I hadn't unwittingly sent her up to do battle with Cally. I collapsed in my chair and let Noah nurse, trying to comprehend what on earth that was all about. I was angry and confused, but I took a few deep breaths, trying to relax so my milk would let down. I nursed my anger with my baby, sitting him up to burp and then transferring him to my shoulder. I hated all this confrontation. At least once a month—and sometimes more often—one of my nieces would call after school and ask, "Hi, Aunt Kelly, do you have any orange juice?" Cody was usually still at the dental office when they got home, and they inevitably turned to me when they wanted to make what they called an Orange Julius and didn't have any juice or vanilla ice cream or whatever it was they needed, and I gave them whatever I had. So that made this tomato thing even more grating. Clearly I was going to have to say something. In the meantime, I decided we'd have my faithful standby—homemade macaroni and cheese—for dinner. Plus, I thought, smiling to myself, I still had those Jolly Green Giant niblets in my freezer.

Andy came home before Cody, and I told him all about the Great Tomato War, as I'd started thinking of it, while he changed out of his sawdust-covered clothes. "First of all, I have no idea why on earth your sister thinks I didn't work hard enough. I picked, I blanched, I peeled, I chopped, I canned, and I paid for my share. The only time I took a break was to nurse Noah or to help the kids if they needed something, so that is ridiculous. And then to tell her kids not to give me a jar of tomatoes, really? Look, I still have tomatoes in my fingernails." I showed him my discolored nails.

"Hmm, are you sure that's what she said?" he asked, looking at my proffered hands and then kissing the back of one.

"Yes, that's what Cally said, anyway. Who knows? But we're not having pasta for dinner like I planned, and Cally definitely refused to give me a jar of tomatoes."

"Why didn't you just go up there and get one anyway?" he asked.

"Because Noah was hungry and I nursed him and put him down for his nap and I just didn't feel like barging up there and snatching a jar of tomatoes. How ridiculous. But I guess you're right—just like the trampoline thing, Cally is a reflection of what she hears at home. I just can't believe the way she talks to me, and I'm so sick of her attitude. Cally talks to me like I'm her ant, not her aunt."

"I know." He chuckled. "Why don't we have a talk with Chris and Cody?"

"Okay, when?"

"I'll invite them out to dinner next weekend," he said.

"But I still want some tomatoes," I added.

The next day, I came home from the store and found a box full of canned tomatoes on my counter. I was happy to see them, but it bothered me that Cody and the girls felt free to come into our house even when we weren't there. The following weekend we went to dinner, Andy and I determined to talk about Cally's disrespect toward us as well as her meanness toward our kids, especially Hannah. As far as the tomatoes went, Cody confirmed that she felt I hadn't done as much work as I should have—as much as she, herself, did—but I dropped it and so did she, having proven her point. It made me realize how differently we sometimes saw the same situation, and I now knew the Great Tomato War was actually only a battle, a symptom of a much larger issue.

We were eating our entrees and making casual conversation, not sure how to broach the subject of Cally, when the topic of school and some issue with the girls came up.

"I've noticed that when people talk about your kids, they really just want to tell you about how bad your kids are and how great theirs are," Chris said. "They just want to dump it all in your lap." Andy and I glanced at each other sideways, examining our own motives and wondering if Chris knew what our intent was—now we didn't dare to bring up the subject of Cally.

We had a good meal and arrived home to find the kids still awake and dancing in the living room with Cassi, who was babysitting.

"Noah was crying and didn't want to go to bed," she said.

"We're playing his song, Mom," Christiana said as I recognized the voice of Annie Lennox filling my living room.

"He does seem to like this song the best," I said, taking Noah from Cassi and dancing with him to "No More I Love You's." I took him down the hall and nursed him to sleep while Andy put the other kids to bed. I thought about our dinner, which hadn't exactly gone as planned. But then we'd come home to such a happy scene. Nothing was ever all good or all bad and I tried to accept that it was part of the package deal with being in a large family. Between the trampoline and the tomatoes, it seemed to me like Cody had something gnawing at her, and I didn't know what it was except that it was manifesting itself in strange ways. When I'd told my mother about the tomato thing over the phone, she'd said, "Well, maybe she's jealous."

"Why?" I asked.

"I don't know. Maybe because you have two boys. You just never know with people." She mentioned my cousin, who had three boys but had always wanted a girl and was jealous of her two sisters because they had daughters.

I thought about that conversation as I crawled into bed with Andy, who always beat me to bed no matter how early I started getting ready. "Hey, do you think Cody is jealous of me?" I asked him. *Certainly*, I thought, *I'd issued no invitation to that green-eyed monster.*

"I don't know," Andy said sleepily. "Why would you think that?"

"Well, my mom said something about maybe she's jealous because we have boys. And she keeps calling me 'Queenie' all of a sudden."

"Yeah, I noticed that she called you that the other day when we were working in the yard. Maybe she's jealous of our relationship. I do help you a lot, and Chris is never around," he said, rolling over and hugging me.

"Help me?" I said, adjusting his heavy arm. "I thought we were just being a married couple. Plus, we like to garden together. To me, your sisters have the strangest relationships with their husbands. I've never understood it. It's like they lead separate lives. The only thing they seem to do together is sleep."

"I know," said Andy. "I don't get that either. I guess they don't really have much in common, except their kids. Plus, my sisters all like to be in control. Like my mom."

"Right. Your sisters raise their kids to be carbon copies of themselves, and their husbands really have no say in the matter. But still, I guess they must like it that way."

"Yeah, but what bothers me is that Cody's kids have no respect for Chris because they hear what Cody says about him, and I know it bothers him. It's not just us they don't respect."

Chris's family was definitely more conservative and proper than Cody's, and he was raised more like I was, so I understood why he might be unhappy. "Still, if it bothers him, then he should be more involved in raising them," I said as Andy began to snore in my ear. I thought about how my own dad had traveled quite a bit to work on submarines while I was growing up, and though he didn't interact with us a lot when he was home, we definitely didn't disrespect him. Andy was much more physically affectionate with our kids, which was wonderful, and I'd always wanted a husband who was involved in parenting. But I was frustrated that we hadn't made any progress in addressing Cally's attitude toward us and our kids, and I decided to keep a closer eye on her when she was around. I fell asleep with an odd mix in my head: Andy's snoring, Annie Lennox's voice singing, "No more I love you's," and Mimi's voice saying, "You have to learn to get along..."

Chapter Seven

ANDY'S BIRTHDAY is November 1 and mine is November 13. We are both Scorpios, a sometimes stinging combination, and for twelve days each year he is older than me. "Me and all the Saints," he liked to remind everyone, having arrived on All Saints Day—a Catholic holy day of obligation. He was busy working on a milling job in his parents' pasture for his birthday and I decided to pack a picnic and drive the two hours to the coast on Saturday so the kids and I could celebrate there with him. The kids had trick-or-treated the night before, with Hannah dressed as a witch, Christiana as a strawberry, and Micah as Robin Hood. Noah and I wore matching witch costumes for his first Halloween. I loaded the kids and their Halloween candy into the minivan, strapping Noah in and making sure Christiana and Micah were buckled up. Then I went back into the house to make sure I had everything, spotted the porta-crib still sitting in the kitchen, and lugged it out to the van.

"Come on, Mom, let's go," Hannah said.

"I know, I know," I said. "I just need to do one more thing." I darted back into the kitchen and started the dishwasher. With the kids so little and so good at getting into everything, I would often shoo them out to play or load them into their car seats and then go back inside to straighten up the house before we took a weekend trip. I didn't like to leave a messy house or return home to one, and I was relieved that whatever I did wouldn't be undone, for a few days anyway, as I shut the kitchen door behind me and hopped in the van.

"Okay, I'm ready," I said, strapping myself into the pilot's seat and backing the van up our sloped driveway. "I hope the sun comes out," I said as we headed up the hill past the Martins'. Cally was in the front yard and ran down the steps to the sidewalk, waving for us to stop.

"Where are you guys going?" she asked, filling her mouth with a yellow Popsicle in between sentences.

"To the coast," I said.

"Can I come?" she asked, slurping on her frozen treat.

"Well, we're staying overnight" I said. "Do you have anything else you need to do?"

"Oh, yeah, I have a birthday party later."

"Well, maybe next time," I said, relieved that I didn't have to make the decision to bring her or not.

"Okay, bye," she said. Since the tomato war she'd been pleasant, but I knew it was only a matter of time before she snarled at me again. Noah fell asleep and the girls played with their Polly Pockets while Micah drove a car or two around his car seat with plenty of sound effects. Every now and again, one of them looked out the window as we drove by a pasture and said, "I call that cow." To which another would call, "I call all those cows." And another would add, "I call all the cows in the world." And so on for each type of farm animal, all of which continued to graze peacefully as we passed by, unaware of the excitement they were engendering in my van.

To get to the coast there were two routes to choose from, one that went due west from Salem and then south down the coast, or one that went south to Corvallis and then west over the mountains. I chose the latter, and we headed south through the Willamette Valley, which lies between mountain ranges. Oregon is like a speed bump on the edge of North America. I imagined that if you were in a runaway vehicle accelerating west across Eastern Oregon, your second-to-last chance to slow down would be the Cascade Range, its snowy peaks rising to our left over eleven thousand feet and running like dotted lines north to south down the state. If that didn't work, you'd descend into the valley we were now in, and your final chance before plunging off the edge into the Pacific would be the parallel Coast Range to our right, running just inland along the coast. We turned west and wound our way up and over Mary's Peak, at 4,100 feet the tallest in the Coast Range, and then dropped down to where the coastal streams all head for the sea. One thing I never got used to while living in Oregon was having the ocean, the reference point of my youth, be to the west instead of the east.

Luckily none of the kids got carsick this trip, as they sometimes did on the switchbacks, so our first stop was Fall Creek Hatchery. Everyone fell out of the car, and I carried the Playmate cooler in one hand and Noah in his car seat in the other to a picnic table by the creek. We ate our sandwiches and chips and watched the Coho spawn, something we loved to observe each year. As a former environmental educator, I looked for any opportunities to show my kids the wonders of the natural world around them, and this was a highlight.

In the fall, the busy salmon-filled stream was a magnificent sight to behold, with hundreds of large red-and-green salmon undulating before us, performing their mating rituals. We watched the females digging their nests, called redds, by using their powerful tails to rearrange the rocky gravel on the creek bottom to form a depression, over which they then hovered. By then, the males had developed a characteristic hook to their snout and sharp teeth, which, along with their coloring, made them look fierce. They also looked half-dead, with their flesh rotting off to expose raw white patches from their journey through fresh water and from fighting each other.

Once her redd is ready, the female releases her eggs, and the lucky male, who has fought off the other suitors in order to be perfectly positioned, fertilizes them with a shiver, covering them with a milky cloud of his milt. They repeat this dance until their work is done and their offspring are ensured. Then the female uses her battered tail once again to cover the newly fertilized eggs with layers of gravel, and the proud parents rest nearby, having fought their way almost thirty miles upstream from the ocean to this place of their birth and this moment of fulfilling their biological purpose. They can finally stop fighting, pointing themselves upstream and letting the cold, clean, oxygen-enriched water pass over their gills until they are too weak to hold their places. Finally, they let the current carry them back downstream, relinquishing first their energy to the river, and then their lives. Their carcasses sink to the bottom, where they will nourish the sweet river water with the salty oceanic elements that comprise their flesh. In a year or so, their alevin, now grown to become fry, will follow the trail their parents blazed in their death to their own new lives.

In the time it took for us to eat our lunch, these marvelous fish did what takes us humans many years to accomplish—namely to mate, procreate, and die. I could have walked up and down the banks of the river watching the fish all day. But we finally got back in the car, and I finished my own journey to find my mate.

At last we turned off the highway at the little blue cabin that sat at the entrance to my in-law's long dirt driveway, and I could see Andy off to the left in the pasture working, the noise of the dusty orange sawmill muffled for him by the bright orange earplugs sticking out of his ears. He stopped to smile and wave; he was coated, like the mill, in a layer of sawdust. Our dog, Huck, was no longer by his side, because he'd mysteriously disappeared from our yard one day that fall, never to be found again.

"Let's go see Bossie and Ben," the kids called, jumping out of the van and running off to the cow barn to play with the bovine matriarch, Bossie, and her latest baby whose name they had chosen. I got out and stretched my arms before sliding open the van door and wrestling Noah, still in his car seat, out of the van. Marcella came out to greet us from the carport that spanned the space between the end of the house and the garage.

"Well, helloooo," she called, and I knew she must be either baking or cleaning, because she had a pair of Bud's old underwear on her head. She used it for a hairnet when she worked.

"We made it," I said, giving her a hug when she got closer.

"Hello, little doll baby," she said in a high voice to Noah, leaning over his car seat and attempting to pick it up. "My, that's heavy," she said.

"I'm used to it. I'll carry him," I said, hefting him up by the handle. Andy's folks were both in their eighties and were going strong, but I thought it was a bit much for her to lift.

"I sure am glad they didn't have those back when I had my babies," she said.

"I'll bet," I said. Andy's parents ran and worked their own business, Kittel Logging, for over fifty years. Bud cut and felled the trees and Marcella ran the yarder, loading and driving their log truck to the sawmill.

"Sometimes I drove that truck to the mill with six kids in the seat next to me," she said, "and when they were babies I put them in apple crates."

"I know, that would have been impossible now," I said, having heard this story many times before but still filled with respect for her tough pioneer spirit and abilities. Andy and his four older brothers all grew up with a chainsaw attached to their wrists, while the girls worked everything from scratch in the kitchen, which we entered now, greeted by the smell of cinnamon rolls baking.

"I made Finneman rolls and baked bread for Andy's birthday," Marcella said.

"Yum," I said, "smells good." I spied six loaves cooling on the counter. In addition to her ability to load and drive a log truck, Andy's mom was an excellent cook. In my family we usually had birthday cake, but Andy's mom was more likely to make cinnamon rolls or a pie using her favorite goose fat for the crust instead. I sat down to nurse Noah while she took the heavenly rolls out of the oven, flipping them over to expose the gooey cinnamon and nuts on top. I couldn't wait to eat one.

"I can't believe that Andy is thirty-five years old already," she said, running a spatula around the pan and spreading the rest of the topping across the block of rolls, which were still attached to each other. "Thirty-five years old," she said. "And I was ten days from my forty-seventh birthday when I had him." She picked up a walnut that had stuck to the pan and ate it, licking her fingers with abandon.

"I know, that's amazing," I said, having heard this story, too, many times. She usually added, "and I kept my figure until that Andy," but she took a different tack today.

"Let's see now, that Joe is seven years older than Andy. And I didn't dare tell that Bud that I was pregnant until the day when I was almost six months along and he found me taking a nap in the living room and said, 'What are you so tired for anyway?'" She chuckled.

"I guess you had a good reason."

Andy was raised like an only child; many of his siblings were gone or on their way out of the house by the time he arrived. They were all reared in a big bunch, with Suzie seventeen years his elder. When Andy came along, his parents had time to engage one-on-one with him, and he had a special bond with them because of it. He was the recipient of a lot of love as well as a lot of advice and a lot of teasing, and he also had more in the way of material things than the others, who often chided him for being spoiled. All of this combined to set him apart from the rest of the tribe.

"You were found in a ditch," his brothers told him.

"You were supposed to be a girl," his sisters said.

"You were our little gift from God," said his mom.

I sat Noah up to burp him, and he sneezed. "*Der gezundheit is besser dan ze krankheit*," Marcella said to him in her kitchen German, which she always followed up with the translation, "to sneeze is better than to be sick." I carried Noah into the back bedroom and changed his diaper; then I returned to the kitchen, sat down, and switched him to nurse on the other side.

"I'm so happy to see that Andy out there cutting wood in the pasture," Marcella said, locking the lid on her pressure cooker and setting it on the stove to cook, "and that Bud sure likes having him around." Andy's parents were both happy about Andy's millwork—a skill his dad had taught him—and they always hoped we'd move to the coast to live near them. I kept a lookout for job opportunities there, but time marched on, and we were getting more and more entrenched in the Salem community in the valley.

"Well, he likes being here, too," I said. "Where's Bud?"

"Oh, he's out there fixing his loader." I hadn't noticed him but could picture him tinkering around with his equipment, something he did often. Andy came from hardworking stock, and they all prided themselves on that. Marcella could tear apart her dryer to fix it, butcher a bear, or make her own soap, and she was known to pop the hood of my van to check things out before we left the driveway.

When Noah finished nursing, I strapped him into his backpack, put a warm Finneman roll on a napkin, and headed out to the pasture to give it to Andy. The hot smell of sawdust filled the air. Andy was in the middle of cutting a board with the giant circular saw blade, and I looked away as his gloved hands guided the wood along, trying not to imagine what that blade could do to flesh and bone as it ripped through a huge log effortlessly. I tried to get used to all the noisy, dangerous equipment that surrounded me always in my West Coast life, but my imagination often got the best of me, and frankly I found it all quite frightening. Priding myself on having certain strength of character, I tried to put it out of my mind. It was better if I didn't watch, so while I waited for him to finish, I kicked around the pasture a bit, cradling the roll and trying not to let it stick to the napkin while bouncing Noah in his backpack. I wondered how fast emergency help could get to us here up in the river valley if that shiny steel blade met the frailties of human flesh, but I hoped I'd never have to find out.

We walked over by the tidal slough that wrapped around the pasture, and I showed Noah some ducks swimming there in the water, checked out the stack of boards Andy had already cut, and then noticed Bud sitting high up in the loader nearby. "Look, Noah, there's Grandpa," I said. Bud gave us a smile and a wave through the broken window of the loader and, as usual, I marveled at the size and strength of his hands—workingman's hands—scarred and callused with each finger easily two or three times the circumference of my own. His hands were tools unto themselves and were usually well oiled with remnants of the day's work.

As usual, I thought about my own family in comparison, marveling at the degree of difference I experienced on a daily basis in my east-meets-west life. I tried hard to adapt, but I often gulped for air like a fish out of water and wasn't really sure what to do with myself, raising my kids in this unfamiliar environment. Sometimes I felt like I followed Andy around. Even on this trip, for example, I followed his trail toward what was home for him, where we hiked through forests filled with giant trees or walked along expansive beaches with driftwood and waves and temperatures that could kill—all of which made me feel small and intimidated compared to the user-friendly beaches and woods I was used to. There weren't many families in these parts who hadn't lost someone in a fishing or logging accident.

Later I would tell him about watching the salmon spawn as if to say, see, I'm fitting in just fine, when I didn't always feel that way. For six years, I'd rooted for the Blazers and attended the Oregon State–University of Oregon Civil War games, even though the Civil War was firmly rooted in the east in my mind. I'd listened to endless holiday hunting and fishing tales while leaning against rigs blaring Jeff Foxworthy monologues, the token environmentalist of the family with nothing to add to the conversation. I ate orange Tillamook cheddar cheese instead of Vermont white and sipped Henry Weinhardt instead of Sam Adams while salmon and elk sizzled on the grill. I sent prewrapped holiday boxes of Sees Candy to my parents and traded my medium Dunkin' Donuts coffee light with one sugar for my custom mocha at Starbucks. I switched my favorite season to the splendor of spring in the absence of fall foliage, surrounded as I was now by endless shades of green, green, green. And I rarely ate the thing I'd so loved as a child—donuts.

Soon Andy would shut off the mill, kiss me, tickle Noah's cheek with a sawdusty finger, and eat his Finneman roll. Later, we'd set up Noah's porta-crib in the back bedroom, where we'd all sleep and I'd tuck my kids into bed, listening to their final tales from playing all afternoon in the barn with Bossy and Ben and the chickens. I'd read *Stellaluna* to them and drift off to sleep, trying not to dwell on how it was mostly left to me to raise them up in an unfamiliar place, kind of like the mama bird in the book raising a baby bat.

Like most moms, I reached back to my own childhood experiences for guidance in raising my kids. Riding a bike? Too hilly. Swimming in the ocean? Not on your life. Driftwood? Drift logs. Quahogs? Geoducks. Horseshoe crabs? Dungeness. White pine trees? Douglas fir. These counterparts were the familiars of my husband and my kids alike. I wondered, *how long do I have to live in this place for it to feel like home?* Or was home an unchangeable, elemental part of me? Was comfort only to be found when I was surrounded by the tastes and smells of my childhood? Was it even possible to replace the lake water and seawater that ran in my veins?

Andy was so comfortable on this coast; and this place, his home, fit him like a glove. Or a mitt. I thought about how Bud's hands were like a baseball mitt. Even though my dad had built our first stereo when he was in college, I came from the suburbs where if something broke, you called on someone like Bud to fix it.

The next day we'd drink coffee and eat Finneman rolls before accompanying Marcella to the Catholic church. We'd have a nice beach walk and eat a Sunday dinner of fried chicken with mashed potatoes and gravy. And then I'd drive the two hours back to Salem and enjoy the welcome downtime, thinking about life while my kids called all the farm animals in the world into their arks.

The calendar flipped to December, and we began getting ready for Noah's first Christmas. One Saturday two weeks before the big day, we bundled up the kids and headed out to a local tree farm, where the three older kids ran up and down the rows playing tag and hide-and-seek while Noah rode on my back, kicking his heels with excitement as he watched them.

"How about this one?" I'd ask, pointing to a perfectly shaped tree.

"Too tall."

"Are you sure?"

"Yes, you have to take the stand into consideration, so that would make it this tall," Andy said, holding his long arm out to demonstrate. One thing I'd realized long ago was that among other things, our height differences contributed to us seeing the world differently. I trusted his judgment, and we moved along. I always had a hard time making decisions and liked to know what all my choices were before deciding on anything, the annual Christmas tree hunt being no different. Eventually, we settled on one perfect noble fir, and I held the trunk while Andy sawed at the stem with the handsaw provided and Noah played with the stiff needles. Unlike a spruce's, they weren't too sharp, and he laughed at the sensation, batting at them with the chubby palm of his hand. The older kids ran over to watch, and Micah slipped and fell in the mud, crying while Andy dragged the tree to the end of the row, where the farmer picked it up and put it in a wagon he pulled behind his tractor.

"Do you want to ride along?" he asked Micah, who immediately stopped crying and clambered aboard. The girls joined him, and we followed their slow progress to a barn, where I sipped hot apple cider while the tree was loaded onto our van.

Once we were back home, the kids asked, "Can we decorate it now?"

"No, it has to rest for a while in its stand," Andy explained, and Micah helped him get it set up, parking it in the corner of the carport. The next night we wrestled it in through the sliding glass doors to our dining room and set it up in the living room. I brought the boxes of lights and ornaments up from the storage room in the basement, and the girls started opening them. "Now, wait just a minute," I said, "Dad has to put the lights on first."

"I'll help you, Dad," Micah said. Andy began wrapping the strings of tiny white lights around and around the tree, passing them to Micah to hold while he made each pass. I could see the pride Micah felt in helping like this. Noah kept scooting over and getting in the way, so I picked him up, and he watched from my lap, clapping his hands as the tree gradually lit up.

"Okay, now the ornaments," I said to them all, and I began passing ornaments out to each of them to hang after making sure they had a hook. "Be careful not to drop these," I said, handing them each their Baby's First Christmas ornament so they could hang them together.

"What about Noah's?" Hannah asked.

"I'll help him with his," I said. I picked him up from where he was playing on the floor and let him help me hold his white porcelain rattle-shaped ornament while we hung it on a high branch.

"See, Noah? Baby's First Christmas," Hannah said, pointing to the writing on his ornament. He reached for it, but I held him back.

"Mom, let's hang some ornaments that Noah can play with," Christiana suggested. Noah was seven months old and sitting up now, so I handed her some of the less fragile ornaments to hang around the bottom where he could sit and play with them, making sure they didn't have any hooks or small parts he could choke on. Once the last ornament was hung, we all sat down and admired our handiwork.

"It's so pretty," Hannah said.

"I can't wait for Santa to come," said Micah.

"I hope he brings us a puppy," Christiana added. And he did.

On Christmas morning the kids awoke to find a new puppy from Santa, and they squealed with delight as it licked their faces. I made them wait to open anything until Andy and I made coffee, and I popped some Pillsbury cinnamon rolls in the oven to bake, feeling a tiny pang of guilt that they weren't homemade Finneman rolls. Then I had the kids pose on the fireplace mantel with their stockings and took their photo before they could empty them, reaching in and pulling out each item until they came to a quarter like I'd always found in my own childhood stocking. Noah had a new stocking my mom had made for him, with his name embroidered across the top. The kids helped him empty it, but mostly he wanted to chew on the felt tab used for hanging it.

Once the final quarter was retrieved, they set their stockings aside, and we moved to the tree where Hannah picked out one gift for each of them. They opened them together, one at a time, while I took photos. Noah was more interested in eating the wrapping paper that piled up around him as the other kids unwrapped their gifts and Andy and I sat and sipped our coffee. After all the work of planning and buying and wrapping, I liked to savor these moments and enjoyed watching their reactions to each item. Christmas was a big tradition in my family, with stockings overflowing on the fireplace mantel and presents spilling out from around the tree, but Andy had grown up with much less emphasis on holidays and gifts. Before we were very far into the morning, the Martin girls burst through the door and mayhem erupted.

"Hey, what'd you get?" they all asked and immediately began passing out and tearing open presents, interrupting the orderly process I was savoring. I tried to redirect them to no avail.

"Are you done opening your gifts?" I asked, hoping they'd say no and leave.

"Yep," they said, rattling off what they'd received.

"Where are your mom and dad?"

"Oh, they're just getting up," they said.

"They didn't watch you open your presents?"

"Nope."

The idea of having a Christmas gift-opening melee without the participation of your parents was a foreign concept to me. But this was our third holiday as their neighbors so it should have been feeling more familiar to me by then. I tried to reestablish some sense of calm and order when I heard the kitchen door open again, and in came Cody.

"Coffee ready?" she called from the kitchen.

I took a deep breath and braced myself for the onslaught, knowing there was simply no polite way to salvage my dream of a quiet family morning. With the addition of Cody, Andy became distracted talking to her, and the kids finished tearing the wrapping paper off the remaining gifts with their cousins while I watched like I was standing on the sidewalk outside Macy's viewing a holiday window display, snapping an occasional photo like a tourist. I hoped that next year we'd be in a different diorama.

We named the puppy Dude, and Noah was soon pointing at him and saying his first word, "Dooo."

A few days after Christmas I sat rocking and nursing Noah in the living room when Hannah called out from the bathroom, "Mom, I lost a tooth!"

She brought it out to the living room and we were admiring it when I felt something hard on my nipple. *Ouch, what was that?* I wondered, peering into Noah's mouth when he finished nursing. I explored around with my finger and sure enough, I felt his first tooth. Noah had discovered that Andy's ski-slope nose was great for teething and tried to suck on it whenever he could, so I'd figured this tooth was coming.

"Feel this," I told Hannah. We grinned at each other, and Noah grinned at us both in return. "You two really are soul mates," I said.

Noah's second tooth emerged next to the first in time for Hannah's birthday in April. "Look, Mom, he has a little space between his teeth," Hannah noted as I finished nursing him one day.

"I see that," I said. "I wonder if we should make him stop using the binky. We don't want his teeth to be crooked."

Noah was my first baby to be "hooked on Nuk," the phrase my older brother had coined when his first baby became attached to a Nuk pacifier. The other three kids had all sucked one or two of their fingers, and Hannah was the only one who had quit so far.

"Awww, but he's so cute with it," Hannah said, twirling around her finger the red cord that attached Noah's binky to a Winnie the Pooh clip, which was then fastened to the front pocket of his bib overalls. Noah grinned at her and popped his binky in his mouth. I had no doubt he understood exactly what we were discussing. "Can I play with him, Mom?"

"Sure," I said, passing Noah over to her. She carried him out of the living room and down the hall to her bedroom, and soon I could hear the happy sounds of the girls playing house with Noah as their real live baby.

I picked up the Sunday paper, scanning the Homes for Sale section in the Salem area, determined to stop being "just the renters." Andy was in the kitchen making lunch, so I brought the paper out to the kitchen counter and started highlighting properties of interest. We were eating our sandwiches when Cody popped in the door.

"Oh, good, just in time for lunch," she said.

"Help yourself," Andy said.

"What are you doing?" she asked, searching through the refrigerator for the mayo and making herself a sandwich.

"Looking at houses for sale," I said, chewing and trying not to watch her spreading mayo on bread, cringing at the thought of eating that nasty white stuff.

"Well, why don't you just buy this house?"

"Right, how much do you want for it now?" Andy asked.

"Make me an offer." She snorted.

This was not the first time she'd offered to sell the house to us. Every now and again for the past two years she'd say something flippant like she'd just done, but even back when it still seemed like a good idea to become permanent neighbors, each time we came up with an initial sales agreement, she changed her mind and increased the price. We grew tired of being jerked around and had given up. It was time to look elsewhere. I chewed on that along with my sandwich, reading and highlighting while Andy and Cody chatted. I could hear my father's voice in my head say, "Shit or get off the pot."

In May, Noah began to try out his sea legs. "Come on, Noah, come on, you can do it." Andy beckoned from across the room, where he kneeled in front of the couch. I sat in my chair holding Noah's hands over his head while he steeled his legs, holding on as he took a few tentative steps away from me before letting go.

"Go on, Noah, you can do it. Walk to Daddy." I encouraged him from behind as he toddled, stiff-legged, toward Andy's waiting arms and giant grin.

"Come on, atta boy, walk to Daddy," Andy said, moving to catch him before he teetered over sideways or plopped down on his diaper-padded bottom.

"Yayyyy," we said in unison while Noah clapped his own hands with glee. As the days marched closer to his first birthday, Noah toddled between us like this, back and forth on his stiff, chubby legs, almost every day with every chance he got, so proud of himself when he made it to one or the other of us. While he headed toward Andy one day, I noticed that one of the window blind cords had come out of its Safety 1st circle, so I leaned over to rewind the extra cord while Andy caught Noah, hugging him tight. I coiled it back up and snapped on the white cover before taking my turn to catch and hug him in our game of "Noah in the middle." I wondered how on earth a child could hang themselves by skinny blind cords, but I'd recently finished my training through BPA to be a certified first responder and had learned about too many horrible things that could happen, so all of my blind cords were safely tucked away in their tidy round compartments. I wasn't taking any chances.

With four kids, I'd accumulated a large collection of child safety products, and once Noah became mobile, I'd enlisted them all into service, baby-proofing the house wherever it was not already baby proof. I plugged all the unused wall outlets around the house, thinking that made sense because Noah, like most boys, did love to poke and prod. I patrolled bedroom trash cans like a sentry, ensuring they were empty of any potentially suffocating plastic dry-cleaning bags. I double-checked that all household cleaning products were up high instead of installing safety latches on my kitchen cupboards—I didn't want to keep the other kids from being able to open them, plus I was impatient so they drove me crazy. I kept the toilet lids down, since he hadn't learned to lift them up yet. Noah didn't want the big kids to be able to go anywhere in the house that he couldn't go, and I implored them daily to keep the door to the basement stairs closed, even though Noah could turn around and back down them with great speed and agility, grinning up at me when he reached the bottom.

There was no doubt about it: Noah is on the move, I thought, sending him back across the floor to Andy.

"Yesterday when Hannah came home from school, she found Noah hiding up on her bed eating her birthday candy," I told Andy, "and when she caught him he stuffed another piece in his mouth, wrapper and all."

"What did you do, Noah?" Andy said, shaking his index finger and pretending to scold Noah with it as he caught him and hugged him tight. Noah widened his eyes and grinned.

"Right, Noah?" I said. "And when she caught him, she said his eyes got all big, just like they are now, and he tried to hide under her pillow." Andy laughed and Noah clapped his hands. "Some days I find him up on Micah's bed, too," I said. Micah had a queen-size bed with a bookcase for a headboard. "Sometimes he lays there all alone reading books by himself like a good little boy, but sometimes he's standing up and jumping on the bed, right, Noah? No more monkeys jumping on the bed." He grinned at me, and I wondered if he remembered the book by that name that I'd read to him. "The other day I found him there reading books with Micah," I said. "It was so sweet, Micah was reading *Where's Waldo*, and when I walked in he said, 'Hey Mom, we're trying to find Waldo.' And the book was upside down."

Andy laughed and Noah joined in to keep him company. I looked at the two of them together there on the couch and took a mental snapshot of the moment, hoping it would become one of those random moments in life that for some unknown reason you remember forever.

"Okay, time for your nap," I said, taking Noah from Andy and sitting back down to nurse him before laying him down. He fell right asleep after all that exercise.

While I was putting him in his crib, I heard Cody in the kitchen talking to Andy. I wanted to take a nap myself, but I went out to see what was up. Our neighbor, Mildred, had recently fallen and broken her hip, and Cody was discussing her with Andy when I walked in. Because our houses were located diagonally from each other, Mildred actually lived across the street from both of us.

When I walked in, Cody turned to tell me, "Mildred's being moved to a nursing home to recover." Mildred was a spinster and an only child and had no close relatives, so Cody had elected herself to take over Mildred's medical care and, by default, control of her house.

"For how long?" I asked.

"I don't know. That depends on how she does. She may never get out," Cody said.

"Wow, poor gal," I said, knowing how independent Mildred was and that she probably wouldn't like this very much.

"Right," Cody said, heading for the door. "She'll probably be there for a while, so your aunt and uncle can stay at her house when they get here."

"Oh," I said, digesting that bit. My parents were on a cross-country tour with my aunt and uncle in their motor home, and they were all due to arrive any day now in time for Noah's birthday. I had planned to put my folks in Micah's bed, and my aunt and uncle would sleep in the RV. "I guess that would work," I said to Cody's back as she walked out the door.

"Oh, yeah," she said, turning her head to add, "I'll be moving the trampoline up to Mildred's front yard."

She shut the door behind her, and I nearly jumped up and touched my toes in celebration.

"Did you hear that?" I asked Andy.

"Finally," he said.

"No kidding."

I called down the stairs to Micah and Christiana to come up for their nap, and they moaned a little but came running up from the basement to gather books and blankies, and we all snuggled into Micah's bed with Noah already snoring from his crib where we'd set it up at the foot. I read *Froggy Gets Dressed* and *Guess How Much I Love You*, and as we all fell asleep with the words of the little nut-brown hare and his mama in our heads, I listened to the quiet sounds of my kids breathing and thought with joy about the uninterrupted nap times ahead of us when that trampoline was finally relocated.

My parents arrived, and my aunt and uncle were happy to sleep across the street at Mildred's house, taking a break from the confines of their motor home and probably my parents, too. But in the midst of their stay, they loaded back into it, and we all headed to the coast for a family overnight camping celebration for Andy's aunt's birthday, which happened to coincide with Noah's. I'd baked cupcakes to bring along and on Sunday, I put one lit candle in Noah's and we all sang Happy Birthday to his beaming face. The kids all helped him blow it out, and he clapped his hands.

Noah was thrilled to have his own cupcake, and while they all ate, Mom said, "Look what I bought for him on the trip," unfolding a white T-shirt with a colorful Noah's ark on the front. "I thought he could wear it today."

"Well, let's wait until he's done with his frosting." I laughed, seeing the shirt he had on slowly being transformed into something vaguely edible. When he finished, I stripped off the frosting-coated shirt, wiped him down, and pulled the clean shirt over his head.

"Happy Birthday, Noah," Mom said. "Look at all the animals." Noah looked down and pointed to his belly where they all rocked safely, two by two, while his grandma named them all.

The day was warm and sunny, and my mom lined up all the kids on the picnic table. She began with her Girl Scouts repertoire. "We're going on a lion hunt. Got your hat? Got your gun? All set? Let's go," She proceeded through the song, taking them through grass and swamp and up and over trees and stumps to find a lion for Noah.

That night we all stood on the beach and watched the horizon light up. "What a beautiful sunset," we all agreed. "Happy Birthday, Noah," we said, kissing and hugging him in his new birthday T-shirt as the sun sank into the Pacific Ocean.

We'd bought Noah a red Little Tykes ride-on toy for his birthday that he could stand behind and push around, and when we all returned back home from the coast we gave it to him. He immediately tried to follow Micah around on the front lawn with it, but it was difficult for him to push it across the grass. Still, he persevered until he reached the sport court, so happy to find that playing with the big kids was finally within his reach.

"Mildred has some lovely things," my aunt remarked one day. By then Cody had started taking an informal inventory herself, as it seemed Mildred might have to stay in the home permanently. Mildred's house was filled with antiques and treasures from her world travels and her family's Midwest history. She reminded me of Mimi with her hat and glove boxes, china cups and button shoes.

"I know," I said, "I wonder what will happen to them all."

My parents stayed for a few more days and then they all loaded back into their RV, heading east toward Yellowstone on their national parks tour.

"Where'd you get that tea set?" I asked Cody as Mildred's treasures began appearing on Cody's shelves and Mildred's magazines on her tables.

"Mildred," she'd reply. "I figured she didn't need them."

"What's the Dumpster for?" Andy asked her one day, noticing the new addition in Mildred's driveway.

"Oh, I'm cleaning out Mildred's house," Cody said, as she discarded Mildred's family heirlooms at her discretion and anything else that she deemed rubbish. "I'll probably have to sell it for her soon. Do you want to buy it?"

"No," Andy said. We frowned at each other, thinking how this conversation would inevitably head down the same path as the one about buying our rental. We shuddered to think of moving to the new home of the trampoline.

One of Cody's mottoes was, "I invest in people." But increasingly, we realized that "invest" was the key word and that wealth was really the most important thing to Cody. We'd witnessed her loaning family and friends money, effectively buying their friendship and loyalty with gratitude and interest payments.

The more accurate version of Cody's motto would have been, "I control people by investing in them." This was further confirmed as we watched Cody take over Mildred's house and the Dumpster gradually fill with her prized possessions.

Chapter Eight

THE HAPPY, carefree days of summer stretched their arms out again, beckoning us to come and play all day, then holding us spellbound in their warm, nightly embrace. One Friday evening in August, when Andy was milling at his parents' house on the coast again, I took the kids to the waterfront park to enjoy an outdoor festival. I wished Andy were there, but I was used to coming up with things to do in his absence and was proud of myself for planning the upcoming week-end in Salem without him. This time, I was determined not to simply follow him to the coast.

(I'd wanted to go camping with the Returned Peace Corps Volunteers in Eastern Oregon. But Corporate America had come call-ing and offered Andy a job in telecommunications that he couldn't refuse; he was busy finishing up his milling jobs before switching the machine to idle permanently—and I definitely wasn't up for camping with the kids on my own.)

The three older kids skipped ahead while I pushed Noah in his stroller, stopping to chat with friends along the way. Noah loved to ride, sitting up on the edge of his seat with his feet crossed and his hands on the bar, pointing at everything in his path.

I thought back to a month earlier when Hannah, Noah, and I were in Rhode Island. We'd stayed with Erin, since my parents were already in Maine, where we would eventually join them for the Fourth of July. Unable to afford the time for our usual lengthy summer visit or the airfare for all of us, I'd brought only Hannah and Noah with me for a weeklong visit over the holiday weekend. Andy had to work, so we'd hired a college student to babysit for the summer, and she had stayed with Christiana and Micah while we were away.

His sea legs firmly underneath him, Noah had been determined to climb up the ladder to Erin's pool slide; we had to watch him every minute. He pulled her dogs' tails whenever they were within reach. This year, he loved the water, playing happily in the ocean and ending each day covered in sand. We ate Dunkin' Donuts and went to our favorite ice cream shop, where I ordered one black raspberry cone, not daring to buy Noah his own for fear of the mess he would certainly make. But it was love at first taste for him, and he grew very impatient, insistently screaming at me for his next bite before I could even get a lick in myself. Erin called him "Screech" because of the way he sounded, and the nickname stuck like the purple ice cream covering his face.

Now Noah's screech brought me back to attention until I acknowledged what he was pointing at. "Yes, Noah, I see the squirrel," I said. He quieted, relaxing back into his stroller seat; he was content until something else caught his eye and then he'd screech again.

I called the kids together while the shadows lengthened across the park and spread a quilt out on the grass for us to share during the fireworks display. The three kids gradually adjusted their arms and legs around each other and I sat on the edge next to Noah, who was content to remain perched in his stroller. The sky grew black, and the streaming lights infused the air with excitement. With each burst of pyrotechnic color, Noah clapped with great gusto and then put his arm around my neck, hugging me with his little head on my shoulder. When the next blast came, he sat up, clapped, and then hugged me again. I loved the way he clapped, usually just twice but with emphasis and enthusiasm.

What remains with me of that night is a beautiful summer memory. My skin retains the sweet feeling of Noah's loving arm hugging me, and the weight of his toddler head still rests on my shoulder. Noah was growing into a lovely little boy and showed us glimpses of the person he was becoming—stalwart and sturdy, he could wrestle with Micah and hold his own, but he was also mild-mannered and sweet like his sisters. He had the safety of his family's loving arms to hold him while he discovered his place in the world, toddling around the yard after them, playing with rocks and dirt, and touching everything with his pointer finger. Noah loved to swing, and he loved to dance, either with us holding him and twirling him around, or by himself, bouncing on his sturdy legs and clapping while we danced around him. He stood in his high chair and played with the light switch, grinning and stomping his feet daringly. He was so proud that he could now sit up in the shopping cart, and he laughed when it bounced across the pavement. I tickled him when we shopped, and he giggled with delight, making even a mundane trip to the grocery store a fun outing.

When we got home, the phone was ringing, and I rushed to open the door and grab it before the answering machine clicked on. "Hello," I said, out of breath.

The voice of my sister-in-law hit my ear. "Can you come down tomorrow and help Mom?" Cody asked. "I want to come home for my birthday." Cody was at the coast, along with Cassi and Chane, helping Marcella, who'd tripped over the living room rug the previous weekend and fallen, injuring her leg badly enough that she had to use a walker for a while. "And anyway, it's Micah's fault that Mom got hurt in the first place."

"What?" I said, stepping aside as the girls stumbled past me and headed down the hall to their beds.

"Well, Mom said Micah was playing with his cars on that rug and the edge got folded over and that's what she tripped on."

I could see Micah sound asleep in the van in the glow of the carport light and couldn't believe they were casting blame on a four-year-old. I knew from experience that that round Oriental rug was always getting caught up in the reclining chairs and often needed straightening. "Well, I'm sure it was an accident however it happened," I said.

"So can you come?" she said, ignoring my comment.

"Okay," I managed to say before she hung up. I mentally erased the plans I'd made for the weekend in Salem as I traipsed back out to the van and carried my sleeping boys to bed, one at a time. Micah was getting heavy, and I struggled to pull the covers back with one hand before laying him down on the cool sheet. I pried a matchbox car out of his fist and kissed his cheek, smoothing his hair off his damp forehead. I wondered who'd decided that the accident was Micah's fault and sure hoped nobody had told him that he was to blame for Grandma's injury. *Tomorrow I'll see the likely perpetrators and find out*, I thought. But I never did.

"Mommy loves you," I sang in a whisper.

The next morning I phoned across the street to see if either Cally or Charissa could come down and babysit for me while I went to Jazzercise, determined to get that in before my trip to the coast. Cally came. When I got home, I started packing and asked her, "Do you want to come to the coast with me? You can stay the weekend or you could even ride back home later with your mother."

"No," she said and walked home.

I loaded the van, feeling a little relieved that she'd declined my offer. I asked the kids to go outside and play while I finished cleaning up, putting Noah in his crib so he would stay out of trouble while I vacuumed the house. As I turned on the machine, I wondered if he would love motors as much as Micah did. Noah was being such a good boy, and every time I glanced up at him he was standing in the corner of his crib, watching me with a quiet intensity as though he was memorizing the moment. I stopped the vacuum for a minute and we simply looked at each other in the sudden silence. Right before my eyes, he seemed to mature way beyond his one year.

I bent over to move Micah's matchbox cars out of the way and was about to turn the vacuum on again when the phone rang. It was Cally. "I changed my mind, I wanna go with you," she said. I finished cleaning, thinking about my niece, who was sixteen now. I felt a little tense knowing she was coming along, but I was also hopeful as I spent a lot of time puzzling over how to make our relationship better. I knew it would be helpful to have her along for the two hours in the car with the four kids. Andy and I hadn't made much progress in talking to either Cody or Chris about Cally's behavior, and any overtures we made fell on deaf ears.

One day when we were out walking, Cody had confided in me

that she felt guilty because she hadn't spent enough time with Cally when she was a baby, since she and Chris were busy then—she with nursing school and he with his dental practice. Charissa had been an easy baby, the perfect first child, but Cally was fussy and demanding. She'd grown into a defiant and chubby girl, which drove her fitness-fanatic father crazy. "Chris was chubby when he was little," Cody said. That perhaps explained why he was always biking or golfing or doing something active. And why Cally's weight upset him, which I could understand.

I picked up Noah and walked into the kitchen just as Cally was coming through the door, her bag and pillow in her hands and a sandwich stuffed in her mouth. Cally was as rebellious about her eating as she was about everything else and deliberately stuffed food in her mouth like Augustus Gloop in *Willy Wonka & the Chocolate Factory.*

"You can put your stuff in the van; we're just about ready to leave," I said, following her out with Noah. A few years back, Cody had taken Cally to a therapist because of her attitude and weight. The gal had decided that Cally didn't crawl enough as a baby and prescribed crawl therapy. As I followed her, I remembered the disturbing sight of her crawling around her living room after school and thought, *so much for that.*

I strapped Noah into his car seat, and Cally decided she'd sit next to him instead of me, even though Hannah was already sitting there. Hannah moved to the backseat, and I thanked the kids for waiting so patiently. On this trip I decided to drive east from Salem and then south down the coast, which was sunny and warm, a rarity in the summer. Typically the Oregon coast is blanketed in cool, misty fog when it's hot in the valley due to the coldness of the ocean and the barricade of the coastal mountain range, which traps and cools the air. But this was a perfect summer day—the kind of magical day that leaves you wondering, *why don't we live here?*

Along the way the traffic stopped while a bicycle race went by, and Noah began to fuss. He was old enough to face forward in his car seat now, so Cally and I played peekaboo and this-little-piggy with him until we got moving again, and I was glad I didn't have to stop to nurse him. By the time we reached Newport, all the kids were tired of being in the car, so I pulled into the Oregon Maid ice cream store.

"Mom, buy Noah his own cone," the girls each pleaded.

"Okay." I considered getting the black raspberry he'd loved in Maine but instead ordered him a tiny bit of less-staining vanilla on a baby cone. We ate outside and Noah sat up straight in his own chair, so obviously proud of himself to finally have his very own cone. He proceeded to eat it from the bottom up, making a huge mess, and we all laughed along with him while his orange Old Navy onesie began to resemble one of the Orange Juliuses his cousins loved to make.

Proceeding south to Waldport, I headed for Patterson, our favorite beach park. I strapped Noah into his backpack, and we headed across the wide beach for a walk. The kids darted in and out of the freezing cold ocean, seeing how long their feet could stand the pain and squealing when their toes felt like popsicles. "Look, kids, a seal," I said as a familiar head popped up in between waves to watch us. I thought about how different the Pacific is from my familiar Atlantic. There would be no floating or swimming here.

A stream of fresh water flowed across the sand that was a bit warmer than the ocean and when we returned to it, I freed Noah from the confines of his backpack, and the kids all splashed and played with their beach toys in the perfect combination of sand, salt, sun, and summer. Noah vroomed his boats in the water, and I took his vanilla-flavored onesie off and rinsed it. He screeched with joy, stomping around in the water naked and free. I watched my children frolicking and was happy we'd come after all.

By the time we drove upriver to Andy's parents' house, the sun was heading for the Pacific. As it dropped towards the pointed tree tops lining the river, it filled the spaces in between the giant fir trees, setting the national forest aglow. The temperature was always warmer away from the ocean, even just those seven miles inland. We turned in at the little blue cabin and continued down the long dirt driveway. Seeing us, Andy turned off his sawmill for the day, brushed away the sawdust, and pulled out his orange earplugs.

"Hey, why don't we take the kids up to Hootenanny?" he called.

"Yayyy, we want to go to the swimming hole," they all cried. A flurry of activity ensued as they searched for bathing suits and towels and climbed all over Andy's pickup.

"Can we ride in the back?" my nieces begged.

"Oh, all right," Andy said, throwing a bit of caution to the wind because it was a warm evening, and riding in the back of a pickup with summer air blowing in your hair was a memory we both treasured from our own youthful summers. We felt carefree.

"I don't think the kids should ride back there," Cody said when she walked out of the house to find her three girls sitting in the bed of the pickup.

"Oh, they'll be fine," Andy said.

"Leave Noah with me," she said.

"Aren't you leaving?" I asked as I handed Noah over.

"Oh, I'll go later when you get back," she said. I wavered; Noah began crying, his arms stretched out to me. But I relented, knowing it would be easier without him, since the swimming hole is deep, and Micah still needed to wear a life vest and be watched.

"It's okay, honey, Mommy will be right back," I said, climbing into the cab. We had seven kids along to lifeguard, but I felt a pang of guilt watching Noah from my side-view mirror as he squirmed in his Auntie Cody's arms, crying and reaching after us, while we headed down the driveway in our truck overflowing with happy kids that didn't include him.

"I wish we'd brought him along," I said to no one in particular, my voice drowned out by the giggles of children. I knew how much he wanted to be like his older brother and sisters and felt his anguish at being left behind as if it were my own.

We had our three kids in the cab of the pickup along with another niece, Courtney, the only child of Andy's brother, Steve, who lived nearby. Courtney had arrived at the house with her mom, Diane, just in time to join us. We drove eight miles up the Alsea River and parked along the road near a house called Hootenanny, for which the swimming hole was named. Everyone tumbled down the embankment to the sandy beach formed by an eddy and we had a lazy swim in the gathering dusk of early evening. The river was cool and clean and carried our dust and doubts away downriver. We waded upstream, where a set of rippling rapids beckoned, leaning our backs into the smooth rocks and letting the water run its fingers over and around us, massaging our muscles.

"Look, Dad, a crayfish," Micah called, holding one of the bright orange creatures up against his red life vest. He had no fear of grabbing crabs at the coast or crayfish in this river or at our lake in Maine, where they were greenish brown instead of this neon color.

"Cody saved me from drowning here when I was five," Andy said as we watched the older kids launching themselves off the rope swing that hung from a big tree limb on the opposite bank. "I was floating on an inner tube, and she was teaching me how to swim. Buster was on the beach and yelled, 'Andy, you'd better start swimming!' and then he dove in the water and pushed me off the tube. It was right over there." He pointed to the middle of the river between the beach and where the kids were jumping. His story was momentarily interrupted by Cally screaming as she hit the water with a big splash.

"I remember watching the sun shining down through the green water and my bubbles rising to the surface as I sank deeper and deeper until I hit the bottom," Andy continued. "It was really peaceful. But then I saw Cody diving down and she grabbed me and pulled me to the surface." He said this just as Cally came up for air, laughing. I knew that Andy sank like a stone, and I'd heard plenty of stories about how Andy's four older brothers had tortured him, but I'd never heard this one before. We were both happy that our kids seemed to all have inherited my ability to float.

We shook off the river water and loaded the kids back into the truck for the ride home. We all felt rejuvenated by this perfect ending to a summer day—when life is blissful, and you might even stop to ponder your good fortune, happy that your husband didn't drown when he was five, and content with all that you can see and hold around you, wanting nothing more. The frogs began to sing and night colored the air, but it still held enough warmth to caress our skin on the ride home.

We returned to the house to find Cody well into a bottle of wine— her usual nightly beverage and the part of her Catholic faith she embraced religiously.

"Noah received his first communion on my birthday," she joked as his arms reached me at last. I kissed his wine-tainted lips and sat down at the kitchen table to nurse him, both of us relieved and happy at our reunion.

"I changed my mind. I'm not going home tonight; I'll leave tomorrow," Cody announced with the blood of Christ on her breath. So, my trip from Salem to relieve her in caring for her mother hadn't been necessary after all. I was surprised that she didn't want to spend her birthday evening with her husband, but I chalked it up to one more thing about their marriage that I didn't understand. Normally her tendency to change her mind with no thought toward others, like me, would have annoyed me more, but the river water was still dripping off our laughter, and dinner was ready to fill our hungry bellies. We were together as a family, and the happy memories of the day infused our thoughts. It was a lovely summer night. This was not the time for regrets.

When dinner was over, and it was time to put the kids to bed, Cally announced, "I'm not sleeping in the cabin," and she marched into the living room to watch TV.

We'd had such a nice day together, but now that she was back with her mother she reverted to her snotty attitude. I felt betrayed and disappointed that no matter what I tried to do to change things with Cally, the spinner continued to land on the same place—right hand, red—in our game of Twister. I looked at Cody and she shrugged, drank her wine, and said nothing, as usual—left foot, green.

Marcella said that Andy and I could take the kids up the driveway and sleep in the blue cabin. Now that the birthday girl and three of her girls were staying over, the bedrooms in the main house would be full, so we were left with no choice. But that cabin gave me the creeps. It was very small, with one tiny bedroom, a kitchen, a bathroom, and a mini front room. I'd never slept in it before and had only set my foot inside once or twice, which was enough for me. Marcella usually rented it to some down-and-out person with gaps instead of teeth, who inevitably fell behind on the rent and had to leave. Like Cally, I was not keen on sleeping there. The tidal slough flowed behind it, and I half expected to find a rat in the bathroom. I was glad we'd brought our own pillows.

"Come on, it'll be fine," Andy said, and he began gathering up our things.

"Just for one night, right?" I said as we trudged up the driveway with all our gear. Andy and I made beds for the kids on the floor of the front room with the noise from Highway 34 right outside their door. The kids brushed their teeth, and I tucked them in without reading a book, as it was too late, and we were all tired. I prayed some errant logging truck wouldn't come careening into the cabin while they slept, and I sang "Mommy loves you," with Andy chiming in his part, "And Daddy does, too." Then I wished them sweet dreams, like I did every night—those two simple words the last they heard before falling asleep.

By the time I entered our tiny room, Andy had Noah's porta-crib set up at the foot of our bed—there was barely enough space to squeeze it in—and he was snuggling in bed with Noah, who was wearing his Lion King pajamas. I climbed under the covers, and Noah settled down between us. He nursed greedily, then gulped more slowly as his belly filled and the milk and the day knocked him out.

I eased my nipple out of Noah's parted lips after he drifted off, watching a tiny rivulet of milk dribble out of the corner of his mouth and seek its own course down his cheek before I stopped its progress toward my pillow. Watching my kids sleep was my just deserts, and I paused to admire him. Even after the most trying days as a mom, the moment any of my children closed their eyes and saw their own dreams instead of my frustrations, I forgave them all of their trespasses, praying they would do the same for me. I kissed Noah's cheek and moved him gently into his porta-crib.

"Sweet dreams," I whispered. He smiled in his sleep.

Chapter Nine

SUNDAY MORNING DAWNED. Andy and I made love quietly, and I was actually happy for one aspect of the cabin—privacy. Noah stood up and grinned at us over the rail of his porta-crib, wanting to climb into bed with us but unable to get his leg over the edge.

"Baba," Noah said. "Ba Ba."

Andy sat up and reached his long arms to meet Noah's, pulling him into bed between us. Noah snuggled in and closed his eyes in contentment. While he nursed he kept pushing Andy's face away from him with his hand. "Hey, I want Mommy, too," Andy said, laughing and teasing him. Having never woken up in that room before, I looked around me in the new light, trying to change my mind about it. But it smelled musty and was not improved by closer examination. I was relieved that we'd soon be leaving it.

"How long did Buster and Debbie live here?" I asked Andy, remembering that his brother and first wife had slept in this room long before I'd come into the family. The room felt depressing to me, and I couldn't imagine what life would be like, waking up in it every morning.

"I was in high school," he said, staring at the ceiling. "I think they lived here the whole time Debbie was pregnant and after Chad was born. After Chad died, Debbie couldn't bear to be here anymore, and they moved out soon after. She went a little crazy and started saying his death was the work of the devil."

One morning, when Chad was only a few months old, they had

woken up in that room to find their firstborn son dead in his crib. That was all I really knew about it.

"My family blamed Debbie for everything," Andy continued. "Chad was born a month premature, and they used to say maybe he died because she didn't carry him longer or that she had put him to sleep in the wrong position or even because she'd fed him honey."

"Honey? I've only heard your mom say that he was never quite right, like he wasn't meant to be," I said.

The only noise came from Noah's gulping while Andy and I looked around the room and wandered away in our thoughts, the enormity and sadness of Chad's death infiltrating the blissful mood of our morning. I could certainly understand Debbie not wanting to live here, but I couldn't imagine the rest.

"My family took over," Andy said, turning to look at me. "Buster and Debbie were just so sad, and Mom quickly arranged for Chad to be buried in Newport. Mom was friends with the Batemans from the funeral home, and Mom paid for everything. They had a service there for him and everyone went but Dad. 'This is what you deserve,' he told Buster."

"What?" I looked at him and frowned in horror, trying to reconcile these ugly words with the quiet man who set the oatmeal to cook in the double boiler each morning before heading to the barn to milk Bossie with Micah following in his footsteps.

"Well, Dad didn't like Buster. When he kicked him out of the house for disrespecting him, Dad thought Buster would come crawling back and ask for forgiveness. But the Nickels took Buster in, and Dad was mad at them for interfering with his family."

"Buster was only what—fourteen then?" I asked. I could not imagine not liking your own child or kicking them out of your house, raised as I was to believe that you had to learn to get along with everyone, especially family.

"Yeah," he said. "And he never moved back home until Mom let them live here, which Dad didn't like. Dad didn't want Buster around and he didn't want me to hang around with him either. When Buster got bigger, I watched him and Dad fight so many times. When everyone came back to the house after Chad's funeral, Dad disappeared until it was over. After that day, Mom told Debbie she had to let Chad go, like she could just forget about him. She told her, 'You can always have another one.'"

Buster and Debbie did, in fact, have two more children, but their marriage had ended before I'd joined the family. *No wonder*, I thought after hearing this story. Buster was what you'd call rough around the edges, a unique character with a full red beard who always looked like he'd just rolled out of a bed of sawdust. He now lived the closest to his parents of all of Andy's siblings, which I found ironic. He and Bud had grown to tolerate each other, and Buster had his own logging business and so was often around the property, borrowing or fixing equipment or hauling logs out of the slough and storing them in the pasture.

Now it felt even creepier to be in that room.

"I'm so glad we don't have to sleep in here again," I said to Andy. With Cody leaving, we'd sleep down in the house that night. I shivered at the unimaginable horror of losing a child, squeezing Noah just a little bit closer to my chest and stroking his fat fist with my thumb while he finished his breakfast. I smiled across his blond head at my lover and gave thanks that we shared such a strong bond. Two of Andy's brothers were divorced by then and Andy said repeatedly, "I never want to get divorced."

The other three kids woke up, got dressed, and ran down the driveway to the main house. The hens had had chicks and they were so excited to get to the barn to play with the fluffy, peeping balls. I got up and picked out Noah's clothes for the day: his denim overalls, his Noah's ark T-shirt that my mom had given him for his birthday, and his lime-green saltwater sandals. I tossed them all to Andy and sat on the bed. I loved watching Andy's big hands wrestle Noah's little clothes onto his toddler's body and tickle and play with him. I could have sat there all day, watching them giggle together.

All was well in the present tense of our world. Andy and I loved each other and our four children. We had good jobs and a big loving family. The sun smiled on us, and the morning beckoned with its fingers-crossed promise of another lovely day to follow. Andy clipped Noah's binky onto his overalls, and Noah popped it in his mouth as we headed out to the sunshine and down the driveway into the day that would change all days to follow.

"Oh, I like your cute sandals, Noah," Cody said after breakfast. I pulled him out from the high chair where he'd finished eating one of my homemade blueberry muffins and some Cheerios, most of which now littered the floor. He looked down at his feet and stomped them a few times, slipping on the Cheerios and the shiny Formica floor while showing off both his sandals and his newfound agility. He grinned like the star of the show, so pleased with himself.

The coffee pot was emptied and refilled a few times, and Cody started cleaning out the china hutch which occupied the entire dining room wall opposite the table, piling jumbled treasures from the large, cluttered cabinet—plates, cups, saucers, photos, and assorted knick-knacks—on the floor. It reminded me of what she'd done at Mildred's house, and I knew once she got started, she wouldn't stop until the cabinet was empty of all things she deemed junk. Marcella was a Depression-era hoarder, so this immediately set her on edge. "Now why are you doing that?" she asked as her treasures stacked up all around. "Now don't you throw anything away," she said, watching Cody's every move like a hawk while Cody carried on, ignoring her.

Noah was also watching his aunt, attracted to all the shiny and breakable things emerging from the depths of the cupboard and wanting to touch them all. Cody grew frustrated with him, and he with her constantly snatching everything away from him, so I decided to put him down for his morning nap. Rather than hang out in that creepy cabin while Noah slept, I asked Andy to get his porta-crib and set it up in the back bedroom where we'd be sleeping that night. Leaving Noah in the house, I walked outside with Andy and watched him head between the parked cars and up the driveway, stopping on his way to pet Dude, who was lying down on the other side in the shade. The air was heating up, and it looked like it would be another perfect day, but suddenly I felt so tired, like all the energy had just been sucked right out of me.

Micah and Christiana ran up and asked, "Can we go with Cally, Mom?"

"My mom said I can take the kids to the beach," Cally said as she walked out of the mudroom door behind me and into the carport. She was proud of her driver's license, which was only a few months old.

I hadn't really formulated a plan for the day and was thinking maybe I needed to lie down with Noah, too. "I guess that would be okay," I said. The foot-numbing cold of the ocean meant the kids wouldn't be swimming, and I thought they'd have fun splashing around in the stream we'd played in the day before, which would be easy enough for Cally to handle.

"Okay," I said, thinking I should go inside and get their beach toys. Micah's red life jacket hung on the clothesline out back, drying from our river swim the evening before, and as I walked back toward the door I heard him calling, "Mom, Mom, get this, get this." I could see him across the backyard, jumping up and down, trying to reach the jacket and pull it off the line.

"You don't need your life jacket," I said, walking across the grass to him.

"Yes I do, yes I do!" he said, his frustration threatening to escalate into a temper tantrum.

"All right," I relented, fetching it off the line just so he would stop. "You don't need this," I said, wondering why on earth he wanted his life jacket for the beach. I held on to it while we walked across the yard and through the back door into the mudroom to get their toys, crossing to the windows that lined both front walls and overlooked the driveway.

Still arguing with Micah, I happened to look up and out the window and noticed Cally playing with the stereo in the driver's seat of Cody's green Tahoe, which was parked right outside the windows. I glanced back down toward Micah to continue the life jacket debate when a sudden movement caught my eye. I looked out the window again and saw Chane jump out the back door of the Tahoe on the passenger's side, the side nearest to me. I saw her look behind the car and jump back in. I was still wondering why she'd done that when my eyes traveled around to the front of the car, where I noticed what looked like Noah's shadow by the driver's side front tire. *Is that Noah? Is he standing on the other side—the side I can't see?*

I stood riveted in the mudroom, holding Micah's red life jacket while he pulled at my side yelling, "Mommy," as if now from a great distance away.

And then I realized that the car was running.

And I saw Cally start to reverse, turning the front tires sharply to the right to back the vehicle around.

And I saw what Chane had not seen when she looked behind the car.

And I saw what Cally would have seen if she had looked out her window.

And I saw what someone in a smaller car would have been able to see from closer to the ground.

And I saw what Dude could see from his spot across the driveway in the shade.

I saw the shadow of one small sun-kissed boy with little green sandals who loved cars and trucks.

And then I saw first his shadow and then my son disappearing under the left front tire of that five-thousand-pound vehicle.

"STOP, Cally, STOP!" I screamed from inside the house, through the double-paned windows and the walls that I couldn't burst through—the door was miles away down the hall behind me.

"STOP!"

"STOP!"

My breath was wasted. I was completely powerless to stop her. I could not move from that spot. I could not put two thoughts together or make two muscles move to wrench myself into motion and reach my baby in time. I could not save my son. And she did not stop. She kept going.

So I stopped. I stopped breathing. I stopped watching.

And the world changed.

Behind all that summer sunshine, darkness had been lurking. Now I saw it. I saw it clearly. And I could never again pretend it didn't exist.

I ran out of the house, through the carport, and picked up my sweet still boy in his dusty overalls and Noah's ark T-shirt. He was not bloody. He was not moving. I crushed him to my chest, wondering too late if maybe I shouldn't have moved him in case he had a neck or spine injury. I ran into the house with him as fast as I could, through the mudroom and into the kitchen, where I stopped, summoning the courage to extend my arms so I could look at my baby. He still wasn't moving. I felt a sickening wave wash over me.

You're about to collapse, my brain managed to say to my body.

Just then, Cody appeared at my side, and I quickly handed Noah to her, putting my hands on my knees and doubling over—trying to get some blood flowing, trying to breathe while the life was sucked right out of me.

"Oh, God," I said, turning to look at her.

"His head," Cody said. She held him at arm's length, then turned and ran outside with Noah in her arms. I straightened up and followed, briefly wondering where she was going and catching up to her at the bottom of the back steps, where she handed Noah back to me and simply said, "Oh, Kelly."

And just then Noah touched my arm with his left hand. "Mommy," his tiny voice groaned from somewhere already far away.

Cody and I looked at each other and sprang into action, trying to save Noah's life with the life-saving skills we'd learned, trying to do this one thing together. I laid him on the grass and Cody started CPR; she did the chest compressions while I gave him mouth-to-mouth.

Cally ran into the house behind us, saying, "Now everyone will hate me!" Andy had appeared outside behind us but he quickly turned away. I found out later that he had followed Cally inside to call 911, but in the moment I wondered where he was going, thinking he was following *her*—and thinking, *We'll deal with the living later.*

Soon I realized that Bud and Buster had materialized and that the kids had all gathered around us and were watching. Even in the midst of performing CPR, I searched my mothering mind to think of something for them to do. In between breaths I said to my poor crying kids and their cousins, "Hold hands! Hold hands and pray!"

Then Noah groaned again. He threw up. Cody rolled him on his side and I watched the blueberry muffin I'd fed him for breakfast dribble into the grass along with the breast milk he'd woken up to that morning. I tried to believe he was coming around and resumed making my desperate attempts to breathe for him, praying all the while, *Breathe, Noah, breathe, breathe, damn it, please, God, make him breathe!*

After what seemed like forever, an ambulance siren filled the air, adding a welcome cacophony to our quiet counting and compressions. The family circle was split in two by the paramedics who appeared by our sides and took over. In one swift motion they sliced that little Noah's ark T-shirt right down the middle—a decisive, destructive act that shocked me to my core. I clutched at my own chest, catapulted into the gravity of our situation, where all things we might have considered precious before, like preserving a cute first birthday gift from Grandma, were shredded. They strapped Noah onto a body board much too big for him and lifted him up in a well-rehearsed choreography. I didn't know how they could possibly move with the weight of all the hope I had piled on their shoulders. But they did, carrying Noah to the ambulance in a practiced rush, with me in desperate pursuit.

"Ma'am, you can't come with us," one of them said as they passed Noah through the door.

"I'm a trained first responder," I replied, trying on Cody's boldness for size. One look at my eyes told them that I was going, and there was no time to waste arguing. I jumped in, they shut the door behind me, and our siren shattered the peaceful prayers of every church service we passed that Sunday morning.

Once we were underway, the medics jabbed a long needle into Noah's leg. I held his hand and stroked his arm like I always did when he got a shot. But he didn't even flinch.

"Look at him," I said to nobody in particular. Noah always cried when the doctor gave him a shot. "He doesn't even care," I murmured. Usually I'd have tried to quiet him down; now I desperately wanted him to scream and cry and hold his arms out to me and to bother everyone. But he was being such a terribly good little boy. The ideal patient. The paramedic looked at me with her professionally neutral eyes and said nothing, which spoke volumes.

The emergency system had been activated, and the 911 operator had radioed the ambulance to meet the Life Flight helicopter down the coast at a grassy airstrip called Wakonda Beach Airport, from where Noah would be flown to a Portland hospital—his only chance at survival. Andy was following somewhere behind us in the sheriff's car. But while the ambulance rushed westward, there was a change of plans—it was not, after all, another perfect day. That damned summer fog had returned, smothering the coast like a wet blanket. The visibility kept shifting, making it impossible for a helicopter to land, so we received instructions to go north to Newport Hospital instead, where the Life Flight team would meet us. With our sudden change in direction, Andy and the sheriff lost us, and at the Newport Hospital I found myself alone with Noah and the emergency medical system in action. They wheeled him out of the ambulance and into the emergency room and shunted me off to the admitting desk to fill out paperwork.

"You can have a seat here in the waiting room," the desk lady informed me.

My body trembled, but I steadied my gaze, channeled Cody, and said, "There's no way in hell I'm going to sit in the waiting room and read magazines while my baby is in there fighting for his life."

She conferred with a nurse, who capitulated. "You can come in as long as you remain quiet and stay out of the way."

Just then Andy arrived, so they escorted us both to Noah's room. As we entered, they were receiving another update from Life Flight: now the fog was too thick for them to land at Newport; they were forced to land seven miles inland in Toledo, and Noah would have to be transferred yet again by ambulance. All of this was wasting precious time. Noah's life was ticking away. Our son's life depended on the fickleness of fog.

As the fog rolled in and out, Andy and I stood against the wall at Noah's feet, watching helplessly while the doctors resuscitated our baby two or three times. We held hands silently, desperately, and prayed. On the wall next to Noah's bed was a backlit X-ray of his head. His skull was cracked in three places. I could only glance at it, not wanting to commit this picture to memory.

The doctor asked to speak with us privately, and we followed him to his office, reluctant to leave Noah. He said, "I need you to understand that your son has sustained a severe head injury. It's your decision whether or not to send him to Portland."

I couldn't accept that they might not be able to put Noah back together again, even though this was no nursery rhyme. I looked at Andy and he looked at me and neither one of us needed to say a word. "Send him," we said without a moment's hesitation.

"Okay, well, then you might want to say good-bye," the doctor said. There was no room in the helicopter for any passengers. But that wasn't the kind of good-bye he meant.

Andy and I did what we were told. We were living now for the moment—one moment, and only one, at a time. And these were monumental moments—moments that were off the clock and an eternity longer than they used to be, yet were never long enough. How long should the moment be, after all, when you say good-bye to your son? How much time should you get?

While they prepared for his transfer, we crouched down by Noah, who looked so small in that big boy's bed, and we stroked his hands.

"Mommy loves you," I sang quietly into his ear, noticing a trickle of dried blood and licking my finger to wipe at it.

"And Daddy does, too," Andy said.

Our voices cracked along with our hearts. "I love you, Noah," we said over and over, wishing he would wake up and push Andy's face away, wishing we could laugh with him, wishing we could start this day all over again by returning to that creepy cabin and never leaving it again.

"You're going for a helicopter ride, and Mommy and Daddy can't come. Be a brave boy," Andy instructed our silent, Saturday's child.

We both looked at his broken body and forced ourselves to say words we didn't know. Words we didn't have. Words we couldn't say.

Gathering the strength of my ancestors, I laid my lips against his ear and whispered, "You go and find Mimi. She'll take good care of you. She always wanted a redheaded baby."

Noah still had sand in his hair and saltwater on his skin from our combined tears and the ocean beyond.

"It's okay," Andy and I both lied to him. "You can go if you have to."

And they took him away.

We staggered out to the waiting room where some of our tribal members had gathered.

"He's gone," Andy said and I cringed, hoping he hadn't uttered an unintentional double entendre.

I realized I needed the bathroom. Cody and Diane came in with me. I waded across the room, numb and disconnected, collapsing on the toilet with the weight of the day pressing down on me.

"Look," I said, realizing I had Noah's blood on my hands and I didn't even know where it had come from. But I clenched them into fists anyway and vowed to myself, *I will never wash them again.*

Then I shuffled over to the sink and washed them.

Andy and I managed to get back to the house to pick up our other kids so we could begin the long drive to Portland. All the kids had stayed with Bud and Marcella, and we returned to learn that Andy's sister, Suzie, had shown up and had taken it upon herself to drive Cally to the sheriff's office in town for questioning, and that for some reason she'd also taken Christiana with her—a classic nonsensical Suzie move. Cody was furious and flew off to rescue her own child. We were distraught but had a long drive ahead of us and had already wasted precious time going back to the house—we couldn't backtrack yet another hour to collect Christiana. So we gathered up Hannah and Micah and had to leave without her, just one more thing to be upset about. Once I'd been forced to look up from Noah's hospital bed, I wanted to glue the rest of my kids to my chest and never let them go. I desperately wanted Christiana to come with us, but I had to tear myself away and once again surrender to a reality I didn't want. Now part of me was in the car, rushing to Portland, while another part was left behind, sitting in the Lincoln County Sheriff's Office, and yet another part of me flew away from me as fast as he could in his first helicopter ride.

Hannah, Micah, Andy, and I drove the three hours to Portland in silence and shock. The kids fell asleep, but I couldn't. I felt like I'd been run over, but I would never use that particular figure of speech again and would cringe inwardly every time others did. I started to pray, but I couldn't hold more than two or three words in my head at a time, resorting to simply, "Please, God," and hoping He could fill in the rest. Neither Andy nor I spoke the entire trip, except for once when Andy answered a brief phone call from his brother and said, "That was Joe."

Outside of our deathly quiet van, that promised sunny summer day proceeded as planned, only without us. We passed animals grazing and happy families sitting down to Sunday dinners, blessing their food and giving thanks to God for their good fortune. We were becoming different, apart, and separate, watching while others cavorted in the warmth of normality we had once relished.

How could they?

How could they eat?

How could they give thanks?

How could they frolic in the sun?

How could the sun conspire with all these strangers to magnify our cold, dark pain?

Why was this sunny day not meant for us?

It was all so cruel and so impossible to fathom. And we had to drive through it and watch. We had to hurry.

When at last we were crossing the Fremont Bridge over the Willamette River, the kids woke up. They stretched and asked where we were. I turned around and looked at my firstborn girl and boy, Hannah and Micah, reluctant to start this conversation.

"We're almost at the hospital. I want you to know that Noah might not be okay. He might be paralyzed. He might be a vegetable."

I was explaining this so badly.

"What? A vegetable? Do you mean like a carrot?" Hannah asked.

"Celery?" Micah added.

It might have been funny hearing them name the green and yellow vegetables I'd been counseled by my mother to eat every day had we been crossing over any other river on any other day, had our destination been any other place than our son's bed at Emmanuel Hospital on the opposite shore. But now we were pulling up to the door, and I failed to answer them, unable to add a new word to their young minds that would clarify the horrifying possibilities that awaited us on the other side of that hospital entrance.

Andy parked the car, and I dragged myself from the vehicle, stepping through the portals of the revolving door, which delivered us all with a *swoosh* into another realm. The four of us entered the hushed sanctuary of the children's emergency room. Everyone tiptoed around in their silent shoes as if any noise would send us all right over the edge. The nurses greeted us with screaming solemnity and led us to a curtained-off room. They asked Hannah and Micah to wait on one side of the fabric barrier and then led Andy and me through to Noah's side. Overwhelmed by relief to see Noah again, I allowed myself to breathe a bit deeper, inhaling the antiseptic odor of despair. Noah was hooked up to so many machines, but no alarms were going off, and that seemed good. His eyes were closed. I stepped up to look at him more closely but hesitated to touch him, afraid of disturbing something. I clenched my fists instead. Naked but for a diaper, his body was covered with all kinds of tape and tubes and gauze and monitors. I examined him from his feet up, slowly, as if I'd just delivered him, coming at last to rest on his head. Swollen. Way too big. Another terrible thing to see on a day filled with terrible sights.

The nurses and doctors looked at us with their professional pity and their carefully controlled selves while trying to make us understand that they'd kept Noah "alive" until this, the moment they were waiting for—our arrival. Yet another doctor entered our lives, introducing himself as the pediatric neurologist, and doing his best to get it through our thick heads that there was too much pressure on Noah's brain and in his body. And no way to relieve it. Andy and I suddenly reverted from highly educated adults into people who couldn't comprehend anything, who needed a lot of explanation, a lot of repetition, a lot of very simple words. The neurologist said that Noah had some other broken bones, like the arm he'd managed to reach out and touch me with for the last time.

My brain imploded.

Too much pressure? My head was filled with the same. Too much pressure. And no relief was in sight for me, either.

We may have attempted a few questions beginning with "Umm" or "What if," but there were no question marks in this doctor's mind. He had other lives to save, other parents to talk to. He was there to deliver a message and move on with his skills. He was a highly trained specialist who billed top dollar by the nanosecond. He was the deal-closer, the guy in the back room who makes all the important decisions. They'd kept Noah warm for our lips and our hands, for our farewell, and that was final. Period. They asked us if we'd like to donate his corneas, but I said no, not his eyes; I couldn't bear to think of them snipping away at his beautiful blue eyes. The doctor concluded with the standard parting words that we would hear again and again, forever after. Words we didn't want to hear. Words that spoke volumes but meant nothing at all and yet meant everything there ever was to say. Words that allowed others their exit: "I'm sorry."

That simple phrase, those two little words, thus entered into our lives, replacing our son's name. They would be spoken in hospital rooms and churches, and they would be mailed and handed to us disguised as flowers and food. They would mean so much and also so little. And sometimes, when we were most ready to hear them, they would be withheld. But that was all yet to come.

Right now they meant that Noah wasn't coming to the beach with us or to the lake with us, or even home with us that sunny summer day. Or ever again. I remembered Noah's outstretched hand as we headed for Hootenanny without him just the night before, and his pain at being abandoned by us socked me right in the gut. Now that I was the one left behind.

Noah was already gone. He had left without us. We had told him he could.

The nurse appeared and said, "You can bring the children in to say good-bye, but maybe they'll just want to touch his foot or hand."

I guess she thought maybe they wouldn't want to see Noah's head all big like that. But we had lost our ability to speak and so gave them no warning. Hannah and Micah, Noah's brave big sister and brother, were having none of that, anyway. They marched right up to their No-wee's bed and climbed aboard. Hannah caressed his face. Micah kissed his cheek. They talked to him. They loved him in the way they had loved him since the day he was born. One last time.

The nurses asked us all to wait on the other side of the curtain while they silenced the beeps and whirring of all those machines and what was left of Noah. Andy and I hugged each other and covered each other with the tears of the "be" people—the bewildered, the bereft, the bereaved. I soaked the shores of Andy's shoulder with the first waves from my ocean of grief—me, who hated to cry. And while I cried my heart out, I could see the nurses through a gap in the curtain working to disconnect our baby, our son, our Noah. I watched them removing all that tape they'd so recently covered him with, adhering Noah to the earth until our arrival. Now his family was here. Now they could detach all that held Noah's body here with us. With each pull of the adhesive, they wrenched him away from us. With each rip, each tear, each tiny blond hair they pulled from his body, my own heart ripped and tore. I watched until they unhooked Noah from the question marks of the present and placed him firmly, finally, in the past. Until nothing was left but the sounds of their footsteps.

The nurses called Andy and me back in. They wrapped Noah's body in a blanket and handed him to me like he'd just been born. It was 6:15 p.m. They ushered us into a quiet room with a minister we didn't know and who could offer us nothing if not a miracle. I sat down in a Papa Bear–size wooden rocking chair that made me feel small and inadequate, automatically adjusting the body of my baby in the football hold as though we were preparing to nurse together for the first time instead of rocking for the last. I held him and looked down at him. And then I stopped rocking. This was not Noah. He wasn't there. It didn't feel like him; it didn't smell like him. And I knew immediately, right then and there, that this was only Noah's body. The body Andy and I had created out of our love for each other. The body I'd grown inside of me and pushed out into the world only fifteen months prior. The body I'd nursed from my own every day. The body Andy and I had cuddled and tickled and bathed and fed and walked and sang to and pushed on the swing so many, many times. The body we'd all loved and cared for. The body that was broken. I felt nothing. Noah was gone. And I did not want to hold this shell of him any longer. I handed him to Andy.

"This is not Noah," I said.

Andy cradled his son's body in his long arms for a moment and agreed, "No, it's not."

We looked at each other with wonder as Noah taught us both in that moment that we are not our bodies. They say the soul weighs twenty-one grams and we both felt its absence. We held his body but not his soul. Noah was not in that room.

We went back to the treatment room and laid Noah's body on the bed. The kids came in.

"Can I give him his first haircut?" I asked.

The nurse handed me a pair of scissors, and I cut some of the strawberry-gold locks off the head of my dead baby. Then I rinsed off the traces of blood and sand in the sink, the cold tap water mixing with my warm tears. The faceless nurses handed us a bag with Noah's torn, dirty clothes, his saltwater sandals, and a souvenir from his short visit—one bright-green, wrist-size Oregon Trauma System bracelet and a card with his dead handprint on it, slightly smudged. There was nothing more we could do, and we were made to understand that standing there forever was not an option. Somehow we gathered the will to turn and take that first baby step away. Away from our baby. Never having been away from him for more than a few hours, we stepped away from him forever.

The trained professionals who were still thinking logically brought me back to the present, asking, "Do you need to call anyone?" Before I could answer, I found myself seated at a desk with a phone receiver in my hand. I dialed one of the few numbers I knew by heart. "Mom," I said, taking a deep breath, "Noah is dead."

I immediately wished I could snatch those three words right back and clasp my hand over my mouth so as never to let them escape from my lips again. I could feel my mother's smile collapsing in horror through the receiver. I could hear her mind spinning, trying to deny the words she thought she'd just heard. I would have countless future experiences of wanting to spare others from the news I had to share. Over time I would learn how to break it to them gently. Over time I learned to comfort those who wanted to comfort me. But this time was the first time. I was brand-new to this—the speaking of the three short words that would make this all forever real.

I don't know how much I told her. I don't remember the rest of the conversation, the details, the questions, the future plans. We had no future plans. I know that when we finally hung up she was faced with telling this terrible news to my dad and my older brother, Brian, and his family and their friends who were all visiting. She, in turn, destroyed the peacefulness of their fine summer evening while they rocked on the porch listening to the frogs and loons calling happier news across the lakes to each other. Noah had played in those same lake waters one month earlier. He had skimmed across them happily in boats, big enough this summer to enjoy his Mickey Mouse life vest. He'd slid down an orange plastic Little Tykes slide at the beach, landing bravely with a splash in the waters of his ancestors, laughing. But the places that knew him would know him no more.

We limped down the hall through the pediatric ICU, too numb to wonder if that would have been a better place for our son. The revolving front door pushed us back into that same sunny day, still relentless in its intent to shine brightly for everyone else. We shielded our eyes and limped along, even sadder and more broken than when we'd arrived. All hope for a happy ending was sealed by its final *swoosh* behind us. We managed to find our van, and Andy unbuckled Noah's car seat and moved it to the back so Micah and Hannah could sit together, even though they didn't ask, didn't fight over it. I hoped Christiana was on her way home with the Martins but didn't have the wherewithal to call and find out. We drove the hour home to Salem, beginning to test the replay button of this most terrible day, daring to search for the highlights and begin to comprehend.

How on earth could God have been so unavailable to us on a Sunday morning at ten o'clock? Surely that should have been a safe moment for us, when the power of the Holy Spirit moves among us, and our God, who is an awesome God, draws nigh for just a closer walk with thee? Ten o'clock, the time when our church service began, when I'd normally rush in to sit in my favorite pew after depositing my children in their respective Sunday school classrooms to learn about Jesus, after prying my little boy's clutching hands from my Sunday dress and extricating myself from the nursery with a smile and a promise. "It'll be okay, Noah, Mommy will be right back." Or so it would have been—that is, if I hadn't left Salem and gone to the coast to help my mother-in-law, skipping church that day.

Our absence had violated God's commandment, "Remember the Sabbath and keep it holy." Was this our punishment for skipping that one little commandment? One out of ten wasn't bad, was it? We hadn't spent the day taking the Lord's name in vain or coveting our neighbor's ass or stealing or bearing false witness or carving minia-ture idols out of wood. Given the opportunity, we could even have argued that we were actually obeying the commandment to "honor your mother and father," which surely extends to injured mothers-in-law as well. But we'd had no opportunity to mount a defense, cut off as we were from God's mercy, our verdict delivered with terrible finality.

I thought about God as Andy drove down I-5 from Portland to Salem. And I thought about Jesus. And in light of my day, I thought about them both in a whole new way. When Jesus died, he returned to the heavenly home of his Father and dwelt with Him there, for-ever seated within His reach at His right hand—I'd memorized and mumbled this creed so faithfully at all the Saturday night masses of my youth. But now I wondered, so just how terrible was Jesus's death, really, for God, his Father? Because when my son died, he was taken from me so suddenly and finally, that all I had left within the reach of *my* right hand was the smell of his clothes and his blood on my hands and the toothbrush he'd used and the toys he'd loved to play with and the indent from his head on his little white pillow embroidered with his name, *NOAH*, which we'd all clutch desperately and soak with our tears for many months to come. And I had his brother and sisters, who'd ask, "Where did Noah go, Mommy? Where is he now?" as I clenched my empty fists and searched for answers to tell them.

God isn't always merciful. Sometimes He doesn't even pay attention. Make no mistake about that. And because we'd skipped that sanctuary visit on Sunday, we found ourselves doing a most unimaginably cruel penance there, five days later, on Friday: burying our son.

Chapter Ten

Y OU DO NOT have a good night's sleep after your baby dies. You don't eat or drink or get dressed or shower or walk or talk or make love or pay bills or pay taxes or grocery shop or exercise or breathe or function in any capacity, whatsoever, after your baby dies.

We were sick mentally, physically, spiritually, and intellectually while we walked through the shadow of the valley of death in our living hell. We were like Noah: we looked whole, but we were empty.

There's a phenomenon associated with the loss of a child called "empty arms syndrome," meaning that your arms physically ache because they miss having your baby to hold. My arm muscles had grown proportionately with Noah so they could accommodate his weight perfectly. Now my entire body ached with longing. My breasts did not know he had died and were hard and painfully full of milk, serving as a constant reminder that my baby was gone and there was no relief in sight, no hungry boy to fill his belly while emptying them, making them soft again. Nothing would be completely soft again, including life itself. I missed my baby so much, and I simply didn't know what to do with the void he'd left behind.

Andy and I collapsed into bed each night, where we clung to each other like the two fractions of ourselves could combine to make a whole. I cried the tears I'd withheld for so long as if this were the moment I'd been waiting for. Shadows of our former selves, we hugged and kissed our children constantly. Micah, at age four, was at a stage when he needed to verbalize the events of the day, and he replayed them over and over, unable to rewrite the unhappy ending. "And then Cally ran over Noah; she shouldn't have done that," he said again and again. And again.

I, too, constantly relived that Sunday morning, but silently, to myself. In that terrible moment my life as I'd known it was squeezed right out of me along with Noah's, leaving only what felt like a clenched fist buried deep within my belly. The person I used to be had died in that driveway along with my son. Everywhere was a reminder of him. And of what I had lost. I wandered downstairs to our basement to find my kids watching cartoons and eating Life cereal. They sucked their fingers and clutched their security blankets, and instead of worrying about their habits, I envied them. "If that gives them comfort, they can suck on their fingers for the rest of their lives as far as I'm concerned," I told Andy. I kept finding Noah's binkies stashed all around the house and was tempted to pop them in my own mouth, wishing I had something to comfort me so easily. All of our feng shui had drained right out the red front door.

The things I used to worry about became vague remnants of the past. All my window-blind cords were safely tucked away, and the garbage cans were free of plastic bags. I'd avoided keeping balloons in the house after learning in my first responder course that the Heimlich maneuver can't dislodge them from someone's throat. I'd cut bananas and hot dogs lengthwise, grapes in half. I had baby gates, car seats, door locks, and all those Safety 1st products all over my house. When I finished shopping I always took Noah out of the shopping cart and buckled him securely in his car seat before unloading even one bag of groceries, just in case a car accidentally hit the cart. He had a social security number and was vaccinated for all those terrible childhood diseases. Hadn't I thought of everything? In spite of my best efforts to protect him, my baby had died anyway.

I ached for all those times I'd left Noah in the church nursery or in day care or in the arms of his auntie or his grandma, assuring him, "It's okay, honey, Mommy will be right back." Now I chewed on those bittersweet words and swallowed them like so much regret. Everything was not going to be okay. Mommy would not be right back. Mommy did not know anything. And all that time I could have spent with him was lost.

The next day, Monday, the business of death began. A steady stream of people came that day and throughout the week, asking questions, hugging us, and crying.

"Let me know if there's anything you need. Let me know if there's anything I can do," they'd say.

"Noah!" I wanted to scream, "Bring me Noah. What I need is Noah."

But nobody brought him to me. Instead they brought food I couldn't eat and flowers I couldn't smell.

"What happened?" the brave ones asked.

I tried to speak. I tried to explain. I tried to figure that out myself. What had happened? How did Noah get out of the house? Had someone left the door open? Where was everyone? What was Chane doing? I wondered why the only witnesses to this horrific event were Dude, who could not speak, and me. I wanted Dude to tell me what he had seen from his unobstructed viewpoint across the driveway, but he just looked at me with his wise brown eyes and offered himself up for petting.

I knew I had been busy arguing with Micah about his red life vest when the motion of Chane getting out of the car caught my eye. I knew the horror of seeing that shadow and realizing that shadow was shaped like Noah just as the green Tahoe began to move. I knew that my voice would be forever diminished from the futility of screaming, "Stop, Cally, Stop!" and my body forever found lacking for its utter inability to leap through glass and wood to transform my son from a shadow to a real live boy rescued by my Noah-strengthened arms in the face of danger. I knew that we had woken up happy and whole and gone to bed sad and broken.

Everyone in Andy's family said over and over, "We can't let this split up our family. We all have to stick together and help each other get through this terrible tragedy." And we agreed wholeheartedly.

The enormity of our present loss was more than enough to bear; we couldn't imagine anything worse. Andy and I counted on the loving support of our tribe to help us through these dark, difficult days, and we assumed we had it. Of course we would all unite in our common tragedy.

My family began arriving from the East Coast, and suddenly we had a bunch of people on our hands who needed something to do. So Andy and I came up with the idea of putting in place something we'd intended to do for some time. Under Andy's instruction, they all set to work tearing up the hillside that bordered our front yard to make a garden—Noah's garden. It gave people something straightforward to work on, something to wrap their arms around after the hugging was over, something to talk about for which there were words, and something to focus on so talk was unnecessary. Anyone who came by the house helped; getting dirty and sweaty gave shape to their sorrow and a purpose to their pain. Together, our people from the East and from the West built a rock wall along the edge of the front lawn and cleared the hill, preparing the soil for planting. Then, when somebody asked what we wanted, we had a new answer. Instead of screaming, "Noah!" we said, "Plants." It made sense to us that from death, life should grow. We tried to plant the beauty of Noah everywhere, filling his garden with our sweat and our tears.

We went to the cemetery next door and bought two neighboring plots that were as close to our house as we could get; there would be enough space for Noah and a bench, and anyone sitting there, maybe even Noah himself, could hear the sounds of his brother and sisters playing outside. I wanted Noah as near to us as possible—another terribly quiet neighbor.

People continued arriving from near and far, and we had a funeral to plan. All those terrible decisions to make that we had no prior experience with—there were no guidelines or handbooks, and there was no special chapter in *What to Expect: The Toddler Years* entitled, "How to Bury Your Baby." The only event I'd planned in my life was our wedding, which had taken months. This was like planning a wedding in one week.

Mom, who had always sung in the church choir, helped choose

the music. Cody's friend, Cindy, volunteered to play the piano, and her daughter offered to play the violin and sing at the service. We all met at our church one afternoon to practice. I grew up listening to Mimi "tickle the ivories," as she called it, and was comforted by this instrument above others. But when Cindy began playing, I was overcome by an overwhelming desire to stretch my grief-racked body across the shiny wooden surface. I wanted to crawl inside that grand coffin of a piano, in among the keys, where maybe the hammers could beat some sense back into my life. I wanted to be pounded with real, physical pain to replace this nameless aching void I felt. I wanted the sound to reverberate in my bones and fill my empty aching cells and reteach my heart the rhythm it had lost. I wanted the wood to absorb all my tears and reshape my soul. I had so much to do, and I didn't want to do any of it. I stood there trying to control these urges, thinking these thoughts, clutching the edges of the instrument and willing my feet to stay planted on the floor while I pretended to select music appropriate for honoring the death of my son.

Another friend of Cody's had lost her son years before in an accident, so I turned to her for advice. She suggested that we dress Noah ourselves for the viewing of his body, which would occur before his cremation, for the sake of my family and those who had not seen him getting to be such a big boy lately. I briefly considered washing and mending the last outfit he'd ever worn, now sitting in my closet in a blue GAP bag, but I didn't have the fortitude to fix it, nor would I ever. Instead, I chose the outfit I'd bought Noah at Nordstrom one day in the spring while he'd kicked his heels against his stroller. Usually a sale shopper, I'd splurged, paying full price and buying it a bit big so he could get more wear out of it. He wore it twice—for Easter and for his first birthday photos. But I never imagined, as I justified the price tag, that I would willingly commit it to ashes, along with him, on its third wearing,

On Wednesday afternoon when we went to the funeral home to dress Noah, his body was so swollen and pumped up with embalming fluid that the outfit that had been a bit big when he was full of life now barely fit him. I couldn't squeeze his swollen feet into his first walking shoes, so I set them aside to save. The professionals powdered him and laid him out in the parlor, where we displayed giant photo collages everyone had gathered at home to create and the photo albums I had so meticulously organized. And his Noah's ark baby book with all its forever-after blank pages.

"I'm so sorry," people said as they arrived later that evening.

They came and they looked at Noah. They looked at the photos. They looked at his baby book. They looked at his family. They cried.

And after they all left, I collapsed into a red cushioned chair in the front row next to my dad, finally allowing myself to take a good look at Noah lying there so still in front of us. I looked long, in no hurry to leave him again. We sat there quietly while the room fell away, and all I perceived was the three of us. Dad, so good at being quiet, said nothing. I knew he would continue to sit there beside me for as long as I needed him to stay.

All of a sudden I had an overwhelming desire to take Noah up and devour him. Like with the piano, I felt this as a new, urgent need. I didn't want to literally eat him, I just wanted to crush him against me and absorb him somehow. With the exception of Noah's breast milk still flowing out of me, I felt achingly empty inside. Our bodies were meant for each other, his and mine, and I wanted to gather him back inside me. Back from where he had come. He'd started his journey in this world as a product of the love Andy and I had for each other. I'd carried him inside me for almost one year of my life. My body had nourished and nurtured him as its first priority, even before it cared for itself. I felt every kick and elbow he poked me with, and I knew the spasms of his every hiccup. We had slept, eaten, dreamed, and grown together as one. He was in me and of me first. I had pushed him along the tunnel of me to enter into this world.

And now I wanted him back.

I wanted him to come back through me and be in me and of me for as long as I had to stay here. I did not know how to do it, but I was prepared to sit there forever until I figured it out.

My family's gravestone says, "To live in the hearts of those we leave behind is not to die." And so I will carry him in my heart always. But it's not the same. I hate to lose things, anything, and will tear my house apart searching for whatever it is that's gone missing. This loss was especially hard to relinquish. I wanted to find my baby. I wanted Noah back.

Finally, even my patient dad asked me quietly, "Are you ready to go?"

And somehow I nodded. And I rose from my chair.

And my dad took my arm. And we walked out of that room.

And I left Noah.

Again.

We are Metholic. I was raised in the Methodist church, the faith of my mom. My dad was Irish Catholic, and he went to mass when we were young but eventually capitulated and joined us on Sundays. All my friends were Catholic, so I spent a lot of time at Saturday night mass in my high school years—all the cute boys were there—and from there we went out to party with the body and blood of Christ still on our lips.

Marcella was a devout Catholic, but Bud was Episcopalian and maintained a hearty dislike of the Catholic church. By the time Andy came along, Bud had put his foot down and would not allow Marcella to take him to mass or be otherwise indoctrinated into her faith. So Andy stayed home on Sunday mornings, and his dad read him the Sunday comics while Marcella went to church and prayed for their souls.

On occasion, Andy and I took the kids for mass at Queen of Peace, Cody's Catholic church. Father George gave great sermons, unlike the monotone priests of my youth who'd rushed through their speaking parts, slowing down only to savor the drama of communion and to drink long and two-fisted from the shiny gold chalice. So when it came time to bury our son, we opted to hold the funeral in our Methodist sanctuary and invited Father George to participate that Friday, August 15, three days before Noah would have turned fifteen months old. It felt like a good mix for our families, covering all the bases.

Pastor Scott greeted everyone that sunny morning with, "I

promise you this, if you don't change and become like a child, you will never get into the kingdom of heaven."

Andy and I rose on cue and stood before the large gathering of people. And we smiled! We were the personification of every parent's worst nightmare. Yet we both were filled with a sense of peace and even joy . . . Which is not at all what either of us expected to feel on the day we buried our son. Maybe it derived from the love surrounding us from all of those gathered together. Maybe the spirit of Noah was with us in that sunlit sanctuary. Or maybe God had woken up from His nap.

Whatever it was, I was thankful, and I didn't question the gift as I told the congregation, "The first time I read this poem I felt very angry. But the more I read it, the less angry I became."

Then I read them "A Child Loaned," written by Edgar Guest:

"I'll lend for you a little time, a child of mine," God said, "for you to love while he lives, and mourn for when he's dead . . . I cannot promise he will stay, since all from earth return, but there are lessons taught down there, I want this child to learn. I've looked in the wide world over, in my search for teachers true, and from the throngs that crowd life's lanes, I have selected you. How will you give him all your love, not think the labor vain, nor hate me when I come to take him back again? But shall the angels call him much sooner than we've planned, we'll brave the bitter grief that comes, and surely understand!"

Since the nurse had handed me this poem in the hospital only five days prior, its message had begun to sink in. Apparently, unbeknownst to us, we had made this bargain with God to love and cherish our children while they are here on Earth, understanding that someday any one of them might be called home to heaven. Then it is our task to brave the bitter, painful, all-consuming grief and spend the rest of our lives feeling proud to have been the chosen parents, all the while trying to understand, without hating God in the process.

You discover fairly soon in the darkest hours of your life that you have a big decision to make. You have to decide exactly what you believe and what you don't. I don't believe that this life is a dead end and holding Noah's body had confirmed this for me. I don't know how I could have moved on with my life and not simply quit breathing or sunk into complete despair otherwise. When life gets slippery, you need something to hold on to, some reason to get out of bed each morning. For me, it is much more comforting to have hope in the eternal. I believe in a God that is greater than my own limited capacity to understand Him. I have my list of top-ten questions to take along with me when I go, and I'm expecting Him to have some definitive answers.

Next, Father George said a prayer. "Tender shepherd of the flock, Noah has entered your kingdom and now he lies cradled in your love . . . Comfort us in the knowledge that this child, Noah, lives with you and with your son Jesus Christ and with the Holy Spirit, forever and ever. Amen."

He read Genesis 9, the story of the biblical Noah and the solemn covenant that God has made with us to never again destroy all life on earth with a flood and to set a rainbow in every cloud as a reminder of this promise.

We all sang, and I managed to stay in my seat with no urge to crawl into the piano this time. Pastor Jane turned her Scottish brogue to the words of the twenty-third Psalm: "Yea, though I walk through the valley of the shadow of death, I will fear no evil: for thou art with me; thy rod and thy staff they comfort me."

She looked at us and said, "Look for courage and comfort in these words."

I was desperately seeking comfort and had never felt those words so keenly before. We were literally walking through that valley and it was, indeed, a very dark place. Yet a shower of love and, yes, even comfort rained on us, lifting us up and helping us to get through it all. Surely this was the power of the Holy Spirit that dwells among us. It's what we are capable of doing for each other when we work together to focus our love and affection and energy on each other. Andy and I felt this transfer of energy, tangible and palpable to us. And it was a mighty thing, indeed.

We invited people to share their memories of Noah. When Cassi rose, she talked about how we used to dance in the living room and said through her tears, "This is a song we would play for Noah whenever he was crying, and I don't know why, but it would calm him down immediately." Then the haunting and beautiful deep voice of Annie Lennox filled every crevice of the sanctuary with "No More I Love You's," Noah's theme song. Listening to it, I could almost feel him in my arms as we danced around the living room. So many people rose to share that the pastors finally had to cut it off. I wished they hadn't. What else did I have to do? Nothing is sweeter to hear in your longing for your child than the memories people have of him and how he touched their lives. But the sweetest thing of all was hearing his name spoken again and again. Noah. Noah. Noah. After this day, it would not be spoken much anymore. People would never know if they should say his name or not, afraid it would hurt us. I wanted to shout it from the rooftops for the world to hear and change the church bells to ring it out—No-ah!

The day after the funeral Andy dug a hole in Noah's new garden. The sound of lawn mowers could be heard cutting grass in neighboring yards as we prepared to do a little gardening ourselves, like we might on any sunny Saturday. Only this was to be a bit different from the usual. I approached the freezer with my big silver bread bowl and began fishing around between the frozen vegetables, filling it with a heavy sigh. Then slowly, I began to cut open all the eight-ounce plastic bags filled with perfectly proportioned servings of breast milk that I'd so lovingly and industriously pumped for my baby. I squeezed out their frozen and slushy contents until my fingers grew numb.

"Look at all this waste," I said to Andy as he entered the kitchen. Then I opened the white plastic container sweating in the sink and added the final ingredient to my concoction—Noah's frozen placenta, which floated in the middle of the milky punch like a misshapen ice ring.

Hugging the bowl, I carried my offering out front to the garden.

While a few people gathered around and Andy leaned on his shovel, I carefully poured the contents into the thirsty hole, and we planted Noah's birth tree, a star magnolia, as the voice of Natalie Merchant seasoned the warm air with "Noah's Dove." Star magnolia, with its profusion of star-shaped white flowers, is one of the first trees to announce spring, and I welcomed its blooms each year as it ushered in the season of growth as it had when we brought Noah home from the hospital. We did our best to rise to this unwanted occasion with some degree of grace, and to try to make sense of the unfathomable acts we suddenly found ourselves performing, making it all up as we went along.

That night in a rare quiet moment, I collapsed into my rocking chair, tired of talking and performing for people and happy to be alone to think about my son for a minute. Our friend had made us a fountain with water spilling over rocks on which she'd carved Noah's names and the dates of his birth and death, and it sat on the table next to me where it replaced the sounds of my son gulping his milk with its own gurgling noises. I closed my eyes and listened to the soothing sounds of water, my empty arms missing my nursing son. I knew that Noah's eyes would have widened with glee at the temptation of all that water within his reach, as well as those bite-size stones, and I wished with all of my heart that I did not have these terrible new interior-decorating options.

I opened my eyes and looked across the room, where I noticed a bouquet of huge sunflowers perched on the fireplace ledge that ran around the white brick wall that separated our living and dining rooms. Someone in the steady stream of people in and out of our house had put the bright yellow flowers in a large earthenware pitcher and set them there, their droopy round faces impossibly large for their stems and their heads bowed as if in supplication or sorrow. On the bookcase shelf above the flowers, I could see a framed Christmas photo of the kids sitting where the flowers now wept, as I liked to pose them there on the white surface. Before Noah, I'd kept a profusion of houseplants on this ledge, but Noah loved to climb up and walk along it, so I'd cleared it off for him, knowing that otherwise he'd knock over everything in his path. I thought to myself, *If Noah was here, we could never put those sunflowers there*, and just then, the pitcher toppled over with a crash, spraying water and flowers everywhere.

"Andy, come here and look!" I called.

Andy rushed into the room, took one wise look, and we both said, "Noah!" in unison. We knew immediately at some visceral level by the unbroken pitcher and the puddle of water reaching toward us that this was the work of our son. And the three of us had a good laugh together.

On Sunday, Andy opened the *Statesman Journal* and discovered an article headlined, "Noah's Voyage on Earth Touches Many Lives with Joy and Grief," written by a reporter who had attended our funeral, unbeknownst to us. It began, "Noah Patrick Moore Kittel, with light red hair and sturdy legs still new to the business of walking, was radiant, energetic, a joy to those who loved him. But maybe 'was' isn't the right word. Even now, in the deepest grief parents can know, Andrew and Kelly Kittel are sure of this: The youngest of their four children, taken from them a week ago, is still present, imparting strength, helping to sustain them." I read these words and was relieved that others were paying attention. I clutched this stranger's writing like a big, fat sunflower stem and felt a little less alone, a little less wayward.

Chapter Eleven

Slowly, PEOPLE STARTED to trickle back to their homes and lives, and we five who wanted to be six were left only with each other to cling to. We had become like Noah. We had to learn to crawl and then stand and then walk all over again.

As the busyness gradually subsided, I wanted to call everyone back and say that here, now, this quiet anguish was what we really needed help with. All those arrangements, ceremonies, food, drinks, and plantings they had helped us with were just distractions, the easy part. This was the hard part. If only you could be here now—now when we are forced to stand still and take stock and keep coming up one short. One little bundle of joy was gone from us, and we were crippled by his absence. Burying Noah, it turned out, was easy. Living without him became the hard part.

This was the real grief work. We learned right away that this task could not be avoided. We could not procrastinate and leave it for another day, hard as it was; its lurking presence was too compelling. Grief is demanding and all-consuming. We tried to pay attention, to keep up. It took all our time and energy, and we were incapable of doing much else.

Andy and I and the kids continued to cling to each other for support. We talked and sang and tried to laugh. We scanned the skies for rainbows and cared for each other desperately. But every morning was like waking up gasping from a nightmare with your heart in your throat, a scream in your lungs, and fear in your belly, but without having that moment of intense relief when you realize it was all just a dream. This was not a dream, not even a bad one. It was a living nightmare.

Mimi always said to us when we got hurt, "You can stand any pain as long as you know it's not forever." We would pick our childhood selves up, wipe off the blood, and carry on playing with her words in our ears. But no colorful Band-Aid could cover this forever agony. Every day I would have small panic attacks whenever my kids were outside and I heard a car engine. Every time I got in a car and backed up, I would have to relive that day. Every time I looked at a Tahoe or even just a tire or a blueberry muffin, it all came screaming back. I knew that even the most benign day could turn bad, suddenly, when you were least expecting it. And I prayed we'd never have to do anything like this, ever again.

Cody called one day in those terrible weeks after the accident. "My insurance agent is coming to meet with us tomorrow at two," she said. As usual, she rattled off what she wanted to say, gave a final "okay," her substitute for "good-bye," and then hung up before I could register it all and respond. At the time of the accident, we had given our auto-insurance information to the hospitals since we didn't know what else to do, and they'd billed our insurance company directly. Our policy covered all of the medical expenses up to $25,000. After that, we would have to tap into the Martins' policy.

Andy and I showed up at Cody's the next day, as instructed. The insurance adjustor sat at a round glass table in an anteroom off the kitchen and took a tape-recorded statement from everyone involved. Andy went first, and I sat on a stool in the kitchen, waiting. He had a degree in finance, so I usually let him handle the numbers while I managed the letters in our life. I was half listening for the most part but heard him say, "We want to keep this strictly within the family, nothing legal." As if on cue, Cody bustled in and took a seat next to him at the table. Cally had already given her statement and left the room by then.

"I'm prepared to give you a check for $10,000 today to help with incoming bills," the gal said, her eyeglasses magnifying her kindness, or perhaps it was pity.

"Okay," he said. Bills were starting to trickle in, and the ambulance alone had cost almost this much.

"The extent of this policy is $100,000 for each occurrence, $10,000 for medical, and $2,500 for other expenses," she informed him, flipping her blond hair and turning to include me in her gaze. "I'm also prepared to offer you this full amount today."

"Oh, that won't be necessary," Cody interjected from across the table. "We'll deal with this as a family, and I'll make sure all their bills are covered." She smiled quickly as if to ensure the lady of her sincerity, then turned to Andy and said, "I'll handle all the receipts, so give me anything you have and I'll submit them for reimbursement." Cody had arranged for the cremation and burial services since her friend worked at the cemetery next door to us, and she had already submitted those receipts for reimbursement from her policy. Red flags started waving and I tried to pay attention, but both Andy and I were a bit blinded by the whole situation.

"Well, you think about it, and I'll contact you later," the insurance agent concluded, handing Andy a check for the lesser amount and her business card. Putting anything and everything off sounded good to us just then, and we agreed.

As the days and weeks went by, we received a hillside full of plants for Noah's garden. Instead of playing with Noah on his quilt, we had a baby-blanket rose to prune and smell. We had a new pear tree with four kinds of pears grafted onto it, one for each of our children, only three of whom could eat them. After Noah's funeral we had all convened at our cemetery plot, where we'd sprinkled Noah's ashes in a hole in which we'd planted a second tree, a sweet gum, one of the finest trees in the Oregon autumn for its lovely reddish-orange color that reminded me of Noah's hair and seemed like a fitting choice. But even then I couldn't bear to part with all of him and had saved a portion of his ashes. And so we zealously planted Noah everywhere we could. The Catholic church built a new sanctuary, and we planted his ashes with a new ash tree, of all things, by the front door. Our

Methodist church designed a new garden and we sprinkled more of his ashes there while planting a tupelo tree, which reminded me of sweet Tupelo honey, as did the honey locust tree we planted on the coast for him. But the elk apparently agreed that the locust tasted sweet, and they ate it.

We received hundreds of cards and thousands of dollars in donations to Noah's garden and memorial fund, along with promises of support in whatever ways we needed it. Thanks to the generosity of our friends and neighbors, we had meals delivered for months so I didn't have to cook. But we didn't eat much anyway.

Donations were given in his memory to many charities, and masses were held around the globe in his honor. We paid our bill to the ambulance company, and as a gift in Noah's memory they sent us a letter saying, "We are dedicating a new child-size immobilizer in Noah's name." I hoped they would never have to use it. His godparents had a star named for him in the night sky near Taurus, his zodiac constellation. Friends put together a book fund, and to the library we donated books he had loved and others I would have loved to have read to him, each with a bookplate surrounded by a Noah's ark border, depicting something he would never be—a small boy lying on his stomach with his legs crossed, reading. Our friend expanded the back deck of our house: now it was the perfect place for Noah to cruise around on his new ride-on toys, which lay in the yard on their sides, unused.

In the days after the accident, Chris's cousin had offered to arrange a group counseling session for everyone who was involved. Cody resisted, but as the busywork subsided and I had more time to focus on the questions of that terrible day, I was willing to entertain some answers, thinking I'd feel better.

So, one afternoon in August, Andy, Hannah, and I headed downtown to the large office of a professional counselor where Chris, Cody, Cally, Cassi, and Chane were already waiting. The counselor had the long dark hair and dark skin of some Middle Eastern culture but spoke without an accent when she made some general remarks about grief and our situation. Then she explained the ground rules for the afternoon: everyone was to take their turn speaking about that day and what had happened from their perspective. We sat in folding chairs in a circle, and the clock ticked on the wall as the story unfolded bit by bit. The chain of events was described by each person, but it did not make me feel better. In fact, it made it all much, much worse.

"I decided not to take the kids to the beach," Cally said when it was her turn. She looked down at the floor. "I told them I was going to take them up the river to Hootenanny to swim instead."

My brain lurched at this revelation and I stared at her in horror, but her eyes would not meet mine. I looked at Cody to see her response but she, too, had her gaze locked down, staring at her favorite tan Clarks sandals as if they contained all the answers. As far as I knew, Cally had not asked permission from any of the adults to take the kids swimming upriver, and none of us were even aware of this change of plans. She had requested and received our permission to take our kids to the beach, which meant playing in the sand or in the shallow stream, and we were all acting accordingly. I remembered Andy's near-drowning story and shuddered. This explained a few things, like why Micah had wanted his life jacket so badly. Cally had told him to get it, and I had insisted he didn't need it. He thought he was going swimming at Hootenanny. Since he was not able to explain himself, in his four-year-old frustration he'd broken down in a temper tantrum instead.

"I was cleaning out the china closet," Cody said, "and Noah kept getting into everything, so I put him outside in the carport and told Hannah to watch him."

This, too, was a shock to me, and I closed my eyes, as if to stop myself from seeing the complete picture as all the pieces fell into place and crushed me with comprehension in my folding chair. So that finally explained how Noah had gotten outside. His Auntie Cody had put him there and told seven-year-old Hannah to watch him while I was at the clothesline with Micah, and Andy, who had returned from the cabin, was in the back bedroom setting up the porta-crib for Noah's nap.

"Aunt Cody told me to watch Noah," Hannah said when it was her turn, and I felt her pain as her voice cracked, remembering the special bond she'd shared with Noah since the night of his birth. "But then Cally yelled at me from the car to go get my bathing suit on if I wanted to go swimming, so I ran into the house to change." She burst into silent tears, and Andy reached his long arm around her shoulders to comfort her.

"Cally told me to get out of the car and check to make sure nothing was behind us," eleven-year-old Chane said, sobbing. "So I did. I didn't know…"

My heart broke again and again, hearing each link connect the chain of events for the first time. Once again, Cally had exerted her will over our children, failing to obtain our consent. Noah's death was the result of yet one more battle for respect and authority in the war Andy and I kept finding ourselves fighting—the war to retain control over our own children. But whereas it used to only puzzle us, we could now see it had a more frightening dimension. There was no way we would have let Cally take the kids to the swimming hole by herself, especially the day after I'd listened to Andy's near-drowning story. And if she'd asked for permission, the chain would have been broken. They couldn't all swim, and it was too dangerous. But she was her mother's daughter, and another of her mother's mottoes rang in my ears: "It's easier to ask forgiveness than permission."

And once again my sister-in-law had proven that she was going to show me who was the boss, putting Noah out of her way because she wasn't going to watch him. That was my job. Her words from the time of sharing memories at Noah's funeral came roaring back into my head. She had stood in front of our friends and family and told them how she was admiring his little green sandals on that fateful Sunday and how he was stomping on his spilled Cheerios and sliding in them. "And I wasn't going to pick them up. I was going to let his mother do it. And she did it!" she'd said, laughing on the altar next to Noah's ashes, as if me doing my job, picking up after my kids, was so unusual.

And poor, poor Hannah. Born on a Wednesday, Hannah's fate, according to the nursery rhyme, was to be "full of woe," but I prayed for her sake that it was wrong. I remembered how the finger of blame for Marcella's accident had pointed to Micah, and I prayed it wasn't digging Hannah in the ribs for this one. I knew how much she tried to win Cally's favor and knew by then that Christiana—always their chosen favorite—was sitting in the car with Chane and Cally.

It all made me sick to my soul and filled me with despair and pain and anger, because the innocent victim of all these human frailties and control dramas was Noah. His parents were pre-occupied. His aunt was frustrated with him and felt the need to prove her point to her sister-in-law, me. His cousin was bossing his siblings around, preparing to defy his parents by taking them swimming. Accidents do happen. But attitudes are no accident.

Chapter Twelve

W AY BACK IN JULY we'd made reservations to fly to Chicago for a Peace Corps friend's wedding later in August. As the date approached, we debated whether or not to go, but in the end we decided to attend, needing some distance from everything, our neighbors included. I hated leaving the kids behind, but their Aunt Phoebe volunteered to watch them at her house near Portland, and we drove them up on our way to the airport. Phoebe had a pool, and they liked going there. "They probably need a break from Salem, too," I said to Andy.

We had a great time seeing our old friends from our carefree Peace Corps days, laughing and drinking rum and playing manically in a brief respite from our grief. We needed that physical and emotional release, and if we appeared to be a little crazy to anyone, it's because we were. At the wedding reception, the familiar beats of reggae and Jamaican dancehall music brought us all back to happier times, and we lived in the past for a few days, barely mentioning the present. "If you can walk, you can dance," I thought, dancing my heart out with my soul mate in the same moss-colored dress I'd worn to bury our son.

A few days after we returned home, I walked out to the mailbox to find several beautiful cards from the friends we'd just seen, each bearing some version of the same message: "I wanted to talk about your loss but was unsure of what to say, so simply said nothing." I dropped the cards on the kitchen counter for Andy to read and went back outside to water Noah's garden. I thought about our friends and their cards and how our family was becoming less human and more reptilian, chameleonlike: Andy and I and even the kids were developing the new skill of sizing up a person or situation instantly and reacting accordingly. With some people we could lay our souls on the carpet and examine them thoroughly. With others we knew we had to shelter them from the terrible reality that was our life and protect them from our pain. Some fell in between—they could start to go in deep with a hug or a word or two but would soon feel discomfort, switching to talk about the weather or something equally benign. We became instant readers of people. Sometimes we got it wrong, but we also became quite good at comforting others and telling them it was all right. Even though it wasn't. People thought we were so brave and strong and admired us for that. And this was true of us, sometimes. But we knew that most people could not handle the full truth. We clung to those who could and would not let them go. And we will remain forever grateful for them.

I appreciated the cards I'd just received, just as I appreciated any time a person made a well-intended effort. A word lover all my life, I now fully realized that words, indeed, can be most inadequate for expressing some feelings, a struggle that people acknowledged over and over in their cards. We received moving messages of love and comfort—even from people we had known only professionally or peripherally before our loss. The utter tragedy of Noah's death caused people to drop their guard, tear down the walls of separation, open their hearts, and pour out the contents in an amazingly powerful show of connectivity. Noah's death forced people to reexamine their lives and served as a reminder to focus on what's really important—loving one another.

And when some of the people we'd expected to be present for us were disappointingly absent or silent, instead of getting hung up on why they weren't there for us, we learned to shift our focus to the legions of strangers who showed up unexpectedly and were a presence to be counted on. In many ways, their efforts held so much more meaning for us because they came from the realm of the unanticipated, which was becoming a more familiar place to us.

I gave Noah's star magnolia tree a thorough soaking, then moved along his new stone wall, admiring the flowers blooming where there used to be only dirt and a few ugly bushes. I am often lost in thought and easily startled, and so I was when Cody said, "Hey." I hadn't seen her approach from across the sport court and had barely recovered when out of the blue, she announced, "I'm not selling the Tahoe, Kelly." Then she turned and walked away, making it clear this was not a topic for conversation. Stunned, I dropped the watering wand, staring at her back as she marched home. I shut off the water and went in the house in tears to find Andy reading the cards, and I told him what had just happened.

"What?" he said, getting up to hug me. "That's really weird."

"I know, and you know what? I'm never riding in that Tahoe again."

I cringed at the sight of that SUV in those mind-numbing days, trying to push it out of my mind as it dragged me right back under the terrible tires of August 10. We'd never mentioned it, but clearly Cody had done some thinking. Now that she had my attention, though, I was absolutely unnerved by her vehemence. Why on earth had she chosen to walk over and announce this to me? And how could she consider keeping that vehicle? In the nine years I'd known Cody, she'd been in two minor accidents with two different vans. "That van has bad karma," she'd said, selling them as quickly as possible following each incident. "I would never keep a car that was in an accident," she avowed. And she hadn't. Until now.

Now, not only did I have to look at that Tahoe every day parked in her driveway across from my house, but I also had to watch my niece driving it and washing it, as usual. Cally wasn't punished or restricted in any way that we were ever aware of for her role in Noah's death and apparently felt no reluctance to drive that car, or any other, afterward. This blew our minds. We wondered if the consequences would have been more serious if she'd been caught speeding or had a minor fender bender.

"If that Tahoe has this effect on me, how can they possibly be so nonchalant about it?" I asked Andy. "I want to move to a place with no cars." I never much liked cars, preferring to bike or walk. I had fantasies of smashing that Tahoe with a sledgehammer, but I didn't dare speak them out loud. I lay in bed some nights visualizing myself getting up, marching up the street, and slashing those oversize tires that took my son's life. Seeing that Tahoe from my kitchen window was like looking at August 10 all over again every day of my life. It was killing me. But I couldn't figure out what kind of tool to use, and just the getting-out-of-bed part of my fantasy overwhelmed me.

Labor Day weekend rolled around, and Andy suggested we go to his parents' house on the coast. For me, any fond memories I had of that place were eclipsed by August 10, 1997, and I never wanted to go there again as long as I lived. For Andy, it was a place that was layered with years and years of memories. It would always be his childhood home. When Noah died, Andy's mom had lamented, "Now you will never come visit us." I was ready to prove her right.

"We'll come, too," said Phoebe, who was babysitting our nieces across the street for the weekend while Cody and Chris had gone somewhere. Initially I was repulsed by the idea of them joining us, but then I sucked it up and thought maybe it would be a step on the path toward healing for Cally and me. For the most part since the accident, our paths had not intersected, and neither of us had sought out the other. I was still reeling from the counseling session discoveries. But Cally refused to go. Andy went over to try to talk to her, but she wrapped herself in a blanket and wouldn't speak to anyone. "Go away," she said. So Phoebe and the girls all stayed home.

I wanted to wrap myself in a blanket and clam up also. But to please my husband, I capitulated. And off I went to prove myself to my mother-in-law.

I hated almost every minute of our stay. Everywhere I looked there were reminders of the last time we'd been there, only a few weeks ago. The cabin, the clothesline, the china cabinet, the porta-crib we'd left behind, the dreaded spot in the dusty driveway, the warm grass where I'd laid Noah down for the last time and tried to make him breathe again. Even those fluffy chicks, one of whom had since been taken by a bald eagle. Everywhere I turned something punched me in the stomach and bruised my soul.

On Sunday we planted a rosebush where Noah had lain in the grass, but it never took root and ultimately died, too, the irony of which was not lost on me. I tried to come to terms with the beginning of the rest of my life, and one sunny moment that afternoon I collapsed into a chair in the backyard, exhausted by my efforts to avoid seeing and feeling everything around me.

"Come sit with me," I said to my three sweaty kids, gathering them into my lap and remembering their smiling faces all crowded into the hospital chair on the day they met Noah for the first time. *I will have to be Noah in this photo*, I thought, and with that idea I started thinking as if I were. We all looked around us quietly at first, not sure what we were going to do next but comforted by the presence of one another. We looked at the field stretching toward the river.

"Look at the trees, Mom," Hannah said.

The crowns of the fir trees surrounding us pointed like arrows toward the sky, drawing our silent gazes until slowly we found our voices and began talking about Noah.

"They must have been what Noah saw, too, when his spirit first left his body," I said.

As our minds allowed us to remember, we began telling one another the story of how Noah had left us, describing how he must have risen up above us just a little bit at first, seeing us all around his body holding hands and praying while our hearts were being crushed like his by the weight of our love for him.

"He saw us crying," Christiana added, and we all agreed that he would have seen our tears of anguish and frustration.

"He didn't want to leave us," I agreed, "and he would have known we didn't want him to go and that we were trying our best to keep him with us. But he knew he had to leave, so he would have risen up a little more, and he would have seen the field with the cows and the baby chicks."

"We showed him those chicks," Micah added, and we all remembered Noah's pointer finger feeling their soft feathers.

"He would have seen the river flowing by," I continued. "He would have risen up a little higher, and he would have seen all the trees growing so straight and tall around Grandpa's farm. He would have risen higher still, peeking over the hills to the ocean and that little stream we played in, remember?"

I thought of the waves breaking on the sand and washing away the footprints from our last beach walk together.

"He was covered in ice cream," Hannah said.

"He would have seen all this," we said, each knowing for ourselves that Noah would have smiled his radiant smile as his beautiful soul was magnified and became one with all that he could see.

We cried and hugged each other as we told ourselves the saddest story we knew, but afterward I felt a little more peaceful in my soul, and our shoulders all lifted a bit. Somehow, something in what we discovered together that day spoke to us and made sense as we began to find the answers to the question "Where did Noah go, Mommy?" Looking at it from Noah's perspective, there was a lot of beauty and peace. Noah had become a part of the trees, the wind, the waters around us. The only problem was that we were not with him. We were all on our own journeys.

And so, just like I tuned in to what my kids were doing here on Earth in my daily Game of Life, I also began to play "Who's in Heaven?" Every day, I picked up the paper and turned immediately to the obituary column to see who was joining Noah. *Surely*, I thought, *Mimi has found her redheaded baby by now*. I imagined Noah graduating from some sort of newcomer's club or freshman orientation.

On August 31, a few Sundays after Noah left, the world reeled at the sudden, tragic death of Princess Diana. I wondered if Noah would be lining up to bow at her arrival in heaven while massive crowds here on Earth lined up to say good-bye. We'd been so consumed with raising our young family and burying our son that we'd missed all the tabloid drama of Diana's fairy-tale love affair and summer vacations on sleek yachts in the South of France. There were rumors of engagement rings and wedding plans, but now all nonrefundable deposits were lost, everything cancelled, while the lovers joined our son.

Viktor Frankl lived ninety-two years and joined Noah and the

Princess on the second day of September. His book *Man's Search for Meaning* had a great impact on me. Frankl survived four Nazi camps and determined that the Nazis could take everything away from him but his own sense of himself and his attitude and purpose in life. He spent his life teaching that "we must never forget that we may also find meaning in life even when confronted with a hopeless situation." I clung to his words and hoped Noah got to spend some time learning from this wise man.

Mother Teresa arrived in Heaven on September 5, and I imagined she had a lot to discuss with Mobutu Sese Seko, the exiled and now expired leader of Zaire, who'd already had his kingdom right here on earth, ruling in a leopard-skin hat and stealing most of his billions from the mouths of his starving subjects. I believe hell is right here on earth, and I loved to picture him coming clean at last with Mother Teresa in some celestial garden while Noah ran around them, playing under Mimi's watchful eye.

Meanwhile, here on earth, school started. Hannah entered the third grade and Christiana began kindergarten. Most people knew of us and of our tragedy, and each social encounter entangled us in an obligation from which we had to extricate ourselves, which was enough to keep me sequestered at home some days. But I mustered my courage, and we entered the school on that bright first morning with fake smiles and heavy hearts. As I stood in the kindergarten class, my new friend, Cindy, approached. She and I had met at kindergarten orientation in July, where Noah had played with her son, Trevor, while Christiana and her other son, Jonathan, learned what to expect in their school debut. I'd liked her immediately and anticipated many happy playdates for our smallest boys. "Where's Noah?" she asked, smiling.

"Oh, you don't know," I started to say, losing the battle to fight back my tears.

"Come on," she said, taking my arm and leading me into the empty hallway.

We sat down on the stairs, and I managed to exhale, "Noah died."

Our souls connected instantly in a wave of grief and gratitude when she responded with two simple words that spoke volumes.

These were not the usual two I'd expected to hear on this day, the two words I was so sick of hearing—"I'm sorry"—but two new words I had not yet heard and that I received like a lifeline. "I understand," she said. "My son, Will, died of leukemia several years ago." My heart lightened instantly. We wouldn't be getting our smallest sons together for playdates, but she became a source of great comfort and kinship to me from there on out.

The bills were mounting, and we were barely treading water. The bill collectors and IRS don't care if your son has died. They might say, "I'm so sorry," but they want your monthly payments and your tax returns all the same. The world went on turning, and people went on with their lives and expected us to function, too. How long can you tell people, "My son has died, so pardon me for fill-in-the-blank"? Some days I could be found sitting in my van at a green light staring off into space and forgetting to go; other days I might be frozen with forgetfulness in the grocery store checkout line by the sudden intrusion of a memory of my baby—like blueberry muffins. We still encountered road rage and checkout-line impatience and all of the myriad public annoyances everyone faces on a daily basis. I wanted to scream or cry or wear a sign saying, "Back off, my son just died."

Cody kept asking for our receipts to submit to her insurance agent until finally the red flags came into focus and we realized that "handling this as a family" meant she was trying to control what got paid from her insurance policy, limiting any checks we were written to the exact amounts of the bills we paid, and submitting her own invoices for reimbursement. Cody had not offered to pay for anything out of her own pocket, and if we'd continued to follow her "receipts only" instructions, we would have received no incidental payment for our loss, our pain, our suffering, or any future expenses.

"You know what? We don't need to negotiate anything with her," Andy said one day as the fog of grief that enveloped us began to lift a bit. He called the insurance agent and told her we'd accept the full amount she'd offered, no receipts required. The insurance company immediately released a check to us after we signed away all future rights to litigate, putting that matter behind us and thinking that would be one more step in moving on. We had no interest in suing anyone, no interest in making anything worse than it already was, no interest in anything that felt like we were somehow profiting from Noah's death. No amount of money could equate to Noah's life or assuage our pain. We wanted only to pay our debts, and accepting the insurance payment even enabled us to pay off a loan Andy had from Cody.

Photographs from that time bear witness to our new survivor look—gaunt with wounded, oversized eyes. I still wasn't eating much and hadn't returned to Jazzercise, but Becki offered to help me can tomatoes that fall and I agreed, happy to assert my independence, happy to have the canners whistling away on my own stove, happy to avoid yet another battle in the Great Tomato War.

Cody called one day to ask, "Do you want to walk?" I'd said no most of the times she'd asked but consented this time, hoping she'd take a break from asking for a while if I went. All conversations ultimately seemed to head right back to her parents' driveway in August, and sure enough, as we walked along Commercial Street, she drove down that path once again. "So I don't get it—where was Noah standing?" She wanted to talk about the accident over and over and kept trying to figure out how it had happened, revisiting every little detail of my nightmare until I wanted to take off running. Noah had suffered from regular ear infections, and I'd pulled many all-nighters in the previous year, rocking him in the living room, sacrificing my sleep for his, and wishing I could go to bed. But now that I could, I still didn't sleep well, and on top of that, I felt sick to my stomach every morning when I awoke. I didn't want to chat about the worst day of my life while I struggled daily and nightly not to keep reliving in my mind what my eyes had seen on that day.

Cody seemed to think the car and the angles of the tires and where Noah was standing presented some interesting trigonometric for which she needed to find the cosine or tangent. But I disliked math, especially this kind. I started to think that she doubted what had happened, what we had all heard in our one family counseling session. She kept trying to rework the equation, making the events of August 10 add up to some brand-new sum that it simply was not. A plus B equals Noah is dead. Period. I kept finding more and more excuses not to take our walks, even though she continued to prove just how difficult it was to "avoid the ones you don't like."

They say there are five stages of grief, but I didn't find grief to follow a linear progression. Indeed, this five-stages theory seemed an idealistic simplification of an intensely personal and chaotic process—a feeble attempt to rationalize the irrational and subdue a maelstrom into a neat step-by-step guide. Grief is a crazy thing that makes you sick in every quadrant of your being: mentally, physically, emotionally, and spiritually. And it arrives in waves and circles, not in goose-stepping lines—otherwise you might be able to sidestep it. On some days it hits from all sides simultaneously and lays you low; on others it eases up and maybe only makes your belly ache and your appetite disappear. Maybe you cry all day. Or maybe you can muster a smile when you feel like crying. Certainly you feel the classic denial, anger, bargaining, depression, and acceptance stages described by Kübler-Ross, but you also feel many others that are indescribable.

Our kids seemed to be weathering the storm better than us and we often turned to them for comfort and even guidance. Being closer to creation, they had an innate understanding that Andy and I had forgotten. And whereas we had amassed all kinds of plans and expectations for our lives and were therefore crippled by so much damned disappointment, they simply did not expect life to be any different. They still had their moments of grappling with the eternal questions of life and death. And they did get angry sometimes and cry out in voices that broke our hearts anew.

"He was only a baby, we never really heard him talk," Hannah cried.

"I think he's in his crib when I get up in the morning," Christiana said, "but he's not there. But he is here, Mom, he's our angel on our shoulders."

"I miss Nowee," Micah sighed.

Grief is like standing immobile in front of a whirling dervish. And in that cyclone is every emotion there ever was. And at any given moment one of those emotions will stick out its muscled arm and punch you in the stomach or the heart or wherever you might feel it most, splitting open old wounds like a professional boxer. Some days you see the strike coming and manage to receive only a glancing blow, and other times it catches you off guard, connecting suddenly and completely, and you find yourself in some strange dark place doubled over with pain, clutching your belly.

They say when you lose your parents you lose your past; when you lose your spouse you lose your present; when you lose your child you lose your future. Thankfully, I didn't yet know about the first two and was very grateful for that. But the last is true. Not only do you lose your child, but you lose all those things you imagined yourselves doing together in the near and distant future, and you have to grieve the loss of each of those anticipated events and the loss of your child anew each time one of those events rolls around. There are inevitable questions about which is worse, losing a child when they are very young and you have not had so much time with them, or losing them later when they have been a part of your life longer. Is it better to have more or fewer memories, photos, experiences, children's drawings, Mother's Day cards, and haircut remnants to mourn? People might tend to perceive that one or the other would be worse depending on their own circumstances, but the cold, hard truth is this: *There is no good time to lose a child.*

And there is no good *way*, either. It is all unfair and unwanted, and you feel cheated and mad and incredibly sad. And responsible. And helpless. As a parent you have failed at the most basic level. You have failed to protect your child from death, be it accidental or not. You couldn't prevent those cancer cells from forming and you couldn't prevent that vehicle from backing up. You ask the entire spectrum of whys and why nots and what ifs, and you beat yourself up endlessly until you come to understand that we are not in control of everything. In fact, we are not in control of anything. Period. You would lay down your own life for your child. You would take his pain for your own, give anything and everything you have for him, including your place here on earth. But nobody asked you for your sacrifice; no one warned you that it was time to run outside and change places with him.

I blamed myself endlessly—for going to the coast instead of camping, for inviting Cally, for vacuuming, for arguing with Micah, for insisting Noah's porta-crib be in the house, for not being right next to him every second of his life, for not bursting through the wall to save him from that tire. Andy blamed himself for cutting lumber, for taking the job that forced him to be at the coast cutting wood on that weekend, for not protecting Noah, for being his father, for everything. Blame is a natural thing, but it's still hard to swallow. We lost a lot of confidence in ourselves and in our abilities—confidence that we would never fully regain, even though it seemed that if we could survive this, everything else in life would be easy.

But if you were going to change the chain of events that killed your child, where would you begin? How far back would you go? All the way back to their birth? And how many times had you saved your child's life without even realizing how close you'd just come to disaster, to being one link too late in a chain of events that would wrap around your neck and choke you forever? How close had you come to knowing this place—the place where you collapse on your knees with one fist in your belly and the other clutching a blue GAP bag containing your baby's ruined clothes, the place from which there is no going back?

The Book of Jonah

Chapter One

WHEN ONE MONTH had passed without Noah, I discovered a tiny vote of confidence clinging to my uterine wall. It grew daily, making me slightly nauseous but reminding me that hope accompanied our despair. In the gravelly depths of my womb, a new alevin had started its journey to join us.

In the days after Noah's death, Andy and I had lain in bed and wondered aloud, "Do you think we can ever have another brother for Micah?" Not that the girls weren't also missing their brother, but they still had each other to play Barbies with, while Micah had lost his truck-and-train-loving playmate. Both of us were too overcome by the present to take any deliberate action for the future. I rubbed my skinny arms. "I don't know. I just don't know," we each said, too unsure of ourselves to make any kind of decision, any plans for the future, this one included.

And so, wasted and sick with grief, I was gobsmacked to discover that life had taken hold inside of me, like a fragile lichen clinging to a cold piece of granite—just as we, too, clung to each other. I fingered my protruding hip bones, astonished that they encased a vital womb when I felt more like Arctic tundra. Making love was one of the many things that reminded us of August 10, and for me it usually evoked a new reaction—spontaneous tears; perhaps they had been watering this new growth all along. The promise of life so soon after Noah's death implied that maybe we had a future. I cradled my delicious secret, this glimmer of hope, this glimpse of a rainbow.

"It's a miracle," Andy said when I told him the news, as surprised as I was that our grief-racked bodies were capable of creating new life. He hadn't always been overjoyed to hear the news that I was pregnant, so I was relieved that we felt the same this time. After the funeral, people had written their remembrances to Noah in his baby book, and now the words Andy's brother, Joe, had inscribed came back to me from one of the pages: *Good thing your dad didn't get the Big V.* At the time I'd found his comment completely inappropriate. I didn't remind Andy how close he'd come to precluding this event, but now I agreed with Joe. It was a good thing, after all.

We planned a memorial service for Noah in October for the benefit of our East Coast friends and family, and as we were making our arrangements to fly east, Cody announced to Andy, "Cally and I want to come to Maine, too."

"Oh, why do they have to come?" I asked Andy when he came home and told me. "I really just wanted to be away from them for a little while."

"I guess they want to show everyone that we're all in this together," he said, though after only one month it was becoming less and less clear that we were.

"Do you want them to come?" I asked.

"Well, she didn't exactly ask me," he said. I had pictured us taking long walks through the woods, healing under the earthy spell of fall foliage and home. Nowhere in my vision were my overbearing sister-in-law and my blanket-wrapped niece. But, as usual, Cody wasn't asking for permission, and I didn't know how to march on up to her house and tell her not to come under the watchful eyes of my polite ancestors. So they came, and Phoebe and Chane also flew out with them.

Even though none of my family has lived in Wayne permanently for several generations now, it's still where we go to be baptized, to play, to boat, to swim, to fish, to eat corn, to pick apples, to get married…and to be buried. The Sleeper bench marks our family plot, where Mimi and Grandpa have their final resting place alongside Minnie and Herbert, Mimi's parents. Every year as children we were made to sit on the granite couch, squinting into the sun while my mother took our pictures to mark our growth—and how the plots had filled up around us. In Minnie's day, the cemetery overlooked the waters of Lake Androscoggin, but pine trees have grown up to block that view. Like so many things on that hillside, the lake shimmers only in the imagination, just beyond the screen of pine needles.

When this unwanted opportunity presented itself, I thought it would be nice to add some shade to the Sleeper bench for the generations of squinters yet to come by planting a tree on the corner of the family plot along with some of Noah's ashes. There was plenty of room, and I loved the idea of having Noah's remains alongside Mimi and Grandpa and his ancestors while his soul met them all beyond the pine needles. Hadn't I sent my son off on his helicopter ride with instructions to go and find Mimi? I was comforted to think that Noah was with her now.

When we lived next door to them, Mimi and Grandpa always made time for me, and whenever I could, I ran over and said, "Can we play our game?" Grandpa was usually in the living room, sitting in his leather recliner next to a crystal dish of Brach's chocolate stars watching sports on TV, and Mimi was usually in the kitchen with her apron on. They rarely refused me. I would wait in the kitchen with Mimi while Grandpa hid a coin for me in the living room. Then, he'd call me in, and if I found it, I could keep it. Out in the kitchen while we waited, Mimi bounced me on her knee, singing "Ride a cock horse to Banbury Cross." She called me "Kelly-o-yu-kalarney-yu-kalay." She'd been a Physical Education teacher back when that included playing the piano while her students and, later, I marched along swinging our trunks like elephants and prancing like high-stepping ponies. She had a repertoire of songs and games that could keep me entertained for hours.

"I'm thinking of something . . . blue." Her blue eyes twinkled at mine while Grandpa took his time hiding the coin, which I now understand was probably his way of keeping me out of his hair so he could watch his game. My dad's father died on Christmas Eve a month after I was born in November (the day before Mimi's birthday), so this was the only grandpa I ever knew. I loved him absolutely. And it broke my seven-year-old heart when he died.

My mother agreed that her family plot would be the place for Noah and embraced the idea of planting a tree there. "I'll tell Uncle Don," she said and casually mentioned it to her brother one day while they were walking home from the beach at the lake, where he had a cabin next door to ours.

"No!" He surprised her with his vehemence. "I don't want any tree roots growing through my body."

Mom eventually recovered her speech and talked with the cemetery keeper, who discovered there was an empty space two plots over. So Mom and Dad bought their own piece of real estate and added a gravestone in the shape of a book, engraved with the words we all knew by heart, words her Grandmother, Minnie, had written in her genealogy book: "To live in the hearts of those we leave behind is not to die." A book. Which was exactly how I'd learned to define death when I met it for the first time.

Everyone said, "He died in his sleep—what a blessing."

But I always wondered if my beloved Grandpa's eyes had snapped open, suddenly alert to the pain in his chest and the subsequent exit strategy employed by his soul. Mimi and Grandpa slept in separate bedrooms, so he was alone with his heart attack on that day before Easter. But he had not risen on the third day, much to my dismay. Sure, he drank too much and he chain-smoked too, but I loved him more than Jesus, as a granddaughter does.

I was usually the first one awake in those days, and Dad and I were in the living room that Saturday morning when Mimi came rushing in, still in her house slippers, my first clue that something was wrong. "Bill, I think Don's dead!" she said. She'd made his breakfast, but he didn't come when she called him, and his fried eggs grew cold while she went to his room to find him of the same temperature. My dad followed her out the door, leaving me alone in the middle of the rug watching cartoons and praying she was wrong. I was crushed.

Later, I stood at my bedroom window, reading over and over the big word written on the side of the vehicle in their driveway. I was the freshly crowned Spelling Bee Champion of my second grade class, encountering yet another new word in my young life: "Ambulance." The sirens were silent. The flashing red lights reflected off each drop of water on the glass as if each memory I had of my Grandpa was being illuminated before rolling down the window and disappearing.

My mother made me go to Janet Galli's birthday party, but I didn't want to pin the tail on any donkey. Grandpa was dead, and I was bereft. This was the first time death carved its name on my heart, creating the memory of pain each subsequent encounter would refer to, and I simply didn't understand it. I could not stop crying.

One day my dry-eyed Mimi sat me down and said, "When you cry for someone who dies, you are really crying for yourself. You should be happy for them because they've gone to heaven and are in a good place now. If crying could bring them back, we'd all sit down and have a good cry."

This did not make me feel better. And I was proving her right, because I certainly cried enough that if she were wrong, Grandpa would have been in his living room hiding a quarter for me right then. I might have tried to suck it up in staunch New England fashion, being a true descendant of the Pilgrims and all, because, as Ron McLarty wrote in *The Memory of Running*, "In New England, and in our home, it was good, very good, to keep things inside. Your emotions were contained. That was why God gave us skin."

My ancestors would have pushed me off the Mayflower with my emotions leaking all over the place. I felt like a disgrace to my genetic forebears, picturing them heartily disapproving of me from their perches above. I missed my Grandpa so much, and I felt like my world had ended. Each night after my mom tucked me in with a final, "Sweet dreams," I lay awake, wrestling with the finality of forever, until one night my young mind seized on the realization that life was just like my beloved books. When you closed the back cover that was it: *The End*. After that, I lay in my bed each night and thought about my book analogy and the lack of Grandpa and his shiny coins and chocolate stars in my life, and I cried myself to sleep for years, wondering who else's book was nearing the last page, hating the ending of Grandpa's story and wishing I could rewrite it.

And so, on a picturesque fall day in Maine, The Book of Noah, which was really more like a short story, became the first entry in our new family gravestone book. We all gathered on the hillside under the foliage and planted a dogwood tree with a granite marker engraved with Noah's name, his dates, and a rendition of Noah's ark his Aunt Erin had drawn. I secretly hoped Noah's tree would grow and grow, nourished by his ashes, until its roots reached his ancestors, after all.

We did spend our remaining days in Maine picking apples and kicking leaves on long walks through the woods. One day, Andy took a walk with his sisters and afterward I asked him, "How was your walk?"

"Well, good, except that I can't believe what Cody said," he answered. "We were walking along when all of a sudden, she said, 'Andy, Cally really needs you to help her heal.' I was stunned."

"What did you say?" I asked. We both agreed that Cally needed help, but neither of us dreamed that we were the most logical choices for that. Andy and I were working full time to heal ourselves and our own little family. As bad as losing my son was, I couldn't imagine losing my soul mate and I needed his help now, more than ever. This was one of the first signs that Andy was being pulled between us and his family.

"I told her it's all I can do to heal myself right now," he said.

One of the many bargains I'd tried to make with God since August 10 was that, okay, if I have to bear this pain, let me be the last. But before Noah had been dead even twenty-four hours, it came to our attention that a boy from Portland had run over his own little brother, both of whom were very close to the ages of Cally and Noah, respectively. So when Andy told me this story, I thought about how much it had helped me to talk to people like my new friend, Cindy, who'd walked down similar paths, and when we returned home, Andy and I met with those parents and tried to arrange for a meeting between Cally and their son. But it ultimately fell through.

We stayed in Maine for a week. On the plane trip home the flight attendants talked and played with our kids, who sat in the row of three seats right behind Andy and me. Perhaps they thought our kids were already on their own in the world at ages four, five, and eight, what with us so seemingly unavailable and distant, each locked in our own silent thoughts.

"So, where have you been?" I heard one of the flight attendants asked them.

"Maine," Hannah and Christiana answered in unison.

"What were you doing there?"

They hesitated, and I could feel their uncertainty as to how to reply, until she prompted them with a lucky guess.

"Were you visiting your grandparents?"

"Yes," they answered with a measure of relief I could feel through the fabric and foam of the seat that separated us. She moved on, and I stared out the window, wondering how she would have reacted if they had simply told her the truth. "We went to Maine to bury our baby brother."

Chapter Two

BPA GRANTED ME five months' leave after Noah's death, and I wasn't scheduled to return to work until after Christmas. Andy had finished with the milling work and started his new corporate job and so needed to focus on getting in the swing of things. I've always said that Andy's perfect job would be hosting his own talk show. One of the reasons I'd fallen in love with him was that he easily expressed his feelings and didn't simply clam up, like the men in my family. He was tuned in to his emotions and honored mine and the kids' as well. But I could see that even he needed the escape to the semblance of order that work provided, and, unfortunately, his new corporate job required him to travel quite a bit.

Please don't go, I begged him silently, trying to control the panic in my stomach every time he got out of bed to knot his tie and catch a plane. I never said a word, not wanting to add my paranoia to the weight he already carried. But I was afraid of every good-bye I had to say, now that I fully comprehended how permanent that utterance could turn out to be.

"Bye, honey," he said with a smile, kissing the cheek beneath my silent staring eyes. I swallowed my fears and winced as he absent-mindedly stuffed his empty dry-cleaning bag into our wastebasket on his way out of the bedroom, another reminder of this hated freedom to be careless we currently had. *Not for long*, I reminded myself, rolling over and popping a lemon drop into my mouth to quell my morning sickness before getting out of bed to get the girls off to school.

Our first Halloween AD rolled around with no mini-witch to accompany my big witch costume like the year before. Hannah took up the slack as a medium-size witch. After the trick-or-treating was over and the witch, the queen, and the Teenage Mutant Ninja Turtle were safely tucked into their beds and dreaming of Skittles, Andy and I went next door to the cemetery. Before Noah's death, we'd planned a family Thanksgiving trip to Jamaica with my parents, siblings, nieces, and nephews—a total of seventeen, but now sixteen, of us. Since our travel arrangements were already in place, Andy and I had decided that we should join the family trip as scheduled, and we were leaving soon. As we sat in the damp grass next to Noah's tree, we discussed it. We'd returned to the sunny island we loved every two or three years since our Peace Corps days. "I think it will be a nice change of scenery," Andy said as we both stared up at the starry sky, scanning the possible candidates and knowing that somewhere up there, near the constellation of Taurus, Noah's star was winking at us. But like everything else we did AD, the trip was yet another challenge—taking our new selves back to a happy place from our past to try it on like last year's bikini, wondering how it would now fit.

While I packed, my tears dripped on the water shoes I'd bought Noah for this journey, remembering the day I tried them on his chubby little feet. In the beach bag I found his Gymboree jacket, still smelling of sunscreen and Noah. I filled a film canister with some of his ashes and packed that instead. I also packed some citrus-scented soaps I'd bought to give to my Jamaican friends. Every pregnancy is different in the foods you crave and those you don't, the latter of which can send you running for the bathroom from their smell alone. With this pregnancy, I craved citrus fruits—lemons, oranges, and especially grapefruit—and I'd become addicted to simply smelling these soaps. I dreamed of picking and eating all the fresh citrus which awaited us, especially the ortaniques, which were a unique cross between oranges and tangerines that I'd never found elsewhere.

When we checked in at the airport we had to explain that the "lap child" indicated on our reservation was simply no longer with us. The gal at the ticket counter carried on without missing a beat and I wondered if she thought we'd decided to leave him behind with his auntie or something. Once airborne, I reminisced with Hannah about our plane ride last July, and we laughed, remembering how Noah had grabbed all the Chinese noodles from my airplane meal, throwing them in the air. And how he'd whined until Hannah poured some of her first Frappuccino into his cup, after which I worried that he would never sleep from drinking that caffeine. As difficult as traveling with him had been, traveling without him was worse. My stomach churned, so I pulled a grapefruit-scented soap out of my carry-on bag, clutched it in my fist, and smelled it over and over, tempted to take a tiny nibble.

When our plane neared the island we knew so well, I saw its familiar shape—like a dog swimming in the sea—and the peak of Blue Mountain sticking out of the clouds at over 7,000 feet. We'd climbed it twice, that mountain, starting in the darkness and hiking up, up, up into another climate, through the cloud forest, past tree ferns dripping with dew in the brightening dawn, until we could see the entire island laid at our feet, with Cuba and Haiti off in the distance.

I'd joined the Peace Corps after college in fulfillment of a lifelong *National Geographic*–inspired dream of traveling to exotic places and helping native peoples. Instead, I ended up in the dirty capital city, Kingston, was labeled a "problem volunteer," and changed my job three times in as many months before landing an assignment teaching environmental education near the country town of Christiana, where Andy lived in a two-bedroom apartment with only one double bed.

I didn't join the Peace Corps to fall in love, but the first time I visited Andy there, he wore the same grin I'd seen during our game of Hearts and said, "You can sleep in here with me or on the floor with the cockroaches." I hate cockroaches, and the rest is history. Seven years later we named our second daughter after this town, and now I held her hand as we prepared to disembark.

As soon as we stepped off the plane, we were kissed by the tropical warmth and hugged by the familiar smells and surrounded by the soundtrack from the place where we'd begun our lives together. Andy always said we'd had our honeymoon first, and it was true. Soon we were seated under the fan of our friends' veranda, sipping cool drinks and admiring their lush, tropical gardens while the kids fed tiny bits of cheese to the lizards. I passed out all the soaps except the pink grapefruit, unable to relinquish all of my new citrus obsession just yet. Our friend Peter is a doctor, and he'd met Noah when last we'd visited, scanning my pumpkin belly with the only ultrasound I'd had of him.

We traveled south to our favorite Treasure Beach to spend time with him and his wife, Margaret, before my family arrived. I'd worked with Margaret in my Peace Corps years and still counted her among my best friends. "Let's go out on the beach and write to Noah," Margaret suggested. It was November 13, the night of my thirty-sixth birthday. We gathered up the kids and stood on the warm moonlit beach, writing messages with sticks in the sand to our fallen one, sprinkling some of his ashes in the warm, extra-salty Caribbean Sea. *No woman, no cry*, I hummed to myself, feeling like Bob Marley had written those words for me.

"We're pregnant," we announced to my family when they landed at the airport a week after us. Even though I'd never had a full miscarriage before, I always followed the common wisdom to wait three months before telling anyone. Before we left, we'd let the news begin to trickle out, knowing that once Suzie caught wind, the telephone wires would be buzzing. This time nobody had offered their opinions nor snorted "no more," which was a relief.

"So are we," my brother Mark's wife, Beth, said to our surprise. We calculated that she was due only a month after me. I was nearing the end of my usual first-trimester morning sickness, and she was, too. That, coupled with our raging hormones, was not a great prescription for a peaceful family vacation, although for the most part it was wonderful. There were a few altercations, though, and one scene in particular I would rather forget.

One night my brothers came back from the rum bar late—and drunk. Erin and my parents and I were sitting around the living room of our rental house talking, and I was soaking my feet in a plastic tub of warm water with a home remedy to try to get rid of my plantar warts. My brothers had broken the window on our rental van, and I was already mad at them for that since Andy and I had rented it and were responsible for returning it in good condition. My brother, Mark, kept badgering me about a bunch of nonsense—rum talk that made no sense—and I felt like he was mocking me and my Peace Corps experience, until finally I lost my temper and stood up and threw the tub of water on him. He was shocked and so was I, and he chased me around the house until, desperate for help, I ran into the bedroom where Andy was sleeping.

The next day I felt completely ashamed of myself and apologetic. Here we were, grown adults, with me pregnant even, acting like children. Mark was seven years younger than me, so it wasn't even a reenactment of anything we'd ever done in our childhood, like the countless fights I'd had with Brian when we were growing up. Displaced anger, they call it. Irish, we call it. Together, an explosive combination.

"You have to tell us how you're feeling. You can't expect us to just know," Mark said the next day when we sat on the beach. I tried to explain myself while I watched the pelicans dive for their lunch and the kids play in the water.

For me, everything was a painful reminder of Noah's absence, which lurked beneath every waking moment and all that we did, including sitting there watching Mark's daughter, Jordan, who was a few months older than Noah and the closest cousin to his age, now playing with her cousins like she'd played with Noah in July. *Hopefully, this next baby will have Jordan's new sibling to play with*, I thought.

Grief is mostly internal. And, we were discovering, it is often mistaken for a lot of other things, like anger, weakness, and lunacy. Andy, the kids, and I all looked okay on the outside, so everyone assumed we were fine on the inside. And when we acted differently, they were confused. I felt like a fragile egg—the least little impact cracked my shell, causing me to leak all over myself and others if they got too close.

Jamaica did her best to wrap me in the shawl of her tropical warmth and rock me, like an old friend would. But it was our first vacation to get through without Noah, like the first of everything we experienced in the year after his death and forever after. Nothing was ever right or complete again—but all the firsts were especially painful.

We left Treasure Beach and headed for the hills of Christiana, where we weathered the first Thanksgiving without our youngest son. Mary, our former landlady, killed some of her prize chickens, and we all gathered around tables under the ortanique trees to eat until we were stuffed, to "mek de belly roll," as she'd say. I sat in a folding chair inhaling the sweet smell of ortaniques ripening overhead along with the sickish smell of them rotting at my feet. I stood up and twisted one of the bright orange fruits from a branch, giving thanks for my years in the Peace Corps. Because I knew I could sit in any third-world country and share the experience of losing a child with nearly everyone there. We might not even speak the same language, but we could tighten our lips, suck on ortaniques, and nod with understanding. Life can be bitter—as known by much of the world. Here in our so-called first world, we tend to pretend otherwise.

Chapter Three

THE NIGHT AFTER our return home to Oregon, I relaxed into a hot bath, welcoming some rare quiet time to just lie there and soak. Andy had taken the kids out shopping. The phone rang, and Cody's voice hit my ear. "Hi," she said, and then without a pause: "Welcome back, do you want to come to the Festival of Trees with me, Chris doesn't want to go and I have an extra ticket and, oh, come on, it will be fun, I'll pick you up in a half hour, or do you want to drive? Okay."

As usual, I could barely get a thought formed in my head, much less out of my mouth and into the phone, before the call was over and I was going. I sank back into the blissful bubbly warmth and rubbed my belly absentmindedly, closing my eyes and recalling the warm buoyant waters of Treasure Beach for a tranquil moment. This was the kind of thing—a party—that I wouldn't have hesitated to attend with Cody or anyone else in the past. Later I would wish I'd said no. But if I said no to everything I didn't feel like doing then, the truth was that I wouldn't have done much of anything. I could have easily stayed in that tub forever. But I was trying to make an effort, to climb out of my grief. So I flicked the lever with my toe to drain the water away, forcing myself to get out of the tub and into a purple outfit that was getting tight. I picked up Cody in my car since I wouldn't ride in that Tahoe.

Once we arrived, we strolled around the room, drinks in hand—the usual wine for her, some kind of nonalcoholic punch for me—and admired all the fancily decorated trees that were up for silent auction.

"Should I get this one for the office?" she asked now and again, placing her bids. Cody was in her element—wine glass in hand, mouth on fast-forward—as she greeted and chatted with the philanthropic crowd of Salem. I was casually acquainted with many of them, mostly through Cody, and many of her fellow doctor/dentist/lawyer wives were shopping for instant holiday cheer to put in their homes and their husbands' offices. But though I normally enjoy socializing and was used to following Cody around at parties, I felt a bit jet-lagged and frumpy in my purple is-she-pregnant-or-not outfit among all that holiday glitter—which included Cody's new silver fur-trimmed vest and her flashing diamonds. I was just wishing I could teleport myself home to float in my tub when we crossed paths with a tall, well-coiffed realtor whom I didn't know.

"Oh, hi," Cody said.

"Hi," the woman replied, and they both agreed they hadn't seen each other for ages.

"Oh," Cody continued, "this is my sister-in-law, Kelly." And before either of us could open our mouths for a perfunctory nice-to-meet-you, Cody added, "Her son was run over by my daughter in August."

The woman and I both stared at each other, horrified and speechless, while Cody took a sip of her wine, smiled a little, and gave her fur trim a half-shoulder shrug. The woman found her tongue long enough to say, "Oh, I'm so sorry to hear that," and we were jostled along in the crowd.

I have been introduced in many ways, but this was certainly a new one. Then I really wished I'd stayed home in my bubbles, and I suggested we leave soon after. Instead of helping me get back in the game, this foray left me feeling like I hadn't even found the correct ball field yet.

Christmas was a huge hurdle. We were all trying to make the best of our new lives. "Can I hang Noah's ornament, Mom?" Hannah asked, pulling his Baby's First Christmas ornament out of the box. There would never be a Second Christmas one to hook on.

"Sure, honey," I answered, wishing I could add, *but put it up high where Noah can't grab it.* We went next door to the cemetery and hung a Noah's ark ornament on his sweet gum tree and decorated it with others that seemed weatherproof enough for the holiday. I wanted to run a long extension cord from our house and wrap his tree in twinkling lights, but even his tree was too far away for a warm embrace.

I realized that I wasn't taking many photos of the kids anymore. Andy had always chided me while I diligently documented their growth, filling their baby books with milestones achieved. "Why do you bother putting yourself through that?" he'd ask when I returned from taking the kids for studio photos to mark their birthdays or having them pose in front of snowflake backgrounds for holiday shots, trips that were often feats of endurance teetering on disaster.

"I am so glad you did," he said after Noah died and suddenly there were no more photo ops to endure. And though I realized the added importance of capturing these moments before they were gone, I kind of lost heart for a while, going through the motions for the sake of posterity as I arranged three kids on Santa's lap when there should have been four.

And yet some magic was in the air that season. On the first day of Christmas, we found a lovely note on our doorstep with a gift. It said, *For the Kittel family, on the first day of Christmas. There are no words that can bring comfort to you this first Christmas without your little son and brother, but we want you to know we care. Each night as we make our visit, we will be praying for you.* The note was signed, *Your Christmas Friends,* and it quoted II Thessalonians 3:16: "Now may the Lord of peace Himself continually grant you peace in every circumstance."

Our Christmas Friends left something every night for the twelve days of Christmas. We never caught them in the act or discovered who these elves were, but their kindness soothed us in a time of great struggle. It was lovely for the kids, and maybe even more so for Andy and me, who needed something magical to believe in. It gave a sparkle of light to those twelve days and a reason to get out of bed on each of those mornings.

We hung Noah's stocking along with the others, just in case. Santa left a letter in it for all the kids saying how sorry he was about Noah and that he and Mrs. Claus missed him also. I thought about next year and looked forward to having a new stocking to hang. I felt the baby starting to swim around inside me, its faint flutter kicks tickling my belly and making me smile.

Chapter Four

AND SO WE ENTERED into the New Year, 1998, with the shadow of death in our hearts but the light of hope shining in our eyes—blinding us, really. We were alone with our grief for many hours of the day, but we were learning to bear it without being crushed. The baby was growing nicely, thanks in large part to the meals we were still receiving from friends and neighbors several times a week, and a box of grapefruit we'd received from Marcella, which I was reluctant to share. I stopped writing in my journal because whenever I tried, it reduced me to tears, and once I started crying, I couldn't stop. When I cried, I worried that my sadness was affecting the new life within me. I didn't want this baby to be sad or bitter or worried, so I tried very hard not to hold on to these emotions for long, lest they be transmitted to the unblemished life within me.

I resumed volunteering at school in both of the girls' classrooms, Micah in tow. I taught Junior Great Books to Hannah and her third-grade classmates, who gathered around me on the circle of assorted throw pillows once a week, munching their lunches. It was similar to a book group, and I belonged to two of those myself. I was reading a lot of books about loss, grief, and death, and I was making good progress on my self-directed study on death and dying and the meaning of life, so a light Rudyard Kipling story was a pleasant diversion.

The kids were getting on well, but we all had our moments. One day I walked into Christiana's kindergarten class to find my bonny girl sitting in the middle of the classroom rug all by herself, crying. I hurried over to hug her tight, asking, "What's wrong?"

"I miss Noah," she said.

It broke my heart to hear her anguish, and I grabbed her backpack and took her home with me.

I also resumed playing Bunco—a dice game—with the Bunco Babes, a group of mostly ladies from the Catholic church that Cody had invited me to join a year or so before. These were all self-proclaimed "Queens of Peace"—simply "Queens" for short—so I guess she figured that I would fit right in. One afternoon, Cody saw me in my driveway and walked down toward our house, calling out, "Queenie, are you playing Bunco tonight?"

When I said yes, she asked if I wanted to ride together.

"Sure," I said.

"Well, I guess you'll want to drive, then?"

"I'll pick you up at seven," I said to her retreating back.

Walking away, she called over her shoulder, "I'll know you're over it when you'll ride in the Tahoe again."

Over "it," I thought. "It" being what? My grief? My son? His death? Her daughter's accident? I was working my way through it, but I was never going to be "over it."

With my allotted months of leave up, I went back to work in Portland, falling right back into my familiar Starbucks routine and enjoying an hour of NPR to and from work. I braced myself for the reactions of my coworkers, thanking them all for their support and sharing the good news that I was now going on five months pregnant, in case they were wondering why my belly had grown so—a welcome change of subject for us all. Back at work, I also found out that our health insurance options had changed, so I had to find a doctor that would be covered under the new plan.

I sat in my kitchen one morning and flipped through the Salem yellow pages, hoping to find a female doctor and chuckling at something I'd heard once: "You wouldn't take your car to a mechanic who'd never owned one." I also hoped to find a midwife to help with this birth. As my belly grew, so did the frequency of Cody's hints about being there for this delivery. I desperately wanted to figure out how to prevent her from coming without having to simply tell her so, knowing that nothing with her was ever that simple and that she assumed her help was necessary and welcome. Every time I tried to push her away, the space I managed to create between us was quickly filled by her stepping into it to assert herself even more, waiting for me to "get over it."

Scanning the ob-gyn page, my eyes landed on an ad for the Salem Women's Clinic, run by a female doctor with a stable of nurse-midwives. Perfect. I called and transferred my care to their clinic in February and throughout the month began to meet a succession of midwives, but not the doctor.

In March, I was working in Portland when I developed a pounding headache. I went to the on-site nurse and found that my blood pressure was elevated, so I lay down for a while, but the headache didn't go away. On my way home I stopped at the clinic, where a midwife took my blood pressure: 180/110—very high for anyone, pregnant or not. She handed me a Johnnie to change into and left the room, returning with Dr. Harmon, who introduced herself and said, "Because of your elevated blood pressure, you're now considered high risk. You'll be under my care only. No more midwives." She wore thick glasses that magnified her eyes, and a wide headband collared her unruly mass of curly brown hair.

"I'm prescribing Aldomet for blood pressure medication," she said, handing me a lab slip and rattling off a long list of instructions without leaving time for questions. I sat, stunned, trying to focus. "You need to go home and lie down. I want you on bed rest for the rest of today. Come back tomorrow for an ultrasound and biophysical profile, and I'll be making an appointment with the high-risk doctor up in Portland because I want you to meet him." She ended her speech with, "You will be seeing a lot of us from now on." Then she pulled out a needle and instructed me to turn around in my easy-access gown so she could inject me in my gluteus maximus with the first of several steroid shots I'd receive, saying, "We need to get this baby's lungs ready in case we deliver you early."

I winced with the shock of both the needle and the realization that I had officially become a high-risk patient. Scared, I went home to bed and cried a little. I called Andy and told him the news. "I don't know anything about premature babies," I said, massaging my aching temples.

"Well, why don't you call Pat?" he suggested. Information always made me feel better prepared, so I phoned Cody's sister-in-law who was a nurse and who was married to Chris's brother, a doctor. Pat worked with premature babies in the Neonatal Intensive Care Unit, the NICU, of Emmanuel Hospital in Portland—the same hospital where Noah had been pronounced dead only seven months prior. Luckily she answered and helped calm me down a bit by informing me of the critical development weeks for the baby from its present twenty-seven weeks of gestation onward.

When I hung up, I felt more assured, knowledge being power, and turned to my *What to Expect When You're Expecting* book to see what else I could learn. By the time Andy came home, the baby was kicking away, and I'd been calmed by the opiate-like effects of Tylenol and reading.

"Hey, honey," he said, coming in and sitting on the bed to hug me. I filled him in on what I'd learned. "It will all be just fine," he said, ever the optimist.

The kids tumbled into the room, asking, "Mommy, why are you in bed?"

"Hey, you guys, let's let Mom rest while we make dinner, and we'll bring it to her in here. Mommy just needs to rest." Andy hoisted Micah over his shoulder and they all left me alone with my worries.

The kids had never seen me eat in bed before, but they agreed to the plan, and I lay in bed listening to pots clanging and my family all laughing and chatting in the kitchen. We had good health care—first-world health care—and the statistics were in our favor; I felt sure we could reach the milestones of the weeks ahead, and the baby would be just fine. In a few months we'd have the feng shui joy of a baby's cry to add to the happy sounds now coming from down the hall.

The next day when I went for my appointment with Dr. Harmon, she said, "I made that appointment for you in Portland to meet the high-risk specialist, Dr. Watson, just in case you end up having to deliver there." Two days later, Andy and I met the kind-looking, white-haired doctor and learned, among other things, that he shared my love for Jazzercise.

"The baby is growing beautifully," he reported following my ultrasound. "All looks well." He explained that since the baby is on the delivery end of the blood supply, the concern with elevated blood pressure is that the baby won't receive an adequate supply of nutrients, so they keep checking the baby's growth to determine how it's doing. "The placenta is a highly vascular organ, and elevated blood pressures like the one you had can cause problems with the blood flow to the placenta, among other things, but the only way we can evaluate the placental function is to measure the end result—the baby. I want you to stay on your blood pressure medication, and Dr. Harmon can increase it if necessary," he advised. "But I also want you to switch from Jazzercise. Do you like to swim?"

"I love to swim," I said.

"Well, that's good, because swimming actually increases the blood flow to the baby," he reassured me, while I thought about how I'd switched from running to swimming a mile almost daily in the latter months of my pregnancy with Hannah. When the other kids came along, it had been too hard to manage child care to keep swimming regularly, but now I only had Micah to find care for, and I knew one friend or another would be willing to have him play for an hour two or three times a week while I increased the blood flow to my baby and kept my gluteus from becoming too maximus.

I made a follow-up appointment to meet Dr. Winkler, his partner, and left the appointment feeling happy. After thinking I would have to be on bed rest for the next few months, I breathed a sigh of relief to have this prescription for staying active. I would have gladly climbed Mount Hood if Dr. Watson had thought that would be good for my baby.

I went home and called my boss, and he agreed I could decrease my work schedule and work from home until the birth. I increased my resting. I had to monitor my blood pressure at home, so we borrowed Cody's cuff, which was a professional sphygmomanometer and, along with the stethoscope, required the use of two hands. Since I couldn't operate it myself, Andy took the readings for me several times a day. But when he was unavailable, that left Cody. She reveled in her nursing role, bursting into the house often and calling, "Queenie, where are you?" Trying my best to rest and relax in bed, I was trapped. Certainly unable to hide under the bed, I took a lot of deep breaths, closed my eyes, and tried to remain calm instead while she sat down next to me, hung her stethoscope on her diamond-studded ears, and set to work. Even this I could endure, I thought, for the sake of this baby. I did need my blood pressure monitored, after all. Mimi's voice echoed in my brain, "You can stand any pain as long as it's not forever."

The next week I went swimming and felt faint afterward. I called the clinic, reported my blood pressure, and they said it was too low, probably due to the medication. The doctor came on the line and instructed me to lower the dosage, adding, "No more swimming. I want you laying down as much as possible for the next two days until your next appointment." Although I didn't know it then, this marked the beginning of what would become a random progression of being on and off bed rest, changing my medication to regulate my blood pressure, and bending over for steroid shots, as well as a regular schedule of ultrasounds and fetal non-stress tests (NSTs). From this point forward, I'd have a medical appointment at least twice a week and oftentimes more. Dr. Harmon was right—I would be spending a lot of time with them, and I'd joke that this was the most photographed baby I'd ever carried. I lay there wondering if I'd be given permission to swim again while all the testing that was to come would confirm one thing: the baby was growing beautifully, swimming like a champ.

I scanned the tower of books on my nightstand, extracting a book of baby names. I was casually flipping through the boys' names, stopping on this name or that to read its meaning, when my focus was drawn like a magnet to *Jonah*. A shockwave ran through me when I read its meaning—*Noah's dove*—knowing instantly that *Jonah* was the name of this baby kicking inside of me, even though I didn't know whether it was a he or a she. *This is the dove,* I thought, *the bird of peace that Noah is sending to us.*

Noah's garden began to come alive for the season, and his star magnolia tree bloomed early outside my kitchen window in mid-March. "Look kids," I said, pointing out the white flowers, "Noah's tree looks like it's full of little white doves."

Chapter Five

MARCH TURNED into April, and Andy had a business trip to Hawaii. "You want to come?" he asked, smiling.

"Fresh pineapple!" I said, still firmly in the grips of my citrus cravings. I checked with Dr. Harmon at my thirty-week appointment and was happily surprised when she noted that my blood pressure was better and bestowed her blessing. I hadn't had any more headaches and looked forward to some time together with my husband before our lives were consumed by the new baby and our family of five being turned back into six.

I loved being back in the tropics and almost forgot that I was in the midst of a high-risk pregnancy and grieving the loss of my son as I lay across our king-size hotel bed in every direction, unused to so much space after our bed at home, sized as it was for a queen. I rubbed my taut belly, reading and napping the day away while awaiting Andy's return from meetings. Then we'd stroll across the street for a beach swim and watch the sunset.

"Can you believe they have a state fish?" I asked Andy while we snorkeled in Hanauma Bay and hovered over the beautiful humuhumunukunukuapua'a, more easily called the reef triggerfish. I can float forever, especially then with the beach ball that was my belly underneath me, and whenever I snorkeled, I'd pick out one fish to follow while it went about its daily errands around its coral neighborhood, imagining the drama unfolding beneath me as it interacted with its fishy friends and family. This was my first trip to a tropical island that was not also a developing nation like Jamaica, and it was nice not to see abject poverty or have to struggle with moral angst when confronted by the ubiquitous beggars of my Peace Corps days.

One day we toured the island in a red convertible, heading for the North Shore and the Banzai Pipeline I'd always heard so much about, having grown up in a surfing culture. We passed plantation after plantation of pineapples. But the big-wave season had passed, so I contented myself with floating on my back in the water at Waimea Bay, humming Beach Boys tunes to my baby, who floated on top of me, both of us enjoying our warm, salty seas.

While we traveled around the coastline, we enjoyed seeing Hawaiians so in love with their ocean—a nice contrast to our experience of Jamaicans, most of who are afraid of the water. The indigenous peoples of the Caribbean were all wiped out by each other or by the diseases brought by explorers like Columbus, so "local" populations of the islands were all transplanted from elsewhere, like from Africa, as slaves. They are therefore not at home in their island environment even all these generations later. Most Jamaicans never learn to swim. Many never visit the sea, as I'd learned in the Peace Corps when teaching school children about coral reefs or mangrove swamps that they'd never seen. Jamaican fishermen have to go so far offshore to catch anything substantial that they don't want to know how to swim, preferring a quick death if they fall overboard. "I'm a lead; I sink," the Treasure Beach fishermen would say with gap-toothed grins on their grizzled faces. *Like my husband*, I'd think. Hawaiians, though, were people after my own heart—happy when wet.

We returned home to prepare for our next great adventure—the birth of our baby. At my next appointment, Dr. Harmon said, "Your blood pressure is beautiful. I think I'll send all my high-risk patients to Hawaii."

But before I could reach my arm around to pat myself on the back, it became apparent that I should have stayed in Hawaii following the humuhumunukunukuapua'a around, because as my eighth month progressed, my blood pressure destabilized. It kept increasing, and Dr. Harmon followed its lead by increasing my dosage of Aldomet. Something about Salem, Oregon, was causing my veins to constrict.

"I want you on complete bed rest at home now," the doctor announced as the end of my eighth month and of April rolled around. So I stopped working completely and canceled all volunteering. Andy got a note from Dr. Harmon saying he needed to stick closer to home until the birth, but since he still had some traveling to do, he arranged for our friends and his family to help out with rides for the kids to and from all of their activities whenever he was gone. I didn't attend any of the kids' spring school concerts or soccer games, and I postponed the party for Hannah's ninth birthday, promising, "You can have your birthday party with the new baby."

I felt bad being so useless to my kids, but we read books, and Micah and I played game after game of Crazy Eights on the wide, wooden arm of my red leather recliner I called the Lazy Girl. One day Cody brought an extra TV/VCR from the dental office and set it up in my bedroom. I have always believed that bedrooms should be quiet spaces for reading and sleeping, but in came that TV, so I resigned myself to having it there for the short term, even though I rarely watched it. It wasn't the first time someone brought me something I didn't need and I tried to be gracious, the way I was raised. I really didn't mind lying around and reading as long as the needs of my kids were being met. This baby was worth all of this and more.

My friends continued bringing us meals, but now they increased their culinary efforts from several times a week to nightly. My friend Cindy did our laundry and had my kids over to play. All of these people who had already done so much for us did even more. We were overwhelmed by their kindness.

The baby was due June 3.

"One more month," I repeated like a mantra to myself whenever I felt guilty about putting our lives on hold. "It will be here before you know it," I said from my bed as I kissed my kids off to one event after another without me. Not one of them ever complained.

"Call any time your blood pressure is elevated," I was told by Dr.

Harmon and the midwives. "If the office is closed, go to the hospital for monitoring." Both the doctor's office and the hospital were only a ten-minute drive from my house, and I went once or twice a week for monitoring to one place or the other. I'd gone back to Portland for my appointment with Dr. Winkler, and weekly amniotic fluid indexes had been added to the battery of tests along with biophysical profiles to check the baby's growth. And though Dr. Harmon had said I was to be under her care only, she was often booked or otherwise unavailable to see me for these many visits, so I usually saw a midwife at the clinic.

And so it was that the first time Andy took my blood pressure on a Saturday and it was elevated, he called in and was told to bring me to the hospital, where a midwife was waiting to receive me, as Dr. Harmon was not on duty that day. I'd met Kate once or twice before at the clinic, and she was one of my favorites. Like Andy, she had smiling eyes, but hers were brown and more squinty than his. She was pleasantly plump with an earthy, Birkenstock feel—the stereotypical midwife in my mind. Kate escorted us to a room, and I could hear her chatting with Andy from the bathroom where I changed into my hospital gown. "We'll start with a non-stress test," she said after I climbed into bed, her long, frizzy black hair tickling my face as she reached across my expanded belly to button the stretchy monitor bands around me.

"I'll be right back," she said once the monitor began beeping away, heading toward the door. "I have a patient I'm concerned about for abruption."

"What's that?" Andy asked. She paused and explained briefly that abruption is the separation of the placenta from the uterus and that smoking and cocaine abuse are contributing factors.

"Are there any symptoms?" I asked, knowing she was in a hurry but curious about this thing I'd never heard about before.

"Well, you usually feel a sharp, stabbing pain in the upper right quadrant of your belly," she replied. "If you ever feel that, you should get to the hospital right away."

She bustled out of the room, and I lay there holding my husband's hand and listening to the reassuring beeps of my baby's heartbeats as it passed yet one more test. I filed her words away in my brain, thinking that even though I'd never felt such a thing, surely I would be able to recognize a sharp, stabbing pain in the upper right quadrant of my uterus, mentally picturing my uterus as a four-square court. No problem, I figured. I hated cigarettes and certainly didn't use cocaine. I pictured Kate down the hall lecturing a pale, undereducated woman with overprocessed blond hair and nicotine-stained fingers about the dangers of smoking and drug use to her and her unborn child. A woman nothing like me.

I went to the hospital two more times that month with elevated blood pressures, including on April 26, Hannah's birthday, when instead of lighting nine candles on a cake plus one to grow on, I stayed overnight for observation. But nobody ever talked to me about abruption again.

"Kelly, I want you to come outside and sit," Cody said one sunny afternoon, marching into the living room where I lay in the Lazy Girl. By this time, I was allowed to be either in bed or in the Lazy Girl in a fully reclined position, and could get up only to use the bathroom or shower. But I also had a whole host of medical appointments to keep, and there was never any question about being allowed to get up for those, which never made any sense to me. "I want to see what your blood pressure does when you get up and sit outside," Cody said.

So I got myself up and out to where she had set up a folding chair on the front lawn. The spring day was fragrant, and the kids were all playing with their friends on the sport court in front of me. I watched them shooting basketballs and riding their bikes around while Nurse Cody got her sphygmomanometer ready. The fresh air was narcotic. After I'd settled in for a few minutes, Cody inflated the cuff and listened. I closed my eyes and let the sun warm my skin, trying to think calm thoughts, as always.

"See, it's low," she said, pulling the stethoscope away from her ears. "And you're not lying down. It doesn't make any sense. Maybe you should sit up more often," she added, contrary to the doctor's bed rest instructions. "The biggest risk with your pressures is stroke," she told me, not for the first time, "and you know I once had a patient who stroked out." I tuned her out, listening to the kids play instead as she rattled on about her experiences in her brief career a long time ago when she'd worked as a nurse in the navy, where she'd met Chris. I had only known her as the one who managed his dental practice and their money.

I did agree with her that it didn't make much sense. Every time someone took my blood pressure, my heart threw a little surprise party. I could never figure out why my blood pressure was high some-times and low at others; it never seemed to correlate to anything in particular and I could see why they named it the "silent killer." But I went back inside to lie down like a good patient and ponder my situation.

Lying around all day made me even more conscious of the baby and what it was doing—sleeping or moving or hiccupping or rolling around. The kids crawled into bed with me, and we all probed the tiny elbows and knees sticking out of my belly and laughed. This was a very active baby, and I did my kick counts faithfully—even if it was still, a few sips of any kind of juice would have it dancing in no time. With the barrage of monitoring there were never any blips on the screen—no signs of slowed growth or decreased movement or any problems whatsoever. The tests were all conclusively reassuring.

They also never showed us what sex the baby was, and we didn't want to know, even though Jonah was the only name on my list. Whenever I worried, Jonah gave me a kick or a high-five to the ribs, and I was instantly reassured. I was confident. Having babies was something I was good at, experienced at, with my proven uterus and my faithful outlook. The baby passed every test they gave it, giving a confident thumbs-up while I studied it during each ultrasound. I was lulled by my past successes and the steady heartbeat during each non-stress test into a false sense of security. This was our just reward, the dove Noah was sending.

Chapter Six

I FLIPPED THE Bob Marley calendar on our kitchen wall to May, and Noah's birthday on the eighteenth appeared, blank and awaiting my attention. Usually I marked everyone's special day with a heart and wrote the number of years it had been since his or her birth. Should I write two? Was he aging wherever he was, or would he forever remain a one-year-old boy not yet steady on his feet? Unsure and unable to stand up for long myself, I settled for a heart and a squiggle line on each side of his name.

May 6, a Wednesday, had a heart around it with the number five for Micah, who mixed his own birthday cake while I instructed him from my Lazy Girl. Two of my friends arrived in time to help him bake it, also bringing me lunch. "Polish soup," my friend said with a wink, "with boiled eggs for good luck."

As I updated them on the latest news of my pregnancy, she asked, "So, are they going to let you go into labor naturally, or have they said they might induce you?"

"I think a natural labor is the plan, but I'm not sure. I guess the baby might be induced early depending on how things go. Maybe it will be born on Noah's birthday," I mused out loud, thinking of my calendar dilemma.

"Oh, no," she said, and her eyes widened with horror at what I'd just said. I knew that many people thought this baby was a replacement for Noah and worried about our sanity, having another baby so soon. But we hadn't even planned this pregnancy, and I knew this baby would certainly not be a substitute for Noah. This baby would be a child in its own right. It had already helped us heal from the loss of Noah by bringing hope into our despair, and it would fill a huge void with the joy it would bring back into our lives. But still…

"This baby needs to have its own birthday," my friend stated emphatically.

"Yes, of course it does," I said, still thinking that if this baby were born on Noah's birthday, that would be a clear sign that it was our gift from God, as Marcella called Andy. And it would sure help me get through that dreaded first May 18 without Noah.

On Thursday, I had an appointment with Bea, another nurse-midwife, who noted that my blood pressure was up again and told me to check into the hospital for observation. By this time the doctor had increased my medication to four times the initial dosage and it still wasn't controlling my blood pressure. This fifth time at the hospital, yet another midwife, Pat, was on duty and checked me in. But they didn't just check me and send me home as usual. This time they decided to keep me overnight again and ordered a bunch of tests.

Dr. Harmon came by my room and said, "Tomorrow I'm going to try to ripen your cervix and move toward induction. It's early, so it might not work right away."

Andy and I looked at each other, stunned. Tomorrow would be May 8; our baby would be born one month early.

"Why don't you just do a C-section?" Andy asked the doctor. He told her that he was concerned that my blood pressure might spike with labor and that I could have a stroke, something Nurse Cody had also told him all about.

"Stroke *is* a risk of hypertension," she agreed, "but we'll monitor Kelly during labor and if either she or the baby isn't tolerating it, I might consider a C-section. But that's major abdominal surgery, and I wouldn't choose major surgery as the first course of action."

After Dr. Harmon left, the midwife suggested that Andy and I take a walk up to the nursery and look at the premature babies since we had no experience with a preemie. We walked down the halls and took the elevator to stand and stare at the new babies. After so much bed rest, it felt good whenever I could stretch my legs, even though

I was surprised when she allowed me to get up and go. Andy and I arrived at the nursery and stared through the glass at the tiniest babies in their incubators. They looked so fragile in their clear plastic bubbles. After having delivered four big, healthy babies, I felt unsure again. I didn't know anything about premature babies.

"What problems might a baby have this early?" we asked Pat when we returned to my room.

"Well, it might not be able to nurse, or its lungs might not be ready, and sometimes babies born early have trouble bonding with their mothers." I'd dropped my drawers for all those steroid shots and sure hoped they'd served their intended purpose—to mature my baby's lungs. We were scared. But we weren't being given a choice.

Bright and early the next day, Friday, Pat inserted a little tampon of Cervidil into my cervix to soften it so it could dilate, and I had it in all day. I read, slept, played cards, and visited with Andy and the kids. I even got to sit in the Jacuzzi and read. I had some cramps but nothing too severe.

Bea had relieved Pat on duty as the midwife, and she removed the Cervidil that night so I could sleep. "We'll insert a new one and start again tomorrow; have a good rest," she said, and she left me to myself. But I did not rest well. My room was on the labor and delivery floor, so all night I heard my neighbor screaming in labor. And though I'd experienced labor four times already, I felt like a first-timer. Each of her moans filled me with anxiety like the slow ratcheting up, up, up of a rollercoaster to the pinnacle of that first dreaded hill. I can't breathe on roller coasters and, like her, I wanted it to stop. And yet, I was scheduled to be in one of the cars behind her. And though this was the moment I'd been waiting for, still I was afraid of the ride ahead.

I woke up early on Saturday, waiting hungrily until they finally brought my breakfast. My stomach had growled all night, and I was anxious to eat so they could start the induction again. I stopped chewing my Raisin Bran only when the automatic blood pressure monitor, my constant companion, squeezed my arm and flashed the results for my curious mind. "My blood pressures are pretty low," I noted casually to the nurse who came in.

The next midwife on duty, Lisa, came in and introduced herself to me. She was the fourth midwife in Dr. Harmon's practice and the only one whom I'd never met before. I mentioned my nice, low pressures.

"So what do you want to do, then?" Lisa said.

"What do you mean?" I asked.

"Well, do you want to continue with the induction or not?"

My eyebrows raised in surprise, and I was stunned by this sudden choice. As usual, I began asking her lots of questions. We talked at length about which course of action would be better, to continue the induction or to keep the baby in longer so it could grow more.

"Well, how big do you think it is?" I asked.

She felt my stomach with both hands and said, "Maybe five pounds."

I pictured those tiny, fragile babies upstairs.

We talked back and forth about my options, and I listened to all she had to say. She seemed to be more in favor of letting labor follow a natural course.

"Well, the decision is yours," she concluded. "What do you want to do? I'll be back shortly."

She left the room.

As the door closed, the weight of the world descended to settle heavily on my shoulders. I felt paralyzed. How was I supposed to decide what to do? What had begun as a casual remark by me about my low blood pressure readings had evolved into a decision that I was now supposed to make. I was too befuddled then, but later I wished I'd stuffed my mouth with cereal and never said a word.

Before Lisa returned, Andy and the kids stopped by on their way to soccer. I told Andy what had just happened, and he listened to the choices I had. But the kids were late, so he simply said he was sure I'd make the right decision along with the doctor, and he left me alone again. It was Saturday, and the girls were also running in their annual school relay races again, just like on the day Noah was born. And again, I would miss them. And the next day was Mother's Day, my first without Noah. And my parents were arriving from Maine later that week. I wanted my mom there for the birth. Mom, not Cody. All these thoughts and more swirled around in my brain until I felt completely overwhelmed. I must have been the least capable person on the planet at that moment to make a rational decision, and yet that was what I was suddenly expected to do.

It now seemed we were in no hurry to deliver: The baby was doing fine, my blood pressure was low, and they'd said my cervix had only changed about one centimeter with the Cervidil, although nobody ever checked it again. I wanted to do everything I could to make sure the baby was okay. All along, the biggest risk mentioned with the delivery was stroke, stroke, stroke, and in spite of both Cody's and Andy's fears, I was convinced that that wouldn't happen to me. Hadn't I already delivered four children successfully? We had come this far and been so careful. I figured we could just continue along as we were. How many times had I been through this already? In and out of the doctors' offices and in and out of the hospital had become a familiar pattern with this pregnancy, and I'd gotten too comfortable with the routine.

"I guess I'll wait then and let the baby grow a little more," I told Lisa when she returned for my decision, studying her for her reaction.

"Okay, I'll tell Dr. Harmon," she said casually.

I hadn't even known the doctor was there, hadn't spoken with my primary caregiver since being admitted two days before. But soon my door cracked open and Dr. Harmon poked her head and unruly hair in the room. Propping the door open with her clog, she said, "I hear you're going home. I still want you on bed rest and coming in for daily non-stress tests. I'm going to be on vacation but will be calling the office to check in on you and one other patient every day. I'll give you my cell phone number."

Then the door closed, and she vanished as quickly as she'd come, her body never having even entered the room. No advice, no argument, no opinion about my decision, no feeling my belly or taking my pulse or checking the monitor tape or writing discharge instructions or anything. Again, I was stunned, but I figured her nonchalance was a good indication that all was fine and my decision was sound. I waited for her to come back in and give me her cell number like she'd promised, but instead when the door next opened, it was the hospital nurse, Terri. Terri had been my nurse during a prior admission or two, and I was happy to see her. With her perky blond hair and doll-like figure, she reminded me of Hannah's Nurse Barbie. She hooked me back up to the monitor for a non-stress test and chattered away, cheerful and smiling as usual.

The door opened again, and again I expected to see the doctor, but instead, in strode Cody in her running shoes. She was out walking with her friend who'd helped us dress Noah for his viewing, and one or two of my nieces followed shortly. The word was out and they were all excited, thinking I was going to have the baby that day. They were all prepared to settle in and wait for the birth, but I told them what had happened and that I was going home. So they all left. I still hadn't told Cody I didn't want her to be at the delivery, and a few days before she'd said, "And Cally really wants to be there, too. It would really be good for her." That was the last thing I wanted, but I cringed and put her off with an "Oh, we'll see, or something," while screaming silently. I hadn't seen very much of Cally lately, and nothing was resolved between us. I hoped my parents could make it in time and I wanted Christiana to be present after missing Noah's. And she was very excited.

"Your NST looks good," Nurse Barbie said after they left, "but I want you to know that when your family's in the room, your blood pressure goes up. It's stress-related, and even though it's happy stress, the result is the same." I didn't bother to inform her that my family stress was not all happy. On the outside, we did appear to be a loving and supportive family. But my blood pressures were probably a good indication of what was happening on the inside.

I took a shower, changed, and lay back down in bed to wait for Andy to come and get me. But when the door opened, it was Cody, not Andy. "Andy's still at the relay race," she said, "so I said I'd come and get you." What could I say? I collected my things and walked out of the hospital to my waiting chariot—the hated green Tahoe. Again, I was supposed to be horizontal and keeping my blood pressure low for the health of my baby, my number one concern. So I held my breath and got in while my sister-in-law practically ran a few victory laps around her beloved car. "Do you mind if I stop at Starbucks on the way home?" she asked, stepping in—right foot, green—and giving me her best Cheshire Cat grin.

"No," I sighed, meaning yes, of course I do, I mind everything, a lot. I put my feet up on the dashboard in defeat and tried to get as horizontal as possible, feeling like I was betraying myself, my convictions, and my son.

When I got home, I went straight to Micah's room, where Noah's crib and the dresser still filled with his clothes were. I climbed into Micah's bed and pondered my life. "I'll know you're over it when you'll ride in the Tahoe," repeated like a skipping record in my ears.

Chapter Seven

"HAPPY MOTHER'S DAY," the kids said the next morning, kissing me while I lay back in my Lazy Girl chair. I cherished the cards they drew for me at school and opened the gifts they made, reveling in the joy of their three warm bodies and happy to be home with them on this hard day, my first Mother's Day of missing their brother.

My blood pressure rose in the afternoon, so Andy sent the kids up to Cody's and took me to the hospital. This time there were no midwives around and no doctor either—every mother was apparently home with her loved ones. A nurse I'd never met before strapped me to the monitor for a while and then sent me home again. Even though I'd been discharged just the day before, nobody seemed concerned.

Andy made his famous grilled salmon for dinner, and Cody showed up just in time to join in. We'd often shared meals with the Martins in our first year or so of living across the street, which worked out great for a while; but as time went by, I felt that we needed some space for our growing family to come together to talk about our days. After that, we said no to Cody's frequent invitations even more often.

So then she started showing up at our house instead. I got very tired of preparing a dinner, cutting up all the kids' meat and buttering their potatoes, only to have Cody barge in, unannounced, with her manicured nails ready to clutch a fork, asking, "What's for dinner?" In Jamaica, my host mother used to tell me, "Yu mus'n walk wit' yu belly inna yu han'," stuffing me with sweet potato pudding or some other treat before I could walk out the door. She would have sucked her teeth to see Cody walking around, hungry belly in hand. As she grabbed a plate to join us, if I tried to derail her by asking what her family was going to eat, she'd reply, "Oh, they can fend for themselves."

Inviting yourself to dinner, repeatedly, was also a foreign concept to me and was one of those differences that often become highlighted in a marriage, whether east meets east or east meets west. My mom lives to eat and not only does she know when her feet first slide into her slippers each morning exactly what her three square meals for the day will be, *with* the requisite two vegetables, she is already excited about those meals. My dad grew up seated at the right hand of his father, and he knew the back side of that hand well, because if any one of his five siblings did something to annoy William Gerard Moore Sr. during dinner, William Gerard Moore Jr. was the one who got back-handed. To this day, when a plate of food appears in front of him, Dad clams up and eats.

All things considered, our family dinner hour was sacred, not to be interrupted, and presided over by our silent Rhode Island Red rooster. We were instructed never to discuss money, politics, or religion at the table, and conversation was kept to a minimum. We said grace together, "God is great, God is good . . ." to which I added my own silent prayer that the turquoise phone hanging on the kitchen wall across the room wouldn't ring during dinner and if it did, God forbid, it wouldn't be for me.

I resented Cody's intrusion into our day and my Mother's Day dinner, but Andy, sensing my frustration, shot me a look as if to say, *Now, honey . . .* Cody had just watched the kids for us while we were at the hospital, so I sucked it up and shared my portion of salmon with Auntie Cody, even though it wasn't Auntie's Day.

The next day, Monday, I went to the clinic for another non-stress test and ultrasound. As I sat in the waiting room thumbing through parenting magazines, Dr. Harmon breezed in with her own son following behind her.

"I'm off to bake cookies," my primary caregiver sang out to the receptionist, giving us all a little wave as she went out the door to her vacation, and I was called in for yet another visit with a midwife.

When my appointment was over and I tried to book the rest of my daily appointments, the receptionist informed me that there were no appointments available with *any* of the midwives for the next four days, so she scheduled me with a nurse practitioner I'd never met at a satellite office I'd never visited. Apparently my high-risk status had dissipated.

On Tuesday, I found the new office and met the nurse, Peggy Cox. She hooked me up to the monitor for another NST and measured my belly, reporting that the tests from the day before looked great and the baby was in the sixtieth percentile for size. All was well.

On Wednesday, I asked Nurse Cox to check my cervix. "I've been having more painful contractions, and I'm wondering if anything has changed." I said. I was anxious to know if my cervix had softened or dilated any further. Was I moving closer to the roller coaster of delivery after all?

"I'll check your cervix tomorrow," she said.

She never had the opportunity.

The next time I saw her was on the witness stand four years later.

Chapter Eight

THE NEXT DAY—Thursday, May 14, 1998—Andy kissed me awake early. I drew in my breath, realizing my contractions were getting more uncomfortable. My parents were arriving that afternoon and I was excited, thinking they might make it in time after all. "I hope these contractions are working," I said, kissing him back. "That nurse better check my dilation today, or you'll have to."

"Gladly," he said, grinning.

Easing out of bed, I followed him to the kitchen. After all the waiting and worrying, I was ready to have this baby. I definitely did not call Cody, thinking maybe I could simply sneak in and have the baby without telling her and avoid the whole birthing-room discussion.

"Have a great day," I said, kissing Hannah and Christiana. "Maybe today we'll have a baby." For the first time in ages, I watched from my kitchen stool as they skipped off to school, and that felt good, like I was getting back to where I should be. The sun reflected off their blond hair and the dew in the grass, the spring air sparkling with new growth and possibility.

Andy and I headed back down the hall—I to shower, he to dress Micah—and soon I heard them arguing from Micah's room: "Pleeeeze, you only have to wear them for an hour."

Micah skipped in, dressed in the corduroy pants he hated, saying, "See, Mom? They swish when I move. Are you coming to my music?"

"Yes, I wouldn't miss it." I laughed, ruffling his hair and taking care not to hit his red-framed eyeglasses. I'd missed so many of my kids' milestones over the past few months. I didn't think it could hurt to ride three houses down to Joanne Ellis's home to see Micah's final performance of the year. My appointment with the nurse was at ten and his music program at nine; I'd stay for a half hour while Andy had a conference call and go directly from there. I could sit there as easily as I could sit in my Lazy Girl at home to wait, and it was certainly no more activity than my daily medical appointments entailed.

I took a quick shower and pulled on the clothes I was tired of wearing: my favorite oversize navy-blue cotton shirt, with stretchy red cotton leggings underneath—red, the color of the day. Since I stayed in good shape, lived in the era of Lycra, and was on the small side, I could get away with wearing regular, non-maternity clothing a size or two larger than usual, pulling the elastic waistbands below my belly as it expanded, just like so many men with beer bellies do. I often rubbed my protruding belly and preferred to have nothing but skin between Jonah and me while I massaged the numb spot where my belly button had flattened out, caressing his bumps.

Andy drove us right up to the front door of Joanne's house and said, "I'll be back for you in half an hour."

Micah and I eased our way down the stairs to the basement, where Joanne taught the local kids music once a week. I sat down right away and put my feet up, trying to get as horizontal as possible.

"I hope my water doesn't break on your couch," I joked with Joanne, who was busy setting up.

"Oh, it's an old couch," she said, a casual retort she would later recall on the witness stand.

My friend Linda arrived and sat next to me. She excitedly asked, "So, do you think today's the day?"

"I sure hope so, fingers crossed," I said, rubbing my belly. I'd already arranged for Micah to go home with her to play with her son after the program while I went to my appointment. The music program began with the kids singing songs and playing rhythms on their miniature instruments, demonstrating their new music-reading ability. Then Joanne said, "Now grab a partner for the circle dance."

"Come on, Mom!" Micah said, pulling on my hand to help me

up. I stood, feeling a pending sense of freedom, since I was hoping the nurse would soon say it was time to have this baby. All the other parents were joining their kids, so how could I say no to Micah? I waddled the three or four steps to our place in the circle. The song began, and we all shuffled around together like a large, undulating amoeba in a small Petri dish. Whenever the music paused, we were supposed to touch our elbow, stand on one foot, or do some other motion. I did only the hand and arm movements, happy to just stand holding Micah's hand while the other parents touched their noses to the carpet. When the song finished, Micah ran back to his chair, and I eased myself back down onto the couch.

Andy arrived soon after and caught my eye, gesturing from the stairs. I rose and was taking the five or six steps to meet him at the back of the room when I felt a gush between my legs, and thought, *Oh my God, my water* has *broken!* I scooted into the bedroom that was there at the bottom of the stairs and whispered to Andy, "Quick, get me a towel." I perched on the edge of the bed. He tossed me a hand towel from the adjoining bathroom, which I stuffed between my legs, not wanting to leak all over Joanne's bed. Leaning forward, I pulled the front edge of the towel away, tentatively, expecting to see the telltale wetness of my baby's bathwater.

The white towel was bright red with blood.

Andy and I exchanged wide-eyed looks of panic. I managed to get on my feet and up the stairs without creating an incident, our crisis unfolding to the sweet voices of five-year-olds singing "Slow Poke Fred." Nobody missed a note as we made it out the door and into Andy's red Blazer, speeding off to the hospital while Andy phoned the doctor's office on his cell phone.

Inside, I was screaming, but, "Hurry," was all I managed to say as I clenched my legs together, trying to seal my leaking cells, my fingers pressing firmly against my baby's life, now ebbing into a towel.

We arrived in about ten minutes—an eternity—and parked at the entrance. I was just starting to tell the admissions gal what was happening when I spotted our favorite Nurse Barbie. "The Kittels are here," she sang with glee.

"Terri, I'm bleeding," I said, wiping the smile right off her face.

She rushed me into the nearest room, handed me a Johnnie, and pushed me into the bathroom to change.

I hope I haven't ruined Joanne's towel, I thought, pulling it from between my legs and tossing it in the sink. *What am I doing in here? Hurry, hurry, please God, hurry, hurry*, I chanted to myself, pulling the gown closed behind my back but not bothering to tie it.

"Get on the bed," Terri instructed. She climbed right up, kneeling over me and palpating my stomach while peppering me with so many questions. "How long have you been bleeding like this? How long has your tummy been hard like this? When was the last time you felt your baby move?"

"I don't know," I said and repeated, "I don't know, I don't know."

I didn't even know my tummy was hard. All I knew was that I was bleeding. A lot.

I couldn't think. I couldn't answer her questions. My mind spun away from my body in panic.

"How long has your tummy been hard like this? How long has it been hard?" she demanded over and over.

I kept saying, "I don't know I don't know I don't know." It was all happening so fast and yet so slow.

"When was the last time you felt your baby move?"

Finally my brain recognized a word.

"Baby?"

"When was the last time you felt the baby move?" Terri repeated, saying the magic word again: *baby*.

My mind snapped to attention, flashing to the night before, me reclining in my Lazy Girl chair, the three kids settling down, ready for bed. The baby was doing its nightly gymnastics inside of me, flipping around, throwing out a knee or elbow. We all felt my belly, laughing and playing with the pointy protrusions. Hannah said, "Mom, I think this is a heel!"

Christiana and Micah danced around until they each grew tired, leaning over to kiss both me and the baby's bumps. "Good night, baby. Good night moon."

"When was the last time you felt your baby move?" Terri's voice interrupted my reverie.

My adrenaline-filled brain managed to stop the video filling its screen, directing my mouth to answer, "Last night?"

While I was busy with my flashback, an ultrasound technician had arrived by my side and hooked up her machine. She had a student shadowing her, who stood at the foot of my bed next to Andy. As her mentor set to work, she turned to Andy, smiling, and crooned, "So, is this your first baby?"

He didn't say a word.

The tech squirted her bluish gel and I felt the coldness spreading in concentric circles around my distended belly while she searched and searched with her ultrasound wand. I prayed it was a magic wand. She paused to turn the screen away from me, then continued examining my baby in its watery world, pushing harder to carve her pattern like an ice skater drawing compulsory circles around the frozen surface of my skin, but selfishly keeping her figure eights all to herself. I held my breath, waiting for her to exhale a sigh of relief. Waiting for her to say something. Her silence was deafening. I examined her face, her eyes, her hands like it was my job, not hers, waiting for her to smile, begging her silently—keep looking, keep skating, don't stop. I beseeched God to get in here. Paging God to my room, *now*.

And I repeated over and over to myself, *This can not be happening to me, this can not be happening, this can not be . . .*

Silence filled the room.

No tiny foot kicked her magic wand away.

Nothing moved beneath the stretched skin and clenched fist of my belly, once so lovely to touch, now as hard as ice, an icy oligotrophic lake—nothing living in it.

I lay there, waiting. Waiting for the inevitable pronouncement. Slamming my ears shut and blocking them to keep my baby in the present tense.

Don't you say anything, don't you dare say a word, I warned everyone wordlessly while I waited impatiently for someone to do something. Whisk me off to surgery, cut me open, save my baby, take my life if you must, but *just do something*!

Instead, everyone seemed to move even slower, like my room had suddenly filled with water and we had nothing to do but wait, rocking in our ark, until God decided to deliver us to dry land. Slowly, slowly, they unplugged and wheeled their machines out of the room, asking no more questions and leaving me lying there with my protruding belly exposed, a dead end covered in bluish gel.

While I was holding Micah's hand, shuffling around in a circle, changing into my Johnnie, or trying to find answers for too many questions, my baby was dying. The flood had returned. My baby had drowned.

Dr. Harmon swam into view and sank all hope as she dared to break the silence. "There's no heartbeat. There's nothing we can do."

I wanted to plug my ears like a child and scream to keep from hearing her terrible words. They had given up. But I hadn't. I was stubborn. I was desperate. I was Irish! But I didn't know how to save this baby. I didn't know what to do. My mind reeled: *No way, no way, no way, this can* not *be happening.*

"I'm so sorry," the doctor said.

I closed my eyes and thought, *Not again.*

Chapter Nine

"I'M SO SORRY," Dr. Harmon repeated while I ebbed away. "There was nothing we could do," she said, switching firmly to the past tense.

She tried to explain that my placenta had sheared off the uterine wall—abrupted. So now we were going to talk about this abruption thing.

"You'll have to deliver the baby," she said. "I'll start the induction."

Now, finally, she was also making the decisions: deliver the baby, no options given, no questions asked.

"I'm ordering pain medication. I don't want you to feel a thing."

I don't think she understood that there was not enough pain medication in the world to numb the pain I had, but I was in no condition to explain. I followed along. Did what I was told. Said nothing. They poked and prodded me with needles, inserting lines into my veins, cranking up the pitocin to kick-start my contractions. I could have morphine or barbiturates or anything I wanted now that they didn't have to worry about how it would affect that baby. Cigarettes? Cocaine? No problem. I could have had a martini and mainlined heroin at that point. Had a regular party in my pajamas with Kate the midwife and her abruption candidate patient I never met.

Instead, she gave me an epidural and we were off. People touched me and talked to me, and Andy answered for me. My mind was on overload and I stopped reacting to anything at all. My baby had no heartbeat and I was going to have to labor and deliver it, and that was more than enough to deal with. It was dead inside of me, and I still had to get it out. The roller coaster paused at the top of the hill, shock set in, and I checked out, letting my cold, heartless body go for its own reckless ride.

I remember only a few minutes of the hours of labor, my pathetic condition, and my horrific existence in that labor and delivery bed. Outside was another fingers-crossed sunny day to mask the insidious darkness in my room. Another of my spring-blooming babies had died. It was too terrible to comprehend.

I didn't want to be there.

So I left.

At some point in my journey away from myself, I nearly succeeded. They'd left Andy and me alone, even though my chart stated, "Watch closely." Fortunately, Andy was staring at the monitors and saw how low my blood pressure had fallen—noticed that his wife bore a striking resemblance to a corpse.

"Honey, are you okay?" He told me later that he'd asked this while holding my hand and looking into my eyes.

"Just let me go," he said I'd replied.

One of the many reasons I'd fallen in love with Andy was that I'd sensed he was a person from whom I could learn and grow. When I'd packed my bags to move to Jamaica for two years with the Peace Corps, I'd brought mostly clothes, towels, and toiletries like sunscreen—I was headed for the beach. Andy came with an iron skillet. He had practical skills, confidence, and a generous spirit, and I knew I would become a better person for knowing and loving him. Certainly, we'd had an intense physical connection from the start, and our children were living proof of our love for each other. But perhaps on top of all that, fate had joined east with west on a tropical island far from home so that one day Andy could save my life.

He ran outside for help.

I was losing too much blood, and my heart lacked the fluids it needed to keep pumping. Struggling to function, my heart rate elevated.

"Come in here *now*," Andy told Dr. Harmon, who was at the nurses' station. She rushed in, and I opened my eyes for a rare moment.

"Kelly?" she said.

I looked at her face and thought disconnectedly, *This will be the last thing I ever see in my life.*

"Patient pale and diaphoretic," she wrote later in my chart. "Diaphoretic" means excessive sweating commonly associated with shock and other medical emergency conditions. A heart doctor stepped up with a long needle, and I closed my eyes again as he injected ephedrine straight into my heart to keep it pumping in spite of my new low blood pressure. So, I lived to see Dr. Harmon again. Lived to hear her say, an hour or so later, words that prodded me into opening my eyes again—"Okay, you can push now."

After all the happy moments of playing with bony elbows and knees, and all the crying and humming and swimming and floating and the bed rest and medications and testing and appointments and consultations and joy and hope and dreams and worry and prayers, so many prayers, I pushed my baby's slippery blue body into the waiting hands of Dr. Harmon with a sad effort and no fanfare. No smiles. A delivery room with no smiles is a terrible, terrible place.

On a much happier day, down the hall from where I lay, Noah had been born at 1:40 a.m.

"Kelly, it's a boy," this doctor said just like Dr. C had. But with no exclamation point. The time was 1:45 p.m. There would be no baby book in which to record all these facts. All the pages were to be blank. For my fifth baby, I took few photos and kept few records.

He was whole. He was beautiful. He was our baby boy. He did not breathe, but he didn't look dead either. He had a head of dark hair and resembled his brother Micah. Somebody cut the cord, and they laid his perfect blue body on the cold scale instead of handing him to me. Nobody spanked him, and he didn't cry. Nothing bothered him at all. He lay on the hard, metal scale so peacefully, with his arms and legs crossed as if he were hugging himself, something he may have done to comfort himself before dying. He was a terribly perfect patient, like his brother Noah, and he let them weigh all six pounds, two ounces, of him, which included no air and was already minus the twenty-one grams of his sweet little soul. Apparently my uterus had two exits and his soul had chosen a different path, going off down its own tunnel to a different light, leaving his body behind for us.

Once again, I repeated my childhood rhyme to see where he landed, surprised to find that with this he was also like Micah: "Thursday's child has far to go." Indeed. He was off and running, leaving one set of slightly smudged footprints behind. We didn't laugh at his blackened feet kicking the air, and nobody attempted to guess at his size. He was nineteen inches long, and he got a zero for his Apgar score, but it wasn't his fault. He wasn't given a fair chance to pass that test, and they didn't evaluate those who had truly failed it for him, like his mother. And her doctor, who later said that even though she'd placed him in the past tense hours ago, even as improbable as it was, she, too, had held out the hope of delivering a living, breathing miracle.

Andy took Jonah's first photo before they swaddled and handed him over, professionally wrapped like all my babies had come to me. I kissed his sweet little cheek, still warm and smelling like me, holding him over my heart, over my breasts, which were filling all the while, ready and waiting for him to drink from.

All he lacked was that first breath. I held my own, waiting, willing him to take it. He was perfect and he was ready to go and we had waited too long because we didn't know any better. There were no words for how much we had all failed him. We were all guilty.

"Would you like me to baptize him?" Pastor Scott asked when he arrived. I suppose we mustered a nod or a word, or maybe he just did what he thought best. We were definitely putting him through his paces.

"What will you call this child?" he asked, holding, with a blessed tenderness, our blue baby wrapped in a white blanket.

"Jonah," I whispered, even though surely this was not the gifted dove Noah had intended for us.

"Emmanuel," Andy added, a name we had chosen so optimistically, because it means "God is with us." Even though God seemed to be napping again or perhaps in Hawaii on vacation. *Again!* Such a painful word to live with. Not, *for the first time*. But, *again*.

"Moore," I said.

"Kittel," Andy concluded.

Andy called Cody, who picked up Jonah's sisters and brother. My poor kids. I'd fed them hope for breakfast and baked them a fresh batch of despair for an afternoon snack.

Why did I have to break their little hearts, *again*?

How could I tell them that everything would be okay, *again*?

Again, they marched forward so very bravely, held their baby brother and cried, their sweet tears falling on his precious face and rolling down the straps of their overalls. Cody held him and caressed his blue cheek with her red-nailed fingers. We all held him and cried quietly. There was nothing to say. Family and friends appeared at intervals and they held him and anointed him, drop by drop, with the living waters of their combined tears. There is nothing sadder in this world than a dead baby. There is nothing more heartbreaking for a mother than to deliver a baby into this world knowing he is no longer of this world, knowing that it is only a token gesture, like closing the cage door after the dove has flown away.

"We saw the most beautiful rainbow over Mount Hood when our plane landed," my mother said when they arrived later that afternoon, too late for one more birth. They held their new grandson briefly and went home with their other grandchildren while I received another blood transfusion.

The placenta is a highly vascular organ, and it circulates up to one pint of blood per minute. Most people don't give it much thought, but it's a pound of wonder, protecting the baby from infections and providing blood, nutrients, and oxygen while removing its waste. The placenta giveth, and the placenta taketh away.

When that miraculous organ separates completely, suddenly, *abruptly* from the uterine wall, like mine had done, it leaves a gaping hole that causes severe internal bleeding. Some of this blood might exit the body through the vagina, like mine did when I stood up in Joanne's basement. Some is trapped and hidden inside. To compensate, the body tries to clamp all those leaking blood vessels by contracting, which is why my uterus was so hard when I arrived at the hospital. Called "hypertonus," it's a continuous contraction of the uterus while it desperately tries to stop the massive internal hemor-rhage and stem the blood flow, just like you might hold your hand over a flesh wound. Just like I'd tried to do with Joanne's towel.

Unfortunately, there was a huge impediment to the process—the baby to be named Jonah Emmanuel. With the baby still in utero, all that contracting and constricting and clamping and clenching is compromised, and the bleeding can't stop. As a second line of defense, the body calls into service its army of coagulants and puts the troops to work forming blood clots. This process, although tem-porarily effective, can ultimately lead to disaster if allowed to con-tinue unabated. If all of the body's blood coagulants are disseminated and utilized, something called DIC rears its ugly head.

My chart stated: "Watch 4 DIC, labs consistent with evolving DIC." DIC—Disseminated Intravascular Coagulation. The prognosis for DIC is grim; its street name is Death Is Coming. With no sticky coagulants left, the newly thinned blood simply leaks out of all veins and arteries, and the patient bleeds to death. I would receive two units of blood, 650 milliliters, to replace some of the more than 1,500 milliliters I lost in the course of labor and delivery.

Once the baby is delivered, the uterus can finally clamp the internal wound, the bleeding can be stemmed, and a huge clot can be built by that army of coagulants. If DIC has begun, performing a C-section carries the risk of exacerbating the condition, and the mom can bleed to death on the operating table. An emergency hys-terectomy might be done successfully to stop the bleeding, but that slams the door to motherhood firmly shut without even a shudder.

So this is how I could consider myself lucky—I still had my uterus.

My door to motherhood was still swinging, even if it did hang slightly askew on bloody hinges.

I had seen the face of death. But I was still alive.

Late that night after Andy had fallen asleep in the hospital chair, Cody showed up. "I couldn't sleep," she said. Obviously, she had talked her way in after visiting hours, and for once she had no jokes and didn't snort about anything, reminding me of a time seemingly so long ago when our relationship was perhaps based more on love and respect. As dreadful as I felt, I appreciated her coming in what seemed a gesture of solidarity and support. The truth was, I probably would not have done the same for her. She stayed a little while in those hushed hours of the night and helped the nurse change me and my bloody bedclothes.

After she left, the nurse said, "Would you like me to take your picture?" I'd been holding Jonah in my arms all night, not willing to relinquish him after so much waiting, so much wanting.

"Yes, thank you," I answered, and she produced a hospital camera.

I was not one for kissing my babies on the lips, especially not a newborn, not wanting to give them my germs. But this time, of course, was different. I kissed Jonah's black raspberry-colored lips, and she snapped our mother-baby photo, handing me the Polaroid when it developed. We both looked like death.

I prayed all night that Jonah would take a breath—that he would open his eyes and look at me with love or hunger or rage and end this nightmare. It was a familiar prayer, one I had prayed just nine months prior but with greater urgency. This time, in the wee hours of the morning, my prayer was more dream than demand, more suggestion than command, more beginning than ending.

Breathe, Jonah, breathe, breathe, damn it, please God, make him breathe.

I prayed for nothing short of a miracle.

I didn't get one.

Only God would ever know the color of Jonah's eyes.

Chapter Ten

A T 6:00 A.M., the nurse woke Andy and me. "We need to move you to the fourth floor because we need this room for deliveries." The fourth floor held the mother-baby unit, but in my case only half of our team was ready to play. Was I a new mother? What was the term for someone like me?

By the time I arrived, my room lacked all things a baby might need—no Steri-Wipes, no plexiglass baby bassinette, no diaper coupons, no stack of New Baby paperwork, no binky, and no matching wrist bracelets to make sure nobody switched babies with me. Instead of a birth certificate, we would receive yet another death certificate to add to our collection with a horrible new acronym to learn: IUFD—Intra-Uterine Fetal Death. Intra—*inside*—inside of my uterus my baby had died. My baby, Jonah, was not allowed on that blissful floor I loved so well since he did not meet the standards of living that were required. He was not, after all, alive.

Andy wanted to accompany me up to my new room, but first he had to do something with our new baby. The nurse bundled Jonah in his white blanket like a real little Kittel doll. A *kittel* is a white Jewish burial shroud, and though Andy wasn't Jewish, when I learned this I wondered if I should have kept my maiden name. The nurse handed Jonah to his father while they wheeled me away. Andy, in turn, walked out to our car parked in the hospital parking lot. When he returned I asked, "Where's Jonah?"

"I put him in the backseat of the van."

"Did you lock the door?" I asked, before I could stop myself.

We looked at each other and began to cry at the terrible irony of our situation. Our sweet little baby, born only yesterday, could be locked in our car unattended.

"Yes," Andy said. But who, after all, would want to steal him?

I rolled my wounded body over into the fetal position for all three of us and tried to escape from the mauve-toned walls that imprisoned me. I wanted to close my eyes and sleep the dreams of the dead, and I didn't want to wake ever again. I attempted to block my ears with waterproof hospital pillows, muffling the squealing of visitors greeting their newborn bundles of joy in every other room on that mother-baby floor but mine. Each cry from all those babies was a caustic rub to my wounds.

I was physically spent, exhausted from the ordeal of the labor and delivery, the blood loss and trauma, my near-conscription into the army of the DIC, and the damned disappointment so huge and unimaginable no acronym could begin to describe it. I didn't want to face myself or my world. I wanted to curl up and go away.

Bea, the midwife, came by with a coffee from Starbucks for me, it being a brand-new day and all. But like everything else, it wasn't quite right—just a regular old mocha. Anyway, the thing I needed first and foremost couldn't be bought and didn't come in a warm, chocolaty cup. A breakfast tray was delivered, which I didn't want either, but I eyeballed the orange juice and the blame game began as I wondered, *had I eaten too much citrus fruit?*

Some stalwart friends and family marched bravely past all those happy new moms to discover me in the last room on the right—the dead end. They were kind to come, but I felt like a total failure, finding it difficult to say anything. What was left to say that hadn't already been said to and by these same loving people only nine months earlier, in August? These were the same good people who'd nourished my baby with their meals and helped him to grow with their love and carpools and laundry service and playdates and prayers. My task was to deliver a shining beacon of hope named Jonah Emmanuel, proving to all these good people of faith around me that God is good! Death has no victory!

But death had beaten me fair and square in round two. God's presence was increasingly difficult to discern. Death, on the other hand, was definitely in our corner.

To think that my body had failed my baby so completely made me hate myself. This was the fifth baby my body had delivered, and it should have known the correct order of things by now. *First* comes labor, *then* comes delivery of baby, and *then* comes delivery of the placenta. Simple steps to follow. Delivery for Dummies. One, two, three, basic math, in that ancient order. Me and my "proven uterus" had gotten it all backward.

How many different ways did I have to lose my children?

I didn't have the energy to limp down the hall for a shower, couldn't face passing all those flower-filled rooms or looking at the true crime scene of my body in the small mirror I knew hung in there on the wall. The hospital discharged me that afternoon with a bill for $3,386, which included $950 for a "standard" delivery but no discount for unhappy customers, thank you very much.

Before I left, Dr. Harmon appeared again like the specter of death itself to gaze into my eyes through her thick glasses, her own eyes filled with pity. A few strands of her unruly hair brushed my arm as she sent me home with these words ringing in my ears, "Kelly, I know you can have another baby." *Yes*, I thought, *my uterus and I might just work together again someday.* But the only baby I wanted right then was wrapped in his *kittel* and lying in a hot car in the parking lot.

And so it came to pass that there was another Day After. We stumbled out of Salem Hospital, this time, but fell right back into the same valley of the shadow of death. Once again, the only reward for our efforts was the death penalty which felt, indeed, like a punishment. Was there something I needed to atone for? Did I have some mysterious karmic debt? We limped to our car and crawled home to hug our kids, to smile sadly, and to suffer, suffer, suffer.

And then, of course, I had a birthday party to plan. Three terrible days later, Noah's second birthday arrived. There was no end to the irony, no end to the pain, no getting around the steadfastness of the calendar, no dove named Jonah to escort us through Noah's flood to dry land. On a sunny Sunday, we sat on the hillside in the cemetery next door, which suddenly seemed too conveniently located. We dug around Noah's tree, planting flowers and bulbs. I sat in a low folding beach chair in shorts and a maternity top, feeling fat and weak and pale, watching and trying to make the best of it.

"Look, Mommy, one white balloon and one blue," the kids said, skipping around and tying the balloons my mother had purchased around a low tree branch to mark Noah's two years. We were supposed to have a new baby with us—Noah's dove—a snow-white boy to help ease the pain of facing this terrible first birthday without our golden boy. It would have made all the difference in the world. That I know. But our baby was born blue, like the other balloon.

While I watched my kids dancing in the sun, I daydreamed about sitting on that hillside in front of my son's grave with a hungry new-born slurping at my breast. Jonah was the baby who'd brought us this far out of our grief, and losing him brought it all rushing back to bury us anew in an avalanche of pain. I sat there calmly showing my kids which end pointed up when planting tulip bulbs, wishing my own life was so easily directed —that I could simply plant myself facing up. Instead, I was pointing down, struggling to find my way to the warm and sunny surface. I wished somebody would tie me up in Noah's tree to hang alongside the balloons until I, too, slowly deflated and shriveled up in the sun rather than drag myself through the impending days without my lost babies in my empty arms.

Before I'd gone to the hospital, we'd purchased a large lithograph of Noah's ark, which a friend had framed for us. It had arrived on our doorstep the day before Noah's graveside birthday party. Instead of hanging it in Noah's tree, after we walked home from the cemetery, Andy hung it on our bedroom wall with my guidance. When he was finished, I stepped forward and looked closely at the print: On the bow of the ark stood Noah, his hand outstretched. Flying toward Noah was a white dove ready to land and holding an olive branch in its beak. I looked at Noah and I looked at the dove and I looked at the outstretched hand and I looked at the dove again. Had Noah's dove flown away from me to be with him?

Because maybe then I could accept this rotten situation and begin to turn my bulb around. Maybe if our terrible sacrifice brought comfort to both of our sons, Noah and Jonah, I could glimpse a glimmer of equity shining in an otherwise unfair world. I had three children here on Earth and two in Heaven, and if they were together in their respective places for each other, then that might be okay. We'd conceived Jonah as a playmate for Micah, but perhaps he'd been intended for Noah all along. I might get used to that idea and could draw some measure of comfort from it.

I stood on the barren shore of our bedroom while the flood waters receded before me, watching that dove fly into the waiting, outstretched hand of his Noah. I stared at that picture for a long, long time, until a tiny seedling of peace fell into the cracked surface of my heart.

Chapter Eleven

"HONEY, look at my boobs," I said to Andy through clenched teeth when I woke up the morning after Noah's birthday. On this, the fourth day after Jonah's delivery, my hormones raged, and my normally small breasts were so engorged with milk I could rest my chin on them—yet another painful reminder that my body was ready for a baby, but that there was no baby.

I had night sweats from the hormonal stew boiling within me, and I woke up from nightmarish dreams, drenched in salty broth and shivering with cold. "Come here," Andy said, wrapping me in the embrace of his long arms and holding me against his dry warmth, which I desperately needed. I was a mess. I dreamed my teeth were falling out. I had weird pains in my heart, which raced erratically and beat so forcefully I could see my chest pulsing with its spasms as though it would burst free and run away if it could, trailing errant arteries in its wake. I patted it until it calmed down. Stress? I thought that of all things that can cause cancer, surely losing your children should be at the top of the list. My breasts felt like they could split open any minute, like gigantic, overripe ortaniques. I called the doctor.

"Don't pump. Never pump. It produces even more milk. Use ice packs. Wear two bras. Take two Tylenol, and call me in the morning."

I wore two tight jogging bras with cold packs layered in between them. I took pain relievers, counting the minutes until the next one. The unbearable pressure lasted for weeks and I thought I would go mad, if I wasn't already. But I followed orders, unable to imagine even more milk.

Please, God, I begged silently from my bed, where I lay in the beginning days, recovering my strength and mustering the will to live. *Please, God, please, please, if you can hear me, please just put a baby on my doorstep. Lend it to me even if only for a little while, no questions asked.*

I secretly checked outside my red front door, just in case, but my feng shui doorstep remained empty, joyless.

I let my fingers do the walking and scanned the Yellow Pages, calling for information on milk banks and foster care and whatever else I could find to alleviate my suffering, but I was only met with more dead ends. La Leche League said the only current recipient of breast milk was Canada, which seemed woefully far to mail the milk I wasn't even supposed to start pumping—no pumping, for heaven's sake. They sent me a sympathy card, which did nothing for my aching breasts. I was told I couldn't nurse a foster child because of the risk of transmitting AIDS, even though I had just had a mandatory blood test for the disease with my pregnancy. I would have made the world's best foster mother, but I could not find a baby. I needed a baby and I wanted a baby and my body thought I had a baby and I couldn't convince it otherwise, even though I so desperately wanted it to be true.

Before I'd weathered even the first full week without Jonah, and as I still lay in bed swimming in my misery and recovering my physical strength, Cody burst into the house, and soon I heard her in Micah's room making a racket. Nobody else was home. I dragged myself out of bed and across the hall. "It's time to get this out of here," she declared, refraining from calling me "Queenie," not stopping to even look in my royal direction while she busily dismantled Noah's crib with a screwdriver. I wasn't ready to move his crib yet; it was an act that felt too final while I was still immersed in the immediacy of Jonah's loss. Jonah's expected birth had been my excuse for leaving

Noah's crib and his dresser in the room with Micah. I'd planned to tackle the dreaded task of emptying Noah's clothes from the drawers only when the time had come to fill them back up with the new baby's things—when his clothes would be transformed into hand-me-downs instead of yet another sad reminder of loss.

Apparently Cody had also been fixated on Noah's crib, but with a different motive. She removed bolts and screws as fast as her red nails could rotate while I collapsed into the rocking chair, feeling dizzy and protesting meekly. She completely ignored me. Cody was like a steamroller once she decided to do something, and it took a lot more strength than I had to stop her. All I could do was let her run me over. By the time she was finished, Noah's crib lay in pieces in the basement alongside his dresser. I went back to bed and cried.

When Jonah would have been a snuggly one-week-old infant, I found myself sitting once again in Joanne's basement with Micah, this time for Christiana's music program. Upon arrival, I'd slipped into the bathroom and replaced the towel I'd borrowed, freshly laundered and looking as good as new in spite of my misplaced worry to the contrary. Some stains were easier to remove than others. This time, I chose a hard chair on the edge of the room, avoiding the killer couch, which I also hadn't ruined after all. I focused my gaze on my daughter, avoiding the pitiful stares of other parents, even though I could still feel them. Strapping on a smile, I tried to enjoy my bubbly girl singing, but bubbles pop easily, and it was very difficult. I reined in my mind, determined as it was to keep replaying the raw footage of last week's me, sitting there happily rubbing my extended belly while my baby enjoyed his last moments. I felt happy to be there for Christiana, finally, after all that bed rest. But the repeat performance was torturous.

While I sat in that déjà vu–filled basement listening to my daughter singing so sweetly, it occurred to me that Jonah had probably enjoyed Micah's music program. I pictured him settling in utero and quieting his kicking feet, perhaps continuing some silent toe-tapping against the cushiony wall of our placenta while he clutched the cord that would soon disconnect us. I could almost hear him humming along in his underwater world until the moment I stood up to go. "Hey," he might have said to nobody in particular, "I was listening to that! Where are we going now?" In my head I replayed the last sounds he had heard in his brief life—his brother Micah and friends happily singing "Slow Poke Fred," followed by the receding tones of his parents, praying for his life.

The next day, Andy accompanied me to Dr. Harmon's office for my follow-up appointment. When we approached, the clinic door opened, and out came Lisa—the midwife who'd helped me decide to leave the hospital on the Saturday before Jonah died. Seeing us, she hurried away without a word.

"What was that all about?" I asked Andy.

My appointment was scheduled for late in the day, but still there were happily expectant Moms in the waiting room reading *Parenting* magazine articles about new baby safety products or planning their baby's layettes. Everyone in the office avoided looking at us, but when they called us in, we ran into Kate, the midwife, in the hallway. She hugged me and said, "We all feel just terrible about your loss. You are such a strong person."

"Well, what other choice do I have," I replied, "the insane asylum?"

"Well, that's why they do exist," I remember her saying, and that gave me something to ponder as we continued down the hall.

"I'm so sorry for your loss," Dr. Harmon began when we were seated in her office, "and everyone here in the office feels so bad. You know, we have a beach house on the coast, and you're welcome to use it *any*time." This was a surprise, and I remember thinking, *how nice of her to offer that.* "Your labs show that your blood levels are recovering nicely." *Big deal*, I thought, so not caring anymore about what my blood levels were doing.

"I've been under pressure from the hospital not to perform so many C-sections or deliver premature babies," she continued. *What was she trying to tell us?* I wondered, glancing over to see Andy's raised eyebrows. *That it was the hospital's fault that she didn't deliver Jonah earlier or do a C-section to save his life?* I was stunned by this admission, but she rattled on in her usual way, and I could barely keep up, never mind make sense of it all.

"On Monday I woke up and I just had the strongest gut feeling that I should call you in to deliver that baby," she said. Now she had my attention.

She meant the Monday three days before Jonah's death. I thought back to that day and saw myself sitting in her waiting room for my appointment while she breezed through with her son, cookie recipes on her mind, saying nothing to me. If she'd told me then about this feeling, I surely would have listened. So why on earth did she opt to hold her tongue then? And why unleash it now, when it was woefully too late? Had she really been that eager to get home to her chocolate chips and her cookie dough?

"You know," she continued before I could fully digest her last statement, "Abruption is one of the great mysteries of pregnancy." She reiterated this last statement as if to say that it was nobody's fault, and there was nothing to be done about it. Then she leaned forward as if in confidence and said, "I'll do whatever I can to help you have another baby, Kelly."

Another and *baby* were the only two words she'd spoken that I cared about at that point, and I left her office with them ringing in my ear. But they were the last two words Andy wanted to hear, and as we climbed into our minivan, he said as much, explaining, "Before we even think about having another baby, we need to find out what the risks are. I don't want to lose you."

I agreed and left it at that. I didn't share all the details of my research and my obsession with finding a baby to nurse, and I definitely didn't tell him I was checking our doorstep daily for a gift from God. When you're in pain, all you can truly focus on is getting out of it. I rode home and almost enjoyed the Technicolor treat of Oregon spring blooming all around me thanks to the sweet melody of those two little words, my secret soundtrack of hope. *Another. Baby.* Later, I would have the presence of mind to ponder the rest of the conversation.

Three weeks after Jonah died, we had a follow-up appointment with Dr. Watson, my high-risk doctor in Portland. He gave us even more statistics about abruption and abruption with fetal demise. Now, suddenly, everyone wanted to talk about abruption.

"You have about a 20 percent chance of having another abruption," he said. When he launched into his "abruption is one of the great mysteries of pregnancy" speech, I stopped him and said that all I'd ever known about abruption was what Kate the nurse-midwife had explained to me that day in the hospital.

"Kate said I would feel a sharp, stabbing pain in the right upper quadrant of my uterus," I told him—a pain I'd still never felt.

"Well," said my fellow Jazzercise devotee, looking from beneath his white eyebrows into my eyes in the most memorable moment of the meeting, "she has a lot to learn, doesn't she?"

This hit me hard, the strongest of inklings I'd had to date that perhaps my care providers were not as good as they should have been. Kate's words were as clear in my head as the day she'd spoken them, but now it seemed she'd misinformed me. Maybe mine was not simply a case of this mysterious complication of pregnancy that nobody could have prevented, like we'd been told repeatedly. I reeled from the news that the only information I'd been given about pre-empting the very disaster that had occurred had been incorrect.

Now, in addition to my continued studies on death and dying, I wanted to know all about abruption. I borrowed medical textbooks from Dr. Harmon and asked Pat, Cody's sister-in-law who was the NICU nurse, for information on abruption. Pat sent me pages copied from medical journals. I learned that abruptions are most common in women under twenty or over thirty-five years of age. I sat on the threshold at thirty-six. Of the eight risk factors listed, only two pertained to me: I had hypertension and Jonah was a male. I learned that abruption occurs in 1 percent of pregnancies worldwide but only in 0.4 percent of pregnancies in the United States, and that only one in every 500 to 750 deliveries results in abruption with fetal demise.

Even my math-challenged brain could comprehend the overwhelming odds I'd unwittingly beat: *Zero-point-four percent? And only one in five hundred of those?* Most books are reluctant to even discuss this statistic, focusing instead on the occurrence of partial abruptions where everyone exhales their relief—"Phew, that was a close one"—and lives happily ever after. Even the textbooks that did dare to discuss abruption more fully gave only a nod in my direction, printing a word or two about the very rare possibility that had recently become the story of my life. Having been struck by lightning twice now, I derived no comfort from statistics. I learned that until the 1960s, the decade of my birth, most women died from abruption, because the abilities to induce labor and transfuse blood were not widespread. I learned that even today the leading cause of maternal death in the United States is hemorrhaging after the twenty-eighth week of pregnancy.

After Noah's death we were deluged by a biblical flood of cards and calls and flowers and food and people arriving daily. Following Jonah's death we received more like a light spring shower—just enough to keep the plants from dying. People were out there, thinking about us and praying for us, but they seemed reluctant to speak or visit or engage. They apparently thought we should be left alone. Engulfed as I was by my grief and physical agony, I only realized this as time went by as I came to understand the many iterations of "still" in stillbirth. First, the baby is born still, then the delivery room becomes still, then people's voices are still, and then the rest of your life is silent and still in all the gaping holes where Jonah should have been, from the empty chair at the dinner table to the missing smile in the family photo.

It is my great misfortune to have had this terrible comparative experience, and once or twice somebody has dared to ask, "Which was harder, losing Jonah or losing Noah?" To which I've replied with words I read somewhere: "Which would *you* miss more, your right arm or your left?" Losing a baby through miscarriage or stillbirth or any form of intra-uterine demise is no less traumatic than losing a child who has walked and talked and hugged and thrown up on you. And the physical pain and recovery is, in many ways, much, much worse. When I lost Noah, I had not just run the marathon of labor and delivery, nor had I almost died myself.

I knew this child, Jonah, intimately—as intimately as he'd known me, as intimately as any possible human-knowing can be. He was in me and of me, an inextricably connected unit of me. We were one and the same. He felt the warmth of my hands while I massaged his pointy elbows and knees. He knew the rhythmic beat of my heart and the melody of my internal organs better than I, myself. He knew when I ate or drank or sang or cried. We grew and experienced every moment of many months together and we loved each other completely.

Jonah was no "it," as my mother-in-law now called him. "You just have to look at *it* like *it* was not meant to be," she said after he died, sealing the conversation with her raised palm facing me in a gesture of authority, of finality. But I would not ever, as in *never*, get over "it," either. Because Jonah actually was and always would *be* for me. This time, my loss was greater than Andy's, Hannah's, Christiana's, or Micah's, and certainly Marcella's, in that they never really knew this baby like I did. They were all waiting to meet him. But I already knew him.

And yet I was not ungrateful for what I did receive. I counted as blessings all those who attempted to say or do something to recognize Jonah's passing through our lives. And I especially cherished every instance when someone said his name—Jonah. Jonah. I loved that name, remember? Jonah. And I rejoiced when someone wrote it. Many referred to him as "your baby" or "your loss" and could not, perhaps, bring themselves to say his name. As with Noah's death, many people were stunned speechless and simply did not know what to say—and said so.

Others wrote and admitted that they were avoiding me. I certainly did not blame them. I would have avoided myself, too, if I could have. I felt so pathetic and so unforgiving of myself. Some misunderstood what had transpired; many were afraid to ask; and others confused the two boys. If Noah's death had shaken people's beliefs, Jonah's death rocked their faith to the core. And mine. If Jonah had lived, I imagine that I would have felt like the hand of God, Himself, had dipped me in the river to be born again. Andy would have driven us home to Noah's star magnolia tree, blooming at the end of our dead-end street, where I would have stepped out of my minivan and lifted my lion cub up to the heavens with tears of gratitude and thanks-giving, dedicating my life to shouting the news of my eternal relief: "Look! A gift from God! He answered my prayers!" And I imagine that my life would have been altered in an entirely different direction. But that didn't happen.

Many others tried to make sense of it and sent us what spiritual solace they could muster. We received more donations to Noah's garden and the church landscaping project in Jonah's name, and we donated a stewartia tree to the church garden, which was planted just outside the stained glass window beside our regular pew. While I was in the hospital, a friend filled my house with single peonies, a flower that will always remind me of Jonah—and the day I arrived home from the hospital unable to share their beauty with him. The Heifer International project, whose goal is to end world hunger by donating farm animals, got a flock of chicks in Jonah's name, and we donated another stack of books to the library with a bookplate for Jonah this time; after all, he had listened each day of his life while my tongue twisted around complicated Dr. Seuss rhymes. Jonah was enrolled in masses around the world and would be well prayed for.

One day, as I lay in the Lazy Girl pondering my future, the door-bell rang. "Is your mommy here?" a high, familiar voice asked. My friend Melanie entered and handed me an elegantly wrapped box. "I thought this would make Jonah's life seem a bit more tangible," she said. I unwrapped her gift—a silver child's drinking cup with "Jonah" engraved on it. We placed it in the china cabinet alongside Noah's, given to him by his godparents a few months before he died. Our only two children with engraved silver cups are the two whose lips have no earthly use for them.

Chapter Twelve

We HAD NEITHER the physical nor the emotional strength to plan a funeral for Jonah. My mother and Andy had taken him to be cremated, and he was returned to us in a simple box, which I emptied into his new ceramic urn. We purchased the cemetery plot next to Noah's, and a small group of us gathered for a simple graveside service on another sunny day, a Sunday afternoon, when our baby should have been turning one month alive, not one month dead.

Summer was underway, and the promise of carefree days filled the hearts and minds of most people while we planted our sad little garden of ashes. My friends sang "Amazing Grace," and the emotion caused my breast milk to let down and leak all over the pale, lime-colored silk shirt I'd bought to bury my son in, my body still being Jonah size. The stain proved to be more permanent than my baby; it never washed out, and I finally threw the shirt away. The kids sprinkled rose petals on Jonah's cremains, and we planted another sweet gum tree in the cemetery to keep Noah's tree company. We'd asked for Jonah's placenta after his birth, as usual, but they'd preserved it in formaldehyde as part of their pathological examination, so we didn't think it would be healthy to plant it. Our sons' trees would grow each year, side by side—our earthly reminder of how time was passing. Somewhere, we hoped, our boys were also growing side by side until we'd meet again.

We interred our second son and tried to exhume our lives. Once again, we had to start all over. They say, "When you get to your wits' end, that's where God lives." If that's true, then we were all piled up on His doorstep begging for an audience. But the door was bolted on the inside, and all of our pounding was an exercise in futility; it seemed He was always busy elsewhere.

Slowly, I regained my strength and started taking short walks around the neighborhood. One day I returned home to find Pastor Jane's car in our driveway. I entered the house to find her sitting with Christiana and Micah by Noah's fountain. When I apologized for my brief absence, she said in her lilting Scottish brogue, "Not at all, the kids have been showing me around."

And, indeed, they had.

My now-youngest two children had proudly shown her Noah's and Jonah's things—photos, remembrances, engraved silver cups—chatting with their amazing five- and six-year-old maturity and mat-ter-of-factness about both of their little brothers. She and I looked at each other, recognizing simultaneously that these kids had gained not only the practice of hospitality but also such great wisdom—or maybe they'd had it all along. They were very comfortable discussing the matters of birth and death that scared many adults ten times their age. Andy and I talked about death openly with the kids and showed them our honest feelings, always mindful to never teach them that when life gets hard, you give up. Still, none of this was what we'd intended or wished for them. But these living wonders of ours, in turn, were showing us a way through, with their big brown eyes, their smiles, their hospitality, and their honesty.

Pastor Jane transformed her visit with us into a long and thought-ful article in the weekly church bulletin. It heartened us to learn from it that all of those wonderful people who'd given us so much help felt that Andy and I had helped them instead. She wrote, "In their search for meaning and healing they have shared the blessing with us. That's amazing! That's Grace!"

My parents were staying with us for six weeks, so I signed my mom and myself up for golf lessons, since we both suddenly had all this yawning time on our hands—she still settling into her retirement and me fast-forwarding my fears of the impending emptiness of the house when Micah began kindergarten in a few months. The terrible taste of my unwanted freedom gave me nausea, like morning sickness. "Now don't grip the club, swing steady but not hard," the instructor taught, and I tried to restrain myself. But it was irresistible to refrain from transferring my frustrations to that golf club, swinging as hard as I could at those dimpled balls and sending them flying away from me and out of my life.

After Noah died, we'd attended a few meetings of the local chapter of The Compassionate Friends, a group for bereaved parents, but now I just couldn't go back and face that circle of parents who were hungry for hope and healing and feed them my new story of loss. I had failed, like every alcoholic who has fallen off the wagon. Even among this group, whose 3-D dreams replayed every parent's worst fears, I was their worst nightmare. Their term for me? "Multiple loss."

I continued to experience random pain and offbeat pounding in my heart, so I scheduled a follow-up appointment with the heart doctor who'd jump-started my heart in the hospital. I sat in his waiting room flipping through AARP magazines, surrounded by senior citizens who glanced up in surprise when the nurse called my name, probably thinking I was waiting for someone to come out.

"Your heart is fine," the doctor pronounced, dismissing my complaints after perfunctorily examining me with his stethoscope. "I fully expect you will live a long and uneventful life," he said. I thought perhaps he was in the wrong line of work. Because the correct diagnosis, I could have told him, was that my heart was broken.

In the middle of June I received a letter from Pat, our friend in Jamaica. Seeing her handwriting on the thin, blue airmail paper brought me back to a memorable night during our November visit. In the hill town of Montpelier, high above Montego Bay, Pat and her husband, Tony, the local Episcopal priest, lived in their churchyard home. Pat ran a private school on the grounds of the church property.

"I've had premonitions all my life," Tony, a coffee-with-cream-skinned Jamaican, had said as we sat on their veranda following dinner while all our kids in various shades of brown and white played together. "I have certain dreams that are different from all the others, and they wake me up. I keep a book by my bed and write them down before I go back to sleep. Usually they come to pass. Pat sometimes has them too."

The mountain fog rolled in, enveloping us in its coolness and increasing the surrealism of our setting. Fireflies—peenywallies—winked their bioluminescent calling cards like tiny torches in the swirling darkness. The gothic steeple remained in view, pointing up to heaven out of the rising mist. This stone sentinel had stood for eons, showing the way to whip-scarred slaves, even, as they escaped into the fog while their masters hunted for them atop horses whose hides were rubbed raw by dangling chains and ankle cuffs. Likewise, our conversation turned otherworldly. While we sat in the deepening darkness, some huge Jamaican bat moths visited the lights around us.

"I don't know if you've noticed, but one moth has been hovering around us all night," Tony said in his proper, lilting accent. "You know, Jamaicans believe souls return to earth in the form of moths. I believe that moth there is the soul of Noah." I watched the moth fluttering around us and felt comforted by this thought.

"Souls hang around for a while after death, keeping tabs on their loved ones and making sure all is well," he explained. "When they feel we're okay, their job is done, and they can move on to a different realm."

I dragged my thoughts back to the present of my sunny Oregon kitchen and remembered that listening to Tony had made me hope that Noah felt we were okay, not wanting to hold him back from wherever it was he was going. And how I'd thought, *Maybe he's waiting for the baby to be born.* I carefully unfolded the tissue-thin paper with "fragile" stamped in red, which was an accurate assessment of both the paper and its contents. Pat's British accent spoke clearly to me across climate zones.

I had a strange dream about you all ten days ago. It was a festival meal and we were in a wood-paneled room with a magnificent feast laid out. There were candles and lots of red in the Christmas decorations. Kelly and I were serving the children, and Andy kept saying, "I have this terrible headache, terrible flu. I feel SO ill." There was no baby there, and I woke up with a great shock, knowing that something had gone wrong. I dithered around for days, wondering whether I should write and ask you, and then we heard from Margaret that the baby had died…Allow yourselves to grieve and do not try to be too strong, that is the only feeble advice I can offer.

Chapter Thirteen

IF YOU LOOK at our photos from that summer, you will see us playing in lakes, walking on beaches, swimming in pools, hiking in mountains, visiting with friends, and flying on airplanes. We look like any other happy family enjoying the summer with our children, all beautiful and sun kissed and complete. Along with blueberry muffins, I now avoided all citrus fruits, too. I doubled up on my workouts and slowly began reshaping my body-by-Jonah. I wanted to shave my head but settled for a very short cut instead. I wanted to keen like my Irish ancestors or ululate like an African but, as I'd so recently learned, when faced with a crisis I was more like my Mayflower ancestors—I clammed up. It seemed there should be some outward sign of my grief, and what I really wanted to do was rend my clothes and wander in the wilderness—a woman deranged.

We were invited to camp with some friends at the annual Old Time Fiddler's Contest in Weiser, Idaho, and Andy really wanted to make the journey. I couldn't decide where I wanted to go at any given time, so east was as good of a direction as any. We loaded up the van and headed out across Eastern Oregon. I stared longingly out my window as we drove through vast open spaces, all of which looked like the perfect setting for deranged wandering among the tumbleweeds. I clutched at my armrest to keep from leaping out of our minivan until finally we crossed the Snake River into Idaho. We set up our tent, and the whole scene was all a bit rustic, with sinks and showers and porta-potties set up for the masses who had converged.

The first morning I woke up to the familiar sensation I had not felt for many months. Rushing as inconspicuously as possible to the porta-potty, I shut myself in its blue glow and greeted my first period since Jonah had begun. Another memorable moment provided to me by yours truly, my body. Was there no end to its rebellious torture?

Like the pioneers before us, we headed home afterward along the Oregon Trail, stopping at its museum where we were reminded how hard life had been for the settlers of this land. In a span of fifty years in the early 1800s, some 300,000 pioneers left Missouri to travel over 2,000 miles across endless prairies, scorched deserts, and high mountain peaks. About 60,000 of them came to Oregon in search of their dreams, and the ruts of their wagon wheels can still be seen these centuries later. But a good percentage of them died along the way. Many women buried their newborn babies and children. Many husbands buried both their wives and their children. The audio portion at each diorama recounted voices from the trail. We listened to a mother weeping and wailing for her child who had met the fate of so many others—run over by wagon wheels. I lamented the invention of the wheel and connected with her instantly, even though she'd been dead for 160 years. Then we loaded back up in our minivan and hit the trail once more.

August 10 glared at me from the calendar, the first terrible anniversary of Noah's death. If I were the official timekeeper, I would have declared it the new leap year day and leapt right on over it so I only had to face it once every four years. This year, August 10 fell on a Monday, and it was a different year for sure, only one year later. We'd ordered a smaller version of the Sleeper bench and it was carved and ready, so we arranged to have it placed between the boys' sweet gum trees in the cemetery to mark the day. We listened to the recording from Noah's funeral and cried. The kids attended a church music camp for a few hours, and Andy flew to Kansas in the afternoon for business. Like every day of each year since, I prayed that we would make it through the day without anyone else dying—my new measure of a good day.

My friend had given me a miniature brass urn on a necklace chain into which I'd packed some of Noah's ashes, and she sent another one for Jonah's. I wore the matched set faithfully, comforted by their weight around my neck, fingering them absentmindedly and holding them near my galloping heart. I packed Jonah's ceramic urn with some of his ashes, and the kids and I flew east a week later to bury their brother. Again. Ten short months after burying Noah. Now that four had become three, I managed the flight solo. Nobody asked to come along. Andy joined us two weeks later in Rhode Island, and we all headed to Maine for another week and a half together, where my sister-in-law, Beth, had taken up residence for the month with her new baby, Julia, the anticipated playmate for Jonah. I was happy to meet my niece, but she was as a constant reminder of what I was missing, even though both of their names were freshly embroidered with gold anchors on "Grandma's Crew" sweatshirt.

On Labor Day morning, instead of baptizing our baby, we gathered together for a small family cemetery visit to add another story to our gravestone book. If The Book of Noah was a short story, The Book of Jonah was more like an essay. This time, with our unwanted expertise, we knew exactly who to contact and what to do. We had a matching stone etched with a dove laid for Jonah in front of Noah's ark, and we planted lilies and his ashes around it. Then we all flew home together, so the kids could start school and Andy could fly to Hawaii for another business trip. This time he went alone, which was fine by me since I wasn't ready to face the reef triggerfish empty-handed or to float without my beach ball of a baby. And I certainly didn't want to eat any more pineapple. I stayed home and faced my gaping, empty house.

Andy was working in our yard one day soon after he returned when Cody walked down from her house to put some garbage in the big blue Dumpster she'd installed at the top of our driveway while we were away. Before this, she would wait for her neighbors to wheel their cans to the curb on garbage day, then check them for extra space, which she'd fill with her excess trash. But now she had plenty of space for her office and household waste, and we had to live with yet another big blue object in ours. Andy casually asked how things were going and she replied, "Well, I haven't been sleeping well. Chris and I have been so worried you were going to sue us."

Andy looked at her, stunned, and said, "What? We signed off on that insurance settlement almost a year ago. We have no intention of suing you."

I was as shocked as he was when he came in the house afterward and related the tale. "They've been worried all this time?" I said. "Why the heck didn't they just ask us?"

"Good question," he said.

"Well, what did she say when you told her that we'd never even considered it?" I asked.

"I don't think she believed me," he said. "I think she thinks we'll be like those people who sued Chris."

A few years before Noah's death, one of Chris's patients had died after a dental appointment in Chris's office. I could still remember answering my phone one evening in the kitchen of our first home near Portland to find Charissa sobbing on the other end. I also remembered thinking it was strange that my niece, who was only about ten at the time, was the one calling to tell me the terrible news. Earlier that day, Chris had worked on a young patient whose teeth were so badly decayed that he'd needed to put her under general anesthesia, which wasn't unusual in his pediodontic practice, where he often took on patients that other dentists wouldn't treat. That day, as usual, he had sent the girl home with her mother and with instructions not to let her fall asleep until the anesthesia had completely worn off. Unfortunately, both the mom and her daughter had gone home and fallen asleep. When the mom woke up, she found her daughter dead.

Chris was devastated and he'd voluntarily paid for the funeral expenses, but the family had sued him anyway, and Chris's medical insurance company had settled with them. Cody was mad that he'd paid their expenses, as she said that it looked like an admission of his guilt, and was especially angry that they were sued anyway.

"I really don't think we're like those people," I said as Andy recounted this bizarre Dumpster conversation to me. We were both horrified by the thought of suing our family and had never even discussed it as a possibility. Even after all we'd been through with them, family was still the most important thing to us. We were raised to be moral and decent people and felt Noah's death was unbearable as it was; we were unable to conceive of doing anything that might make it even worse. And now we had our compounded grief over Jonah to weather. Weren't we all trying not to let this destroy our family?

The thought of Cody and Chris worrying about this gave me a glimpse into their mindset, and I realized how different theirs was from our own. And thinking about that lawsuit reminded me how amazing it was to me that my brother-in-law had stood up to his wife long enough to do what I had considered to be the right thing—to help defray some of that poor family's costs. And yet he had offered nothing for his own nephew.

Chapter Fourteen

"KELLY, I KNOW you can have another baby." The words of Dr. Harmon rang in my ears. "I want you to wait at least six months before you get pregnant again," she'd advised. I marked it on my mental calendar, and that gave me the goal that I needed. Six months. I stretched and warmed up in preparation for the November starting line. Unlike Andy, I was in complete denial about my own mortality and was positively obsessed with babies. Everywhere I looked, a new baby or a pregnant mother taunted my desires. Andy was still ambivalent, so we went to see another doctor for his opinion on whether or not we should ever get pregnant again and came away without much in the way of enlightenment on that subject. But we did discover that he, like so many in Salem's medical community, knew all about Jonah's death and was obviously reluctant to talk about it.

Micah started kindergarten and right away made a new friend, Joshua. One day when I picked him up after his morning class, Micah dragged me over to meet Joshua's mother, begging me to ask her if Joshua could come over to play. When she turned to greet me, I realized she was holding a baby. A boy.

"Oh," I said, clenching my fists to capture my pain. "What's his name?"

"Jonah," she replied.

I struggled to focus, asking the usual questions and trying to smile as she answered: "He was born on May 14." "No, I'm not kidding." "Yes, at Salem Hospital."

She and I had been in the same hallway of the same hospital delivering our baby boys on the same day, naming them the same name, and now here we stood, I with my empty arms and she with hers so wonderfully full of her squirming Jonah. I extricated myself from the conversation as quickly as possible, with Micah and Joshua in tow. Fate chose Joshua to be Micah's best friend that year, forcing me to watch their Jonah grow instead of my own while the year progressed and the boys traded playdates—a visceral month-by-month reminder of what I was not recording in a baby book.

Healing my body and spirit and taking care of my family was all that I could manage. In no condition to return to work either physically or mentally, my employer granted me an extended leave period for one year. But I never went back. I busied myself with straightening my empty nest, then looked for ways to fly away from it. Golf was not much help. Jazzercise was, even though I went with empty car seats, no babies overflowing in my Game of Life convertible. I struggled with the sight of all the moms dropping off their kids, so I changed my parking spot to the back of the building to avoid entering the studio past the nursery I didn't need anymore.

One day after Jazzercise, Becki happened to be walking out with me when she stopped by my car and asked, "Kelly, do you ever wonder if Jonah would be alive today if you'd had a different doctor?" Shocked by her question, I half listened while she expressed her misgivings about Dr. Harmon and regaled me with other stories she'd heard about her. If I'd had any doubts, I was unable to entertain them at the time while I maniacally focused on having that next baby. I thought I needed this particular doctor's support to succeed, and that's all I could think about. I didn't even can tomatoes that fall.

Someone suggested I try acupuncture to heal, so I did. Modern medicine had clearly failed me recently, and I thought maybe I needed more ancient wisdom in my life in general. The acupuncturist poked her needles into my skin and burned cups of moxa on my back to build up the areas of my body she deemed weak, in preparation for another pregnancy. "I think you should consider practicing Hatha yoga," she suggested one day. Once again, if this doctor had told me to join the Mazamas, the Portland mountaineering club, and climb Mount Hood, I would have.

Instead, I found an Asian-style studio with a yogi who was an ex-negotiator for the teamsters. As unlikely as his career path seemed, he was a gentle and peaceful yogi, and through him I learned to focus and to bring my whole self back to the basic core of our existence—the breath. Breath, the very thing I'd so desperately tried to push from my lungs into Noah's as I'd prayed, *Breathe, Noah, breathe, breathe, damn it, please, God, make him breathe!* Breath, the essence of life so fatally denied to Jonah by my own body while my soul had prayed its unceasing mantra, *Breathe, Jonah, breathe, breathe, damn it, please, God, make him breathe!* I paid close attention, and I practiced for all three of us, breathing like I was giving birth.

Grief is held in the very core of your being, in the deep recesses of your belly, the hidden parts that never see the sunlight. Our lungs hug our hearts, reaching down toward this place like the roots of a tree with more than 300 million alveoli. But the older we get, the less of our lungs we use, breathing shallowly into the upper lobes and neglecting to inflate the lower ones much at all.

By learning to breathe like a baby again, deeply and fully, I forced myself to oxygenate the dark recesses of my body, which were drowning in grief. I placed my palms on my belly, feeling it rise as I inhaled a big, new Ujjayi, or ocean-sounding, breath. Then I paused, held my breath, and dove straight into those dark waters over and over, exhaling loudly, like an ocean, and forcing the breath of life back into them.

I needed this one quiet hour of yoga to focus only on the moment at hand, forgetting about the past and the future. "Stay here," the yogi reminded us quietly. "Bring your monkey mind back when it wanders away; gently bring it back to the room, back to here, back to now. Focus."

This was a huge effort on my part. I lived daily with so much remorse and regret about the past that it was sometimes difficult even to recognize the present, much less to fully engage in it. I once attended a lecture given by a Maori woman who'd said that her people visualize the future as being behind them because they can't see the future. Like us, they live in the present, but they view the past as lying stretched out in front of them. "We can see the past," she'd said, "and we strongly believe that future mistakes can only be avoided by acknowledging the errors of the past." This reverse timeline made absolute sense to me as my monkey mind swung wildly through the tangled forest of the past ahead of me, falling out of the present again and again. But I was learning to pick myself up and return to the moment, trying hard to avoid stumbling over the tree roots that lay across my path in either direction.

It was hard, but I was learning to be gentle and patient and forgiving of myself. Yoga became the lifeline I tossed to my flailing arms over and over. Over time, I stopped sinking and began to hold my head above the water again, repeating my new mantra: *Breathe, Kelly, breathe, breathe, damn it, please God, help me breathe!*

Slowly I began to forgive both myself and God for allowing my babies to die.

Chapter Fifteen

My PRESENT neighbors, on the other hand, were not so easy to breathe through, and I swallowed a lot of anguish living so close to them and their dreadful car. Cally maintained her attitude of disrespect and negativity toward us, was still sometimes mean to the kids, and continued to drive that Tahoe. One day after Jonah died, she said she was angry at God for letting him die, and I thought perhaps we might establish some commonality there, but any glimmer of solidarity was extinguished before it could glow. I thought that if a stranger had run over Noah we probably would have had a better response. In my idealistic way of thinking, if you had caused so much pain and suffering to someone, especially accidentally, the only decent human response would be to spend your life trying to atone for your actions, however possible. Or at the very least be nice.

My spiritual quest for understanding what had happened to me and my family led me to join a neighborhood bible study, where we held deep discussions that fed my hunger for answers. One shining beacon of God's light who helped lead the study said to me in her front yard one day, with her infectious smile and great joy and excitement, "Kelly, I can not wait to see what God has planned for you. I know he has great things in store!"

"Yes, Mary Kay," I agreed with more sarcasm than optimism. "Let's wait and see what He comes up with next."

Figuring I should cover a few different angles, I also joined the Queens of Peace—the church group of the Bunco Babes. At my first meeting, a priest was our guest speaker. "Jesus warned us about money," he began. We were all gathered around tables with plenty of sugar in our bellies to sweeten the message about Jesus and his life and the topic at hand.

"Jesus warned us about money, not because of what it was, but because of how people would use it," the priest continued. I struggled to listen to his thoughts over the clanging of my own, sitting right next to Cody and thinking how prophetic Jesus had been on that account.

"Love thy neighbor as thyself," the priest said, snapping me back to the meeting of the Queens. "This was the most important commandment according to Jesus." *Guilty*, I pronounced myself as I sat next to my neighbor and struggled with my conflicting feelings about her and my inability to fulfill that very important commandment. It would be easier to move. *Can't you just avoid the ones you don't like?* I still argued silently with Mimi.

Ever the Peace Corps Volunteers, Andy and I kept looking for ways to make inroads, to make things better. Only this went way beyond marketing yams and teaching about sea turtles. Andy asked Cody if she and Chris would come to counseling with us to see if we could improve on our relationship. "Hunh, unh, this is your guyses problem," she said. We still felt very strongly that Cally also needed professional help, but Cody was against it. "We'll deal with this as a family," she said.

I found it increasingly unbearable to be around her, especially if she'd been drinking. When alcohol loosened her tongue, she rambled on and on incoherently about anything and everything, including Noah's death, and it drove me crazy. She was the authority on every subject and dispensed advice from her vast realm of expertise while I looked for a way to extricate myself gracefully. We resumed our search for another house to buy. I hated to think about leaving Noah's growing garden with his placenta tree and all of our friends in the neighborhood and school, but the time had certainly come.

One day in the fall, I was cleaning my bedroom and listening to NPR when a show came on about reconciliation and forgiveness. I stopped cleaning, sat down on my bed, and took notes. Armed with this new information, I decided it was finally time for me to have a talk with Cody about her beloved Tahoe. More than one year after Noah's death, the sight of that car every day brought me right back to August 10. I consulted the calendar, took a deep breath, picked up the phone, and invited her down to talk when I knew the kids would be gone and we'd be alone. Then I rehearsed what I would say.

The radio expert had instructed, "Approach the person by telling them how their actions are impacting you or making you feel. Use 'I' statements instead of accusing them and putting them on the defensive." So I wrote down my sentences, rehearsing them right up to the moment she walked through my kitchen door. We sat down in my living room, and I took a deep breath and began.

"Cody," I said in my calm, rehearsed speech, "I have to tell you how much it hurts me to look at that Tahoe every day of my life. It's a constant reminder to me of Noah's death. And it also hurts me to watch Cally driving it around and washing it in the driveway all the time."

She interrupted me right away with anger. "Right! That's easy for you to say, Kelly, but that means I have to go and do all the work!" I had no idea what she meant by that, other than that she would have to do the selling and buying, but before I could ask for clarification she added, "And are you guys gonna move or what? You guys need to get on with things."

"We're trying to find a house to buy but haven't found anything yet," I said, trying to switch gears from this change in topic.

"Well, somebody has to move on and make a decision here!"

I knew that Cody-in-action voice all too well. We were trying our best to decide where to move to but were just barely limping along with what we had on our plate. Every grief book I read counseled clearly not to make any major decisions or changes for a year after the loss, and we had a couple of them to deal with. Yet just as she'd so clearly demonstrated by packing up Noah's crib, Cody disagreed. She constantly told us we needed to move on, get over it, like we were not doing our best to do just that.

"Please don't do anything to force the issue," I begged, knowing only too well how she liked to take action in spite of her complaints of having to always "do all the work." "We're not in any condition to make a major decision or a move at this point," I told her. "And we're looking. Please don't do anything to pressure us."

She said she had to go, and I never finished my reconciliation speech. From my kitchen window I could see her brain spinning to keep time with the pace of her feet while she hurried home. *That guy on NPR has never met Cody*, I thought.

Suzie proceeded to tell everyone in the tribe that I had "demanded" that Cody sell the Tahoe. This could not have been further from the truth, but Marcella and Suzie both saw fit to berate me for it. Marcella called. Like Cody, she wasn't one for beginning a phone conversation with hello or ending it with good-bye. "Suzie says you're making Cody sell her car. She'll lose a lot of money if she has to sell that car, you know." *Money, the most important thing*, I thought, picturing Jesus hanging from the cross in her living room decorations. "Well, I think it's just terrible. I just don't understand what you have against that car, okay," she said, hanging up. As my mother always says, "The fruit doesn't fall far from the tree."

The tribe acted like I was crazy, and I was beginning to believe them. We began to see that lies about us were circulating and that the family was starting to assign blame and take sides.

In spite of our best efforts, we were unraveling as a family. It became all too clear that Andy's mother and sisters were jumping on Cody's bandwagon, and they lectured us at every opportunity about something or other. We were shocked and dismayed, thinking we were all in this together, pulling for each other. We struggled under the fog of our own denial about the tribe and their motives.

"I just feel so sorry for that Cally," Marcella would say to me every now and again, as if suddenly she were being forced to choose sides.

Not right away, but some time in the months after our meeting, Cody did manage to part with her beloved green Tahoe that had run over Noah, only to replace it with a shiny new silver Tahoe like a gigantic slap across my face. I wondered if the people who bought her old one ever knew its history. Would anyone knowingly buy a vehicle with such bad karma? Phoebe soon followed suit in an act of solidarity by purchasing her own Tahoe in blue. And then I heard through the grapevine that her son borrowed money from his Auntie

Cody to buy a Tahoe of his own. And in the years to come, the silver Tahoe became Cally's car while Cody purchased yet another one. The tribe became one big Tahoe-loving family.

Five years later when I lived clear across the country from Cody's driveway, I heard an NPR interview with Stephen King. He talked about the day he was struck by a beat-up Dodge van and was severely injured while walking on a road in Maine. King freely admitted the anger he felt toward the van that hit him and how he fantasized for six months about smashing it. I wanted to jump into the radio and hug him. I pounded on the steering wheel and shouted out to the radio, "Yes!" Finally, after all this time, somebody understood exactly what I'd been saying and feeling. I wasn't crazy. I wondered how King would have felt if his whole family had started driving old Dodge vans?

Not long after my meeting with Cody, Marcella paid me a rare visit, stopping by unexpectedly while the kids were in school. I made some tea, and we sat at the dining room table making polite small talk, when the conversation suddenly tilted.

"Auntie Marguerite and I were talking, and she said that at the family reunion last time, you went for a walk with Cody and Phoebe and left that Noah for everyone else to watch." Auntie Marguerite was her sister-in-law, Bud's brother's wife, and they lived nearby on the coast also. She was a Jehovah's Witness, which was the cause of some conflict between her and Marcella, a former Catholic Mother of the Year. They didn't exactly see eye to eye.

Before I could respond, she continued, "And that creek was right there, and when I was young I saved my brother from drowning, and we had that river around our house when the kids were growing up, and if it wasn't for me, they would have drowned. It's the mother's job to watch her kids. She can't be expecting other people to do it for her. It's the mother's job—it was your job to watch Noah and you should not have expected other people to do it for you." Now I caught her drift. It was my fault that Noah was run over because I was not watching him. She and Auntie Marguerite had it all figured out.

By this time everyone had lined up their alibis for August 10, and she'd said on more than one occasion, as if someone blamed her, "It wasn't *my* fault, I was laid up." Clearly, she insinuated, if she had not been injured, she would have been right out there to save the day. And her grandson.

In fact, at that family reunion she recalled so vividly, it was Andy who was watching Noah and the other kids while I went for our usual walk with his sisters. But I didn't even bother to mention it. It was bad enough that Auntie Marguerite had concluded that Noah died because, as usual, I wasn't watching him, but what really hurt was that my own mother-in-law would wholeheartedly agree with her, putting aside their differences in one glorious moment of solidarity.

Marcella marched right on, outlining her case. "You're always going walking with the girls." Yes, every family gathering involved the women's walks. But it was also true that I'd logged miles with a backpack and a warm hand on my neck, not minding the extra wiggling weight one bit. Only when my kids were napping or too big to ride would I opt to leave them behind. Often Marcella, herself, would beg, "Oh don't bring him with you, let me watch him," as I headed out the door, strapping one baby or another onto my back. These were not demands I'd made or expectations I had. But the mythmakers were hard at work assigning blame.

I thought about Hannah's favorite animal, the elephant, which we'd been learning about lately. Elephant females raise their offspring communally, and we Kittel women had always acted like one big herd. We'd all pitched in and helped with each other's children, taking them in at any time. Until tragedy struck. After Noah's death, the family conversation made a major shift; I became the lone outcast female, not watching my own, expecting others to do it for me while I sauntered around, carelessly swinging my trunk.

Marcella lectured on while I stared at my tea, wishing I was an elephant. "It's the mother's job to watch the kids. You know, one time we took a trip to North Dakota, and the kids were all in the bed of the pickup under a cover. When we stopped they were all sleepy and sick to their stomachs from carbon monoxide that was leaking in. That

Bud just said, 'Oh well, if we lose these we know where we can always get some others.' He never watched those kids."

My tears mixed with my tea leaves. I couldn't believe my ears. She rattled on and on, oblivious, building momentum. It was bad enough that she'd decided to blame Noah's mother for his death, in spite of the fact that Noah's father was also there that day and that neither of us knew that Noah's Auntie Cody had put him outside before Noah's cousin Cally had—well, we all know the ending. But I found it unbearable that she felt comfortable coming to my house and pronouncing her verdict. Her audacity finally jump-started my Irish blood.

"I can't listen to this any longer," I said, walking into the kitchen, slamming my mug on the counter, and stomping downstairs to find Andy in his basement office.

"You need to come up here right now and talk to your mother," I said, crying hysterically. "I can't take any more." Brimming with grief, I couldn't handle one more drop of any emotion.

As Andy and I headed out of his office, Bud showed up. He'd recently been diagnosed with multiple myeloma, bone marrow cancer, and Cody had strapped on her nurse hat and arranged for him to see a doctor in Salem. Back from his appointment, he let himself in and we all convened at the basement stairs.

"That Kelly lost her temper," Marcella told Bud and Andy, "and I was afraid she was going to hit me."

What? How could she think such a thing, let alone say it? When I told Andy and his dad what she'd just been lecturing me about, Andy quickly came to my defense.

"Mom, I was there that day. I was responsible for Noah, too. But neither one of us was driving that car."

"Well, a mother is always responsible, and if it wasn't for me we wouldn't have eight kids today—" she began, but I cut her off.

"Marcella, the only difference between you and me, is that you were lucky."

Andy chimed in. "Mom, you always tell the story of how someone found me walking on the yellow line of Highway 34 when I was a baby and brought me home. Or when I fell asleep under the boat in the tin shed and you were all out looking for me for hours and hours and you thought I had drowned for sure. Or what about when Suzie fell in the creek and all you could see was her bonnet floating downstream? Or when I almost drowned at Hootenanny?" These were stories Marcella loved to tell and retell, laughing about them now, with the relative safety of years gone by.

"Well, you used to run away all the time," she said, by way of defense.

"Marcy, it's time to go," said Bud, and for once, nobody disagreed.

Marcella was one of many who, upon hearing our tragic tale, immediately sought the shelter of some fabricated reason why such a thing had happened to us but would never happen to her—much like hearing someone has lung cancer and immediately asking, "Did she smoke?"

If you can assign responsibility for every tragedy in life, you can pretend they won't happen to you because you are in control and would never do X. But the reality is this: even if you never do X, someday you may still get whacked on the head by Y.

Chapter Sixteen

ANOTHER HALLOWEEN night found us sitting on our new bench, leaning against the etching of our name carved in the stone behind us, wondering how much real estate we would ultimately need to purchase in this cemetery next door. Thanksgiving came and went, and another Christmas rolled around. Now we had to endure the second of every holiday without Noah and the first of them all without Jonah. The math was wearing on me. We decided to travel to Florida to spend Christmas with my parents for a much-needed change. When the applause died down from the kids' various Christmas pageants—for school, Scouts, church, piano, and ballet—we flew away as fast as we could.

I was a week overdue for my period, and I went to see Dr. Harmon right before we left, happily discovering I was pregnant. I had waited the recommended six months, finished my acupuncture treatments, and was breathing, breathing, breathing my way through my days. I felt that I'd regained some sense of myself and my strength and took my pregnancy as confirmation of this. Andy was still hesitant about rebuilding our family and every now and again would express his thoughts about filing a lawsuit against Dr. Harmon. In his mind, the insurance company and hospital were clearly to blame for Jonah's death. "They took a calculated risk with our baby. And we lost," he'd say. But he agreed that the statistics should work in our favor this time; they were one in five, according to Dr. Watson, and since we'd already had five children, we both prayed that Jonah was our one and we could start over fresh. What a great holiday gift! Erin was pregnant with her first baby, and she and her husband also came to Florida. I told her the happy news as we swam in the pool one afternoon.

Then I woke up on Christmas morning and discovered I was bleeding. A miscarriage. Merry Christmas to me. We went to church, where I kneeled on the altar after communion, cramping, and begged God, "Wake up and pay attention, damn it." The words of Mary Kay echoed in my ears: "I can't wait to see what God has planned for you, Kelly!"

Santa, on the other hand, was paying close attention and managed to find us in Florida. He gave the kids money for Disney World, and we all spent a week at the happiest place on earth, then headed back to the beach. We swam in the pool and played on the powdery white sands of Captiva, where we collected shells for hours. We sat at the water's edge, covering our legs with millions of miniature shells and watching the colorful coquinas rebury themselves again and again after each gentle wave left them high and dry. I was tempted to follow them headfirst into the cool, sandy depths and stay there until I was ready to face the sun of a happier day again. The ospreys cried overhead, and I envied them as they clutched their fresh fish and flew home to feed their hungry babies. Although tinged with sadness, it was still the perfect escape, and later we'd recognize it for what it was—the calm before the storm.

We returned to a pile of Christmas cards and a pink Rent Increase Notice sitting on our kitchen counter. Cody was nearly doubling our monthly rent, and this was how she'd chosen to inform us. When she was hungry, we were family; when not, we were "just the renters."

Andy continued to deposit the customary rent for two months into Cody's account, waiting for her to tell us in person about the increase. Finally Cody called one day when we were out and left a message saying that she was reviewing her bank statements and we owed her the past-due amount. Andy called back and asked for a meeting with her and Chris, and the four of us met at their dental office one afternoon at the end of February. Andy sat at the head of the table, I sat by myself on one side, and Chris and Cody sat on the other, with Chris closest to Andy.

"So, what about the rent you owe us?" Cody asked without much preamble.

"Well, we thought the increased amount was unreasonable," Andy said.

"How much was it?" Chris asked, uninformed.

When Andy told him the new nearly doubled amount, Chris raised his eyebrows and said, "Well, I agreed about an increase, but I didn't expect it to be *that* much. I agree; that is excessive."

I could see Cody's rage buzzing like the refrigerator motor running behind me. I watched Chris, who appeared not to notice as he was focused on Andy and said, "Well, why don't we just split the difference and settle on half that amount?"

"That sounds much more reasonable," Andy said.

Cody sat there, arms folded across her chest, listening to them usurp her authority, and her skin turned the color of her hair. She shot Andy a poisoned look and said, "Fine. But you will always owe me that money, Andy."

"Oh really, Cody?" Andy said, switching his focus to her fury. "And how long will I owe you?"

"Until you can forget about your son."

I had not said a word up until then, and I was struck irrevocably dumb by her heartless response. Nobody said anything, and even the refrigerator stopped running as Cody's words echoed off the walls. I started to cry. The sound of nails being driven into the coffin of our relationship pounded in my head.

"Fine, you can pay that amount," she said, "but I want you out of the house by July!"

The meeting progressed a bit longer, although I never regained my ability to speak, and at one juncture Chris said forlornly, "I just want Cally to have a normal life." I thought, *Yes, that was similar to what we wanted for our son also—simply a life, regardless how normal.* At the end of the meeting Cody stormed off and Chris stood up. His handsome face collapsed around his blue eyes as he looked at us and said, "I feel like we're standing on opposite sides of a deep ravine, and there's no way across."

I never had another conversation with him.

In addition to my research into death and dying, the meaning of life, and abruption, I'd added forgiveness to the list. I read whatever books I could find, examined what the bible had to say, and explored my own heart and conscience as well as my own experience. I understood the wisdom of refraining from harboring hate and holding grudges and was trying very hard to let go and to forgive everyone, including myself. But I was finding it hard to forgive people who didn't seem to be sorry.

I knew rationally that they had to be sorry, that this had to be tearing them up, too. Maybe not like it was doing to me, but in some way. I still believed that Jonah's death had been unavoidable, yet no one had ever apologized for their roles in Noah's death, accidental or not. No one had attempted to make restitution, and there had been no accountability on anyone's part. Denial had worked its insidious charms on the tribe.

All I ever heard from Marcella on down was that I had to forgive, forgive, forgive. Marcella even saw fit on several occasions to recite the Lord's Prayer to me, as if I didn't know it, as if I were unchurched. "Forgive us our trespasses, as we forgive those who trespass against us," she said with emphasis. I bit my tongue, which was becoming quite ragged.

I couldn't figure out why everyone was preaching to me as if I were withholding my forgiveness from Cally. We were often at family events together or in each other's houses, and while I sometimes felt it painful and avoided being around her, I tried to be civilized in deference to my upbringing. Andy tried to talk to her about Noah's death but was rebuffed every time; I found it too difficult and never waded in. She and I had not discussed that day, or much else for that matter, except during that one family counseling session after Noah died.

The tribe acted as if forgiveness were a complete panacea; if I were to somehow grant my forgiveness, then all would be cured. I wished it were that simple. But from what I was learning and living,

I recognized that in order for there to be healing, there had to be accountability. "There has to be common ground where everyone acknowledges what has happened." We needed a time and place for letting go of our individual pain and embracing the pain and loss we all shared together. But Cody continued to refuse to go to counseling with us. Andy and I could imagine how difficult this was for our niece to deal with because we knew how hard it was for us. It troubled us that we couldn't help Cally and that nobody believed she needed professional help.

Because it was so painful for us to discuss that fateful day, we did not feel it necessary to talk about the events surrounding Noah's death with anyone but each other. What we failed to see was that this did not mean others were not talking about it. And, unfortunately, because we did not speak our truth, many untruths were told instead about us as well as about Noah's and Jonah's deaths.

Somehow, sometime, somewhere, a taciturn movement toward blaming the victim had begun. I was the bad mother, the one who failed to watch Noah, who left him "alone." Once I became aware of this, I could relate to every rape victim who had "asked for it" by wearing her skirt too short or her jeans too tight. Instead of dealing with me, it was easier to gather up all the things no one could handle and dump it on me, and then put me out with the rubbish—as I realized later when the trash can lid hit me on the head.

"Forgiveness," I heard on yet another radio program, "is not a justification for wrongdoing and it is not forgetfulness, as in 'forgive and forget.' It's a process, not an instant occurrence."

Well, I was over a year and a half into the process, so this I understood. But I also saw that tribal members were indeed confusing forgiving with forgetting. They expected us to forget about Noah, which would signal to them that we had forgiven Cally.

Not long after our rent meeting with Chris and Cody, we were driving to meet friends for dinner in Portland when Andy suddenly said, "Okay, if we are ever going to move back east, now is the time."

I was so stunned, I almost fell out of our moving car onto the freeway.

"It's your decision," he added.

"Just give me a minute," I said.

"Okay," I blurted, long before my sixty seconds were up.

The Book of Isaiah

Chapter One

ON MAY 14, Jonah's first birthday, Hannah and I flew east to Rhode Island in search of a house 3,000 miles away from my in-laws. There were no balloons and certainly no happy baby boy smearing frosting on his face or eating wrapping paper. But there was this—the tiny flutterings of yet another new baby in my belly, silently urging me on. Andy wasn't completely on board with the idea of another baby, but he knew how important it was for me to heal and was willing to grant me that.

Erin greeted us at the Providence airport with her new baby, Ava, who'd emerged at thirty-six weeks weighing five pounds—another painful reminder of the events leading up to Jonah's death, when I'd agonized about delivering him a month early. No one had told me that babies can make an early appearance naturally, like my new niece did, and that babies smaller than six pounds can be just fine. But here she was, smiling with big brown eyes, clearly not having any trouble bonding with her mother.

We found a house to buy the day before we flew back west to tell the news to my now unhappy husband. He'd been downsized again from his job and was running his sawmill again, which he enjoyed, but he was stressed about keeping our family afloat economically and about the potential new passenger. But those weren't the chief sources of his unhappiness. Ever since our meeting with Cody had set our winds of change into motion, I could feel him sailing away from me. Some days he'd tack toward me with his green eyes smiling; on others I'd be standing alone on the shore, watching his retreat and whispering, *There he goes.*

"I don't want to move," he said.

"But you're the one who offered," I reminded him as we drove home from the airport. Again, I was so stunned I could have fallen onto the freeway. But I was not at all sure that he'd come back and pick me up.

"Well, I didn't think you'd take me up on it," he said. "Maybe we should have looked for another house in Oregon. Now we have to go to the coast and tell my parents." I couldn't believe it. Just as we'd set a firm course for the east, his sail was luffing.

A few days later I arranged for Micah to play with Joshua after kindergarten, and Andy and I took a day trip to the coast, where we found Bud seated at the dining room table, finishing his lunch, and Marcella bustling around the kitchen. We sat down as she locked the lid on her pressure cooker and clunked it down on the stove, turned up the heat, and joined us.

Andy pressed his lips together and looked at me, clearly expecting me to break the news, so I announced, "Andy and I have decided to move back east."

Marcella cried, "How can you leave us?"

"Well, Cody has increased our rent and is evicting us. She said we have to be moved out by July," I said matter-of-factly.

"Oh, I'll get her to change her mind," Bud said.

We knew that she wouldn't.

"Have you found a job for Andy in Rhode Island?" Bud asked me. I knew he was happy to see Andy milling again and realized then that he was probably looking forward to having his son around more often. As if he'd been thinking the same thing, he added, "Oh, why don't you just get divorced?"

I looked at Andy, who was busy studying the wood grain of the table as if he was preparing to mill it but also looked as shocked as I felt by his dad's question. Both of us were too stunned to speak. Bud's words swirled around in the silence like a whirlpool, threatening to drown us all. Tears sprang to my eyes at these angry words from a man who rarely spoke, and I caught a glimpse of the stories I'd heard from the past. But Bud was in a lot of pain from his cancer, and though his words had struck me like a rogue wave, I thought of

Mimi and chalked it up to the forever pain he was in. Once I could breathe again, I could see that we were all doing the best we could to manage our bewilderment. I knew how responsible Andy felt for his parents, and I felt bad for him. I could feel the pressure building in him, the pressure in my own head increasing along with the whistling from Marcella's pressure cooker on the stove, and I wondered if they'd ever dished up a guilt trip like this to any of their other seven kids. Granted, Andy was their baby, but what happened to the idea of a man leaving his parents and taking a wife?

"My own folks have missed us for the ten years we've lived here, too," I said to deaf ears. It was a terrible scene in a long series of them. There was no small talk, and we needed to get home for the kids, so Andy and I rose to leave, his mother following him out the door while I detoured to the bathroom. When I walked through the mudroom, which still made me shudder, Bud was standing there, looking out the window. He turned to me and said, "You don't know how she worries about you. She prays for you all the time."

"That's good," I said, "because I need all the help I can get." We both stood forlornly and looked out the same window where I'd watched my life change two years prior, a window which I avoided and that was now filled with Andy and his mother saying their good-byes. I thought about how our marriage had been sailing through rough seas in the past months, and it dawned on me that perhaps this wasn't the first time Andy had encountered a storm of words from his parents such as we'd just endured. I stared across the driveway at the fence surrounding the pasture, the fence that Andy himself had built, and realized that Andy's family had hoisted him up on the top rail where he was balanced precariously; they were on one side, and I was on the other. Which side would he jump to?

"Andy, we need to go to counseling," I told him on the ride home, thinking of that fence. He agreed, confirming my place on the other side of the rail.

As far as I knew, Bud never talked to Cody, and instead of changing her mind about evicting us, Cody also now suggested to Andy that we divorce, like this was the new tribal panacea for our problems. We'd weathered the deaths of two children—even the death of one child often resulting in divorce for many couples—and now we had all this pressure whistling from his family stove to add to our stress, plus a major move to make. The requisite one-year window of waiting before making any major decisions had clearly slammed shut; push had come to shove. The tribe spoke of love and forgiveness, but their actions spoke another language. Their "love" was killing us. They lured us close with olive branches, then snatched them back and hit us on the head with them instead.

"Do you think I'm doing the right thing—moving?" I asked Karen, our counselor, one day after a particularly painful session when Andy had stormed out ahead of me. Even though all the wheels were in motion for us to leave, I anguished over whether I was making the right move. Andy had sat for the past hour on one end of her couch and I on the other, a cold expanse of leather between us, with his leg crossed away from me as a final barrier.

"You're in a toxic situation," Karen had explained to us during the session, "and it will be difficult for you both to heal in this environment. And if you aren't healing, it will be impossible for you to be present in a positive way for your children."

I'd felt Andy tensing up even more, if that was possible, and watched his foot bending and flexing as though he were preparing to kick someone or something. Like my own name, Andrew also means "warrior" and although I'd rarely glimpsed this in him in the past, it was becoming more evident. I had lived my life around Irish tempers and worried that he would explode. Instead, he'd walked out early without saying a word, which, for him, spoke louder.

Karen stepped closer to me, peering through her glasses and straight into my soul as she said, "Honey, you need to go save yourself."

She was correct. I did.

I wasn't sure our marriage would survive, but I knew that staying near the tribe was killing me. I realized with Karen's help that moving might be the only chance to save our little family. But poor Andy had already lost his sons and now faced losing the love and support of his family—the nine people who'd loved and spoiled and raised him all his life, along with their assorted spouses when they joined the tribe. He was their baby. And he was locked in his own pattern of denial, unable to see how divisive his family had become. It was understandably too difficult for him to face, so I had to stare it down for both of us. But he didn't appreciate the clarity of my vision. The agents of change are never welcome, even when they come in the familiar shape of your loving wife.

"This will kill my father," Andy said as June approached, adding that to my bundle of burdens. "This is your fault," he said, growing increasingly warrior-like toward me in our remaining days in Salem, leaving all of the moving details and packing to me. In the days before we left, he wouldn't look at me or speak to me unless he was forced to, and he spent a lot of time on the coast with his parents cutting wood and working. My communicative husband had suddenly clammed up.

"Why won't you talk to me?" I asked him one day when I woke up to the broad expanse of his back rolling out of bed away from me.

"Because I don't respect you anymore," my soul mate said. I lay there watching him dress to leave me again, wondering if this was what a marriage looked like when it was falling apart. His angry green eyes were crushing me. But I was buried under the load of so many unbearable things that his eyes were just one more weight I had to shoulder. Still, I was having a difficult time standing upright and maintaining my sanity.

I had morning sickness but dared not mention it, since Andy didn't want to hear a word about the pregnancy and the added stress that caused; he was now blaming me as if it were an immaculate conception. I didn't share my news with the kids or anyone, in case of another miscarriage, so any joy I felt I kept between the baby and me. I patted my stomach secretly, comforting the two of us and urging us both to hang in there.

My parents arrived for a three-week stay to help me pack up the house, and when I met them at the airport in Portland, I pointed to my blistered lips and said, "Stress fractures"—my name for the massive cold sores erupting around my mouth from the combination of emotions, hormones, and lack of sleep. Cody mostly stayed away during the whole moving process but came by for the garage sale my mother ran for me. "I want to make sure they aren't selling any of my stuff," she said to my Mayflower Mom, who was shocked speechless.

After all our worldly possessions were boxed, taped, labeled, and ready to go, my parents left, saying, "We'll see you in Maine for the Fourth of July." At least *they* were happy we were coming east, coming home.

Uprooting ourselves from Noah's garden and the boys in the cemetery next door was like tearing out my own lungs. I dug up some of my roses and gave them to friends. I also took some that I thought could survive the journey across the country—like my favorite peony given to me when Jonah died. We said good-bye to so many good friends and our home of six years where we'd been through so many things, both pleasant and painful. People had parties and luncheons and dinners for us at church and in the neighborhood. The kids had all their year-end school activities and plays and recitals, taking a bow for us all while we exited stage right, closing this chapter of our lives.

One of the last social events Andy and I attended was the wedding of the youth pastor from church. I sat in the balcony and cried my way through the whole service, the swirling emotions of the previous months and days washing over me in a tidal wave. I hadn't expected to be such a shipwreck, washed up there in that church where we'd worshiped God, prayed, sang, and buried our son. I could still hear the faint echoes of Annie Lennox singing "No More I Love You's" echoing in the rafters and I cried like I'd expected to do at Noah's funeral until I ran out of Kleenex.

Witnessing the fresh promise of the fledgling love in front of me, I recalled the blissfulness of our own wedding, our early lives together, and how far we'd traveled from the carefree joy of those times. While this new couple stared longingly into each other's eyes, I mourned the innocence that we'd unintentionally lost along the way, with my groom now perched stiffly next to me like a plastic wedding cake topper. I grieved for the marriage we'd once enjoyed, praying we could salvage it in the days and events ahead of us. I prayed for our successful journey east. I prayed for the life of the baby within me. And I gave thanks for the dark glasses I wore out of the church to cover my red, swollen eyes. Then we went to the reception and danced with our friends and our children like we hadn't a care in the world.

The last weekend before leaving we attended the national conference of The Compassionate Friends in Portland. It seemed an appropriate finale for our Oregon residency. We selected sessions entitled "Sudden Death—Vehicular" and the dreaded "Multiple Loss," where I sat in a circle with women who'd lost all of their children, counting my blessings and knowing it could always be worse. There was always more to lose—more pages marked *The End*. Andy and I proudly wore buttons with Noah's smiling picture on them. Jonah's black raspberry-skinned pictures were harder to wear. This was something we could still do together; we still shared our grief over the loss of our sons.

"The emotions remember what the mind forgets," a grief writer assured me while I sat in on her session called, "Telling Your Story." Soon after Noah died, I'd read her book about the deaths of her sons.

"Put your feelings on paper and speak to other people's hearts. Establish credibility with commonality," she said. I noted this, remembering how I'd prayed I would never share the loss of multiple children with her.

"Write for yourself first, but know that it gives other people hope when you share your story." I jotted this down, too, knowing that I wanted to do just that someday.

I raised my hand and asked, "How long should you wait before you write your story?"

"You should wait two or three years to share it verbally, but it takes at least ten years before you can write it effectively."

"Ten years," I wrote, thinking that it seemed like an eternity.

Chapter Two

"I DON'T WANT you guys to leave with all these unresolved issues," Phoebe called to say, a few days before we were moving. "My friend is a counselor, and I want all of us women to meet with her . . . plus Cally."

The only free time I had was the night before we hit the road, which was, frankly, a little late. This wasn't the way I would have otherwise chosen to spend my last night in town. We'd already been evicted, the moving vans were packed, and we were ready to go, so clearly there would be no resolution for any of that. But I agreed to participate, willing to make the effort to leave on better terms, to give it the old Peace Corps try.

And so we all converged in the middle of a field at a riverside park while the June day grew long, gathering our folding chairs in a lopsided circle. The hip counselor with her spiky white-blond hair began with a little lecture, saying, "Forgiveness is a process that requires accountability and remorse and acceptance." *Bingo*, I thought, wondering if she, too, had heard that on the radio, and thinking how those first two steps were still missing, almost two years after Noah's death. "I want each of you to spend some time thinking about the people here in this circle," she continued, "then I want you to write down three things you resent, three things you appreciate, and three things that are unresolved about each person present."

I took the assignment seriously and set to work writing down my thoughts.

When it came time to share, Joe's wife, Zelda, volunteered to speak first. "I'm unhappy that I don't get to host any of the holiday gatherings," she began. "And, Phoebe, I wish you weren't so perfect," she giggled. She blathered on about some other banal issues while I looked at my notes, wishing I could trade lists with her and wondering if I had misunderstood the assignment or was seated in the wrong family circle.

When it came to my turn, I figured I should get the heavy hitters over with, so I turned to Cody first, leaving Zelda to worry over Easter eggs and ham. She was seated a few chairs away to my right, and all I could see of her was one of her favorite Clarks sandals, kicking up and down at the end of her crossed leg. I leaned forward a little to try and see her face but only got as far as her folded arms, then said, "Cody, the first resentment I have is your flippant attitude about Noah's death. Second, I resent your attitude and treatment of me and my family in the past six months. This includes the rent increase; the eviction; your always telling us, 'That's your *"guyses"* problem,' or 'You need to deal with it'; your telling us to get divorced; the issue of selling the Tahoe; and always telling us that we owe you for whatever it is you've done for us yet thinking you owe us nothing. Third, I resent your competitive attitude toward me, calling me 'Queenie' and insinuating that I'm lazy.

"As for unresolved issues," I took a deep breath, looked at my notes, and continued, "they are Noah's death, specifically the lack of accountability and your denial and blame, the issue of competition between us, and lastly your control drama with me and my family." I concluded by saying, "The three things I appreciate about you are the friendship we used to have, the nice things you've done for us, and your presence late in the night after Jonah died, when you stayed and helped the nurse."

Next I looked across the circle at Cally, who sat looking at her feet and sniffling throughout the meeting. She glanced my way but didn't really look at me while I said, "Cally, the three things I resent about you are your running over Noah, your mean-spiritedness toward my kids even after Noah's death, and your competitiveness with me for control of my own kids. The one unresolved issue I have with you is Noah's death. There has been no conversation, no apology, and no forgiveness." At this, she looked up at me but didn't say anything. I continued, "I appreciate your love for my kids and the gifts of time and energy you have given them."

Then I turned to my right again and addressed the last of my top three, my mother-in-law, who was still insisting she didn't need a hearing aid and had spent most of the meeting so far saying, "What? I can't hear."

"Marcella," I said, "I resent you telling me that Noah's death was my fault. I resent the guilt you've placed on Andy for moving. And I resent the lectures you've given me about forgiving Cally, about the Tahoe, and about me not watching my kids. All of these are unresolved issues for us. Three things I do appreciate about you are your experiences with life, your strength, and your love for your family." She didn't say a word, but I don't know if she heard anything I said either.

With those three out of the way, I could breathe a bit easier. I only had appreciative things to say to my sole supportive sister-in-law, Diane, and I told her so, concluding, "Thank you for helping me to understand that I wasn't crazy." I also thanked my sister-in-law Phoebe, seated on my left, for getting us all together. "I only wish it had been sooner," I said.

Then I turned to Suzie on my right and said, "Suzie, I resent you lecturing me about forgiveness. I resent your tendency to muckrake and to misconstrue the truth, and I resent you telling me what a terrible person I was for 'making' Cody sell the Tahoe. I appreciate your good heart and willingness to help and your tears"—I turned further to look her in the eye—"but Suzie, you and I will never have a decent relationship until you can stop lying to me." We never spoke again.

The meeting progressed with everyone saying something, everyone except Cody, who refused to participate, sitting the entire time with her legs crossed and arms folded in what I interpreted as a classic antithetical pose for accountability. When the counselor called on her, she said, "I don't believe in this. Actions speak louder than words. I'll wait to see how people act in the future."

Before the counselor concluded with some parting advice about reconciliation, which mostly fell on deaf ears, Suzie's husband, Foster, who was the only male present, cleared his throat. I don't know why he came to the "women's" meeting, but I supposed that Suzie probably made him come for support. He'd stayed quietly off to the side of our circle the whole time, leaning against his car with his arms folded and working his characteristic toothpick thoughtfully. He said, "I just want to say that, in my opinion, if there was ever a situation on earth that could cause a family to tear apart, this would be it."

I agreed with him that the chain of events could be considered a perfect formula for disaster, but Andy and I felt we'd bent over backward to keep the family from falling apart. We still believed that had we all sincerely worked to keep the family together by holding hands and walking through the valley of the shadow of death and forming circles like the one we were now in and coming to terms with the truth of what had happened, our family wouldn't have become yet another candidate for the Dr. Phil show. While I was pondering this, as if on cue, Marcella interjected, "Well, all I want is to hear *that* Kelly tell Cally that she forgives her."

So I did. Partly because I was curious as to how it would feel. Partly because I was just sick and tired of people saying I hadn't. And partly because I assumed that she was sorry.

Everyone was milling about, gathering their things, and the shadows had grown longer with darkness descending on us. I rose from my chair, noting the full moon peering over the hill that held our houses and bathing us all in its glow. The night air smelled warm and grassy and the crickets were singing. I walked across the circle, hugged my niece, and stepped slightly backward, keeping my hands on her shoulders. Then, despite all my anger, my hurt, and my frustrations with her, I looked into her eyes and said, "I forgive you, Cally." Her tears shone in the moonlight. She said nothing.

We all disbanded. I drove down my dead-end street and turned into my driveway past Noah's star magnolia tree for the last time. Most of the tribe went home and promptly forgot what I had said and done, including Cally herself. As we'd come to learn, it didn't fit with their story and wasn't to be part of their collective memory.

We were leaving. The tribe could breathe a huge sigh of relief and start living out their version of history without our presence as a constant reminder of their discomfort. Instead of Cally running over Noah, they chose to remember Kelly not watching her son; instead of being evicted by Cody and Chris, they chose to remember that we were running away from our problems, taking "their" babies away from them. And then they all pretended to be hurt and angered by these fictitious motives. Cody and Chris gave them free dental care, but we didn't offer them anything money could buy. So they all smiled and waved farewell.

History loves a scapegoat, as Marie Antoinette learned so headlessly. There is within us a deep and primitive urge to blame someone when things go wrong, and being an in-law, a foreigner from the East, I became the obvious choice. The tribe would gladly have pulled Andy back into the familial herd if he'd put me out to pasture with the other scapegoats and jumped to safety on their side of the fence. There they could have all grazed together again, nuzzling each other while the guillotine dropped on my outstretched neck, spraying them all with my warm and welcome sacrificial blood.

We loaded the live cargo the next day and said our final goodbyes. I was heading home to New England to heal my heart and my head, and, I hoped, my family. We drove north and then pointed the vans east at last, heading upstream along the Columbia River. I bid farewell to my job at BPA, having recently resigned, as I drove past my fish projects and toward my natal stream. At one point the road curved, and I looked in my oversized side-view mirror, which perfectly framed a reflection of Mount Hood, its pointed white cap rising into a pure blue sky. Seeing that icon of Oregon and the West retreating behind me, I felt a slight lifting of my heart, inhaled deeply, and exhaled a jump for joy.

Chapter Three

W E RENTED two of the largest U-Haul vans offered and then attached trailers to tow behind us. Much to Christiana's disappointment, we left Dude behind with Marcella and Bud, who'd made their final demand: "He's staying with us." We petted his wagging backside farewell, and Andy promised Christiana she could get a new dog once we were settled. We carted two newts—Sir Isaac and Fig—from Micah's classroom across the country to release them. Like me, they'd been transported from their natal stream in New England.

My U-Haul came equipped with a larger-than-life cowboy covering my flank on his bucking bronco. "Howdy there, pardner," I sidled up each day and said, "and where have you been all my life?" "Wyoming," he answered by way of the large lettering painted next to him on the side of the van. My new Dude and I followed Andy and his Louisiana jazz band for three thousand miles across purple mountains majesty and amber waves of grain, all of which baked under the record-breaking heat that accompanied us. The kids rotated vans at pit stops. We had "America's Moving Adventure" indeed, as our trucks lived up to this U-Haul motto by breaking down twice and getting four flat tires along the way. But these were problems that had easy solutions.

We felt like the Beverly Hillbillies. We laughed out loud and had a great journey. Sometimes we picked up the voices of fellow travelers on our two-way radios, and once we overheard this conversation about us:

"Did you see those two U-Hauls?"

"Yep, I'm sure glad I'm not them."

"Just think, honey," I laughed over the radio, "eleven years ago everything we owned fit in my two-door Honda hatchback."

Andy and I reminisced about the drive we had taken back then from east to west, from our wedding in Maine to our new life in San Francisco, humming the Rice-A-Roni jingle all the way. While we caravanned like U-Haul gypsies, the happy sound of Andy's laughter filtered into my ears through the walkie-talkie. I felt relieved and encouraged to hear his happiness and to see him shaking off his doubt and anger as the family fence fell far behind us. I still tiptoed around him, but his green eyes no longer looked at me with anger. We were in this together. As the odometer numbers spun ever higher and the flat tires scattered in our wake, his mood lifted and he began to regain a slightly reshaped shadow of his twinkly-eyed self.

We crossed into Rhode Island and traversed the Newport Bridge on a warm summer evening, the familiar sights of my Aquidneck Island childhood waiting faithfully on the other side. The white spire of Trinity Church pointed heavenward, keeping watch over all of us lost sheep and the harbor for three centuries, flanked by the guns of Fort Adams—an artillery backup plan. The stone buildings of the Naval War College sat above the geese-strewn lawns, and the sailboats all rested at their moorings. I pulled into Erin's driveway and parked my cowboy at the curb for the last, blessed time.

We settled into our new home located on another quiet street, this time not a dead end, and Andy flew back to Oregon to finish up some milling work and spend time with his parents. The new baby stuck with me; its presence became known to all, growing daily with my reassuring caresses. I floated with my new beach-ball belly in the Atlantic Ocean while the kids swam around me, diving into the waves. The kids caught buckets of crabs, and we inhaled the salty air until our lungs ached. Then we went north to Maine and caught crayfish, fishing and swimming in our lake and resuming our daily pilgrimages to the general store by boat. The loons announced our arrival and tucked us into bed each night. They say you can't go home again but I don't know why because it sure felt very, very good to me.

Our summer activities became memories recorded in "What I Did on My Summer Vacation" essays when the kids began their new-school chapters in the fall. Andy returned from Oregon feeling better about leaving his parents, and we took long beach walks daily while my belly expanded. With each step we slowly mended our relationship, drawing back together as a couple who could hear the faint murmurs of their wedding vows in the silent pauses between crashing waves. Given the perspective of distance and the continued barrage of missiles from his family as they called and e-mailed, Andy began to see a counselor on his own and was able to start to see through the veil of denial with greater clarity. Some days we could talk about the tribe with solidarity, but on others he'd snap at me so I tip-toed around that topic.

Andy found a job with a Texas-based communications company but worked mostly from our house in Portsmouth. I devoted my time to my growing belly. We were seeing old friends and meeting new ones, my obvious pregnancy often the topic of conversation. I tried to duck these waves of inquiry, scared that something terrible would happen again and I'd have to watch their happy faces altered by my bad news. I didn't want to disappoint yet another community. There wasn't enough wood around for me to knock on. Not a day went by without anxiety, and I lived with a tiny knot of fear wedged in the center of my being. We knew uncertainty, and the possibilities were endless; I prayed and prayed for a happy ending. Any last remnants of blissful ignorance had been permanently erased, and I could no longer have confidence in the reliable uterus of my youth.

After Jonah, I could never again swap playground birth stories, and just nodded politely, biting my tongue as other moms laughingly lamented their difficult labors while pushing their happy endings on swing sets. Every sign of health the new baby showed sent a shower of relief over my body. Each kick jump-started my heart; every hiccup was a balm for my wounded soul. But it was ever and always the joy of life shadowed by the specter of death. I had everything to gain. And everything to lose. I switched my urns for a more hopeful silver mother's medal my friend gave me for good luck and dutifully recited A Mother's Prayer every night to St. Gerard—the patron saint of motherhood who shared my father's middle name. I knew I needed all the help I could get.

I transferred my prenatal care from Dr. Harmon in Oregon to Dr. O'Brien in Providence, a kind and quiet man voted one of the top ten ob-gyns in Rhode Island. We determined that we'd give birth at Women and Infants Hospital, which is the teaching hospital for Brown University and is ranked one of the top ten hospitals in the nation for women's health care. We knew enough not to take chances with community hospitals again. Armed with our "top-ten" doctor and hospital list, we prepared for victory but didn't expect it to come without a battle.

Like Dr. Harmon, Dr. O'Brien sent me for a consultation with a high-risk specialist in case we needed his services. The specialist's name was Dr. Carr, and he was a wiry, energetic man with round glasses and intelligent, youthful eyes that contradicted his graying hair. He was a pioneer of in utero surgery, though his demeanor was friendly and unassuming in spite of his obvious brilliance. He reviewed my chart before our meeting and began by asking questions in his curious, forthright manner about my history and health during my pregnancy with Jonah. We talked about abruption and blood pressure and our concerns for this pregnancy.

"Neither Dr. O'Brien nor I would ever let you walk out of our offices with blood pressures like these," he stated emphatically, looking at my chart. He noted that the new medication Dr. O'Brien had prescribed was working beautifully, but that if things changed, they'd switch me to a different one. "For now, everything looks great."

We discussed what our plan should be in case something changed, and he answered our questions thoughtfully. "We can perform a C-section in less than five minutes here at the hospital if needed," he said, alleviating one of our fears.

When the meeting neared its conclusion, he leaned forward in his chair, and what he said then glued us to our seats: "Your baby should not have died. But Dr. O'Brien and I are probably the only ones who will ever tell you that."

Dr. Carr's unequivocal pronouncement shocked me to the core. I began to reexamine my conscience and my assumptions. It was only a year and a few months since Jonah's death, which was still very raw for me, but having this baby was the best solution for healing that I could conceive. For now, I wanted to focus all of my energy on positive things and especially toward the healthy delivery of this new baby. I didn't want to delve into anything negative, and I perceived a lawsuit to be fraught with negativity. I wasn't yet convinced that there was anything anybody could have done differently to have saved Jonah's life. So we continued to walk the beach, and Andy would discuss the matter in the pauses between every so many waves while I did my best to defer the conversation. But the words of Dr. Carr roared in my ears and were pounded into my brain by the surf: "Your baby should not have died."

In early October, Andy went back to Oregon again to spend time with his dad and help him with some woodcutting jobs. He sensed that his father's health was failing from the cancer, and he was right. One evening later that month after Andy had returned to Rhode Island, Cody called to say Bud was dying at home in his bed, and she held the phone to his ear while we each told him good-bye through the silent wire. He was eighty-five. Andy's angry words came back to haunt me: "This will kill my father." I wondered if he would blame me, but he never mentioned it again.

I was entering my eighth month of the pregnancy and was a little nervous about traveling, but my doctor approved, and we all flew out for the funeral. Because that's what family does.

Bud wanted no part of a Catholic funeral service. "Just dig a hole and bury me in the back pasture," were his expressed wishes, and everyone knew it. If you had asked him to attend mass he would likely have said, "Over my dead body." And that's exactly what Marcella arranged. Mass was said, her parish priest gave his usual warnings to us all about heresy, Bud was cremated, and he was never planted anywhere.

Chapter Four

SAFELY BACK in Rhode Island, I marked the thirty-sixth week of my pregnancy in red on my calendar—only three weeks away. Dr. O'Brien agreed he'd deliver the baby as soon as it was ready to go or if any signs of trouble reared their ugly heads. He did a few non-stress tests, but there were no issues of any kind as I moved into the weeks of gestation that had been so problematic with Jonah. Still, I remained hypervigilant under the watchful care of my doctors, eye-balling that fateful week with great trepidation.

"It must be a girl." I declared to Andy during one of our appointments with Dr. O'Brien, basing this assertion on my continued good health. "Let's call her Grace."

"We'll do a late-term amnio to see if the baby's lungs are mature," the doctor said.

"What's that?" I asked ignorantly.

He explained that he could draw out some of the amniotic fluid and test it for what's called an L/S ratio of surfactant, compounds which indicate lung maturity.

"Why on earth didn't they do that last time?" I mused out loud to Andy.

"If the baby's lungs are mature, we'll proceed with induction and delivery," the doctor continued. But as he further discussed the amnio, he informed us that one of the potential risks of the test is abruption. Abruption? Alarm bells rang. He scheduled the test for the first morning of my red-highlighted week, and I packed my bag in anticipation, knowing that once that needle was inserted into my uterus, I was not going home until I delivered a baby.

We arrived at the hospital bright and early on November 29, after counting our blessings around the Thanksgiving table in remembrance of our ancestors. My due date was the end of December—the end of a millennium we were happy to leave behind—but I was anxious to deliver the baby as soon as it was ready and gladly relinquished the free diapers we might win by waiting.

"Now breathe, slowly," Dr. O'Brien instructed, poised with a long needle against the taut skin of my exposed belly. We all concentrated, unblinking, at the image of my womb that filled the ultrasound screen. I felt a poke and watched the thin metal penetrate the wall of my uterus, invading a pocket of amniotic fluid. I held my breath, gaping at my resting baby and praying it would not choose that moment to flex a knee or throw an elbow. Fortunately it cooperated beautifully. The womb invasion ended as the needle was withdrawn, and we could all breathe again, exhaling our relief.

"The first test results take two hours. You can go home and we'll call you, or you can wait nearby," Dr. O'Brien remarked as he expressed the precious amniotic fluid into a clear tube for the lab.

"We aren't going anywhere," Andy informed him, and they agreed to admit me while we waited for the results. We lived forty-five minutes from the hospital, and I wasn't going farther than five minutes away from that emergency C-section Dr. Carr had promised. I would've gladly waited on the operating room table if they'd let me, swathed in Betadine and prepped for surgery with a scalpel poised and ready to slice. When you've been struck by lightning once, you stay away from trees when thunderclouds threaten. When you've been struck twice, you stay away from trees even when the sky is blue.

Unfortunately, the test was not going to go easily for us.

"Well," Dr. O'Brien said after lunch, "the results from the short test are inconclusive. Now we have to wait for the results of the six-hour test for a clearer reading."

"We'll wait right here," Andy said, settling in for the afternoon.

"What are we going to do if the next one is negative?" I asked Andy after Dr. O'Brien left the room, because I wasn't going home, even if the test indicated the baby's lungs were not mature. As far as we both were concerned, we weren't leaving the hospital until I pushed this child down the correct exit from my uterus. We did try to learn from our mistakes.

Fortunately, the doctor returned in the afternoon with a smile. "Good news. The test results are overwhelmingly positive! We needed to see an L/S ratio of at least two, and yours was three point five. We can go ahead and proceed with induction and delivery."

He set to work ordering an IV with pitocin while we caught our breath, asking no questions. And then we were off and running.

My mother flew in from Florida that evening, right on time for the first time in six attempts to be present at a delivery. Andy left to pick her up and they both returned, but as the night wore on he drove her home so she could stay with the kids. Now that the opportunity was at hand, she said she was tired and decided she didn't want to be in the room for the crowning achievement after all. I figured Jonah's birth had probably scared her off.

"I'll just get a bit of sleep," Andy said. "Call me if you need me to come back, and I'll be on my way." He was to bring Christiana, who was not scared and was finally going to get her chance to attend the birth of her sibling. My mom expressed her concern that Christiana would be traumatized by the birth, just like she'd said when Hannah had watched Noah's birth. But when your children have witnessed the death of their brother, any worries about them witnessing the joy of birth fly away.

"I'm starting to get uncomfortable. Maybe you should stay," I told Andy, wincing as the contractions became more and more painful.

"I'll be back soon," he assured me.

After they left, I also felt a bit scared to be on my own with the pain building and the roller-coaster labor ride looming ahead. I turned on the television and tried to focus on a documentary about the life of Jackie Kennedy, learning that she'd lost two baby boys before John Jr's birth because they were born too early and their lungs were immature. I listened through my cramping contractions with great empathy, weeping a bit for the magnitude of loss Jackie had faced in her life. I was happy that she had not been alive to bury her only surviving son, whose plane had crashed in the nearby Atlantic just as we'd moved back a few months before. The nurse came in to check on me.

"This story is so sad," I said to her, teary-eyed.

Later Dr. O'Brien told me that the nurse had left my room and woke him up to say I was crying because of my contractions. Though they were not the culprit, the contractions did continue to build and my labor ratcheted higher until the nurse decided to move me to the labor and delivery unit. I called Andy at home and on his cell phone, but he didn't answer. It was the middle of the night and I couldn't raise anyone in my house; I pictured them all snoring away. Off I went to the delivery floor, alone and annoyed, with Andy's words, "Just call me," fueling my distress.

After I was settled into my new bed, I asked the nurse to help me to the toilet. I always shake uncontrollably with the pain of labor, and my legs were trembling like a new fawn's so that I could barely walk. "Can I have an epidural now?" I begged through chattering teeth, climbing back into bed and pulling the heated blankets over me.

"No, you're not dilated to five centimeters yet. We have to wait. But I can give you something to take the edge off," the nurse offered before I broke down. She left for a moment and returned to inject some magic into my IV. The cool liquid moved through my veins, erasing the pain in its wake. *So this is why people become drug addicts*, I thought while my teeth slowly stopped chattering and my body ceased its incessant shaking.

My head collapsed back onto my pillows, and I closed my eyes, unable to move, murmuring "Ahhh," and sounding like the dope coursing through my veins. I didn't care about anything. I was filled with this pleasurable new feeling like I'd been suddenly thrust back to the 1960s; all thoughts were infused with sunshine and happiness. Suddenly a realization intruded on my flower-powered bliss: I was alone. I managed to drag myself out of my stupor long enough to dial my house one more time. This time, Andy answered. "We're on our way," he said before I could even form a word, much less a sentence, sinking back into my narcotic haze.

No traffic was about at that hour, and the twinkling eyes of Andy and Christiana appeared in my doorway before the sun rose. By then, Dr. O'Brien had been replaced by Dr. Manning from his practice, and my cervix had passed the dilation test. Andy distracted Christiana while I hunched over, immobile, trying not to flinch as the anesthesiologist inserted the epidural needle into my spine and I grew even more enamored with the numbing powers of drugs—drugs, beautiful drugs. After they finished taping and taping the catheter to my back like I'd have to wear it forever, Andy and I both fell sound asleep. I'd been up most of the night and was so tired and now so blissfully numb. We slept while Christiana watched cartoons and ordered cranberry juice and snacks from the nurses, who found themselves with a new seven-year-old customer while their old one snored away.

Dr. Manning came in to examine me but I barely noticed, even though she was down there exploring around my ying-yang.

"Okay, if you want to sit up now, you can have this baby," she said.

What I really wanted to do was roll over, pull my white cotton hospital blanket up to my neck, and get back to my drug-induced dreams. But I reluctantly opened one eye, consenting to participate. I managed to elbow my belly and half-numb body into some semblance of a seated position with the help of my mechanical bed while the nurse covered every surface with a blue impermeable barrier.

"Wake up," I called to Andy.

"Turn the TV off," he told Christiana. "You're not missing school this morning to watch cartoons."

"Okay, you can push now," the doctor said calmly. I gave one simple push, and out slipped our baby. It was so easy. No time for mirrors. No need for good-byes. Every delivery is the most incredible moment in a parent's life. But following on the heels of the last one, this was every synonym for "momentous" in the thesaurus. Instead of a giant roller coaster, Andy and I stepped off what was more like a Magic Kingdom ride. He and I were now fully alert and overcome with emotion, hugging each other and crying, so the doctor turned to Christiana instead.

"Would you like to cut the cord?"

Christiana stepped right up and stood confidently by my side with one hand on her hip and the other hand grasping the scissors, and she neatly snipped the fat cord like it was just another day in second grade. All those years of craft-making had paid off. She was good with scissors.

The baby cried. It was music to our ears, and we rejoiced at the sound, which was all we needed to hear and all we wanted to know—our baby was breathing. One and a half years had passed since we'd experienced the terrible silence of Jonah's birth, and every baby noise stitched our broken hearts back together.

"Well, don't you want to know what it is?" the doctor finally asked.

We paused from our private fiesta, remembering that other guests were present at the party, and said, "It's a girl, right?"

"Nope—it's a boy!" she announced.

We were stunned.

"Does he have a name?" she asked, placing him on my healing heart.

"Grace!" we said almost in unison, staring at the miracle looking back at us.

The familiar smell of my son and his weight on my chest was instantly comforting, like taking joy and applying it directly. He felt like so much more than a gold medal this time. His skin was fair and his hair a reddish blond, like Noah's, and his eyes squinted up at me from pink oxygenated skin. "Look, Mom," Christiana said, watching her new brother, "he has brown eyes like me." We all stared at each other, unable to squeeze much language into this moment, happy simply to be alive and breathing together.

"Let me just weigh him quickly," the nurse interrupted, perhaps thinking we didn't know what to do with a newborn baby. Or perhaps because she knew things that we did not. Because even in our blinded state of bliss, we, too, should have known by then that you just never know. And before I could attach his mouth to my nipple and never let him go, she put him on the scale, and we rejoiced in the miracle of his flailing arms and feet as she announced, "He weighs six pounds and four ounces and is almost twenty inches long." But as she was writing down his excellent Apgar score, our son, whom we still thought of as "Grace," began struggling to breathe.

When she finished his test, someone covered in blue said, "We're just going to wheel him down to the NICU for observation."

Andy hadn't even taken our son's first photo yet, but lost as we were in our sense of celebration and relief, we didn't feel concerned. We had never before delivered a baby at this excellent teaching hospital; maybe this was what they did with all the babies? Who knew? We shouted out the happy news to our waiting family—"It's a boy!" We were elated.

"Can we please keep the placenta?" Andy asked Dr. Manning as she wrapped up her work with us. She looked at us questioningly, a look we'd seen five times before on the West Coast, but nodded and instructed the nurse to mark it with a "K" before it went to the lab.

"All placentas go to the lab for examination first," she said, "but you can collect yours from them when they're finished."

Just then the door opened, and a short Indian doctor came in. He walked right up to me at ear-level, quietly introducing himself as Dr. P from the NICU. Then he wiped the smiles right off our faces.

"Your son is very sick," he said in a slow, practiced, accented whisper. "His lungs are not ready. He is unable to breathe on his own." In spite of the "overwhelmingly positive" lung-maturity test results, he explained to our disbelieving ears, our son who had recently serenaded us with his new cries was now lying in the NICU, intubated and hooked to a ventilator with a machine doing all of his inhaling and exhaling for him. Our baby was silent. We all became still.

"He will be receiving his first dose of surfactant shortly," he patiently explained, listing escalating potential medical procedures that we could barely focus on.

My baby can't breathe, my brain repeated over and over as if it were the first time I'd had to comprehend such cold, hard facts.

Later Dr. O'Brien would tell us that this was only the second time in his long career he'd seen erroneous lung-maturity test results. Our happiness turned to dread while we robotically signed paper after paper, authorizing the intensive care of Baby Kittel, trying to digest all the information being imparted to us about his emergency care and the possibility of his transfer to Boston, where they had machines that would not only breathe for him but remove his blood and externally circulate and oxygenate it for him if necessary.

"We'll gladly take a baby with a little lung dysfunction over a dead baby any day," we'd told Dr. O'Brien weeks before when discussing the early delivery of this baby. Now we were eating those words for breakfast. We tasted their bitterness and chewed on each and every syllable—"a little lung dysfunction," indeed. Like Jackie O, we, of all people, should have known better by now. Life is not to be trifled with.

Chapter Five

ONCE AGAIN I was wheeled to a room on the mother-baby floor without a baby. Again that word, *again*. Fortunately, our baby wasn't lying alone in the car this time; he was lying in limbo, two floors below me in the NICU, with a machine breathing for him. I was put to bed to contemplate his sickness and choose a new name.

"Isaiah or Grayson?" I asked, thumbing through the baby-name book anew while my sister was visiting.

"Definitely Isaiah," Erin said. Andy agreed, and we named our new son Isaiah, meaning "God is my helper." If he couldn't be with us, we hoped He was at least paying attention and would live up to the task at hand on this, a Tuesday. Even though I no longer believed that God was much of a hands-on kind of helpful guy.

"Tuesday's child is full of Grace," I recited to myself, smiling at the irony.

"I'd like him to have my dad's name," said Andy, and I agreed, so we gave him Martin for his middle name.

The news of Isaiah's birth spread from coast to coast, and my room phone rang later that day. Cody's voice hit my ear, and I immediately wished I hadn't answered. "Oh, you named him Martin after us?" she snorted. After planting her nurse's cap firmly on her head and pressing me for all the medical details she said, "Why do you keep doing this to us?" *Doing what?* I thought. *Creating all this stress for you by having babies?* But before I could ask, she hung up. *Why, indeed?* I thought in response.

"You will need to scrub your hands and arms here in this sink before entering," we were instructed when we approached the NICU through a scrubbing anteroom. I searched for hope in the faces of other parents as they shuffled in and out of the NICU sanctuary, preparing to become one of them. By the time we were allowed to see our baby for the first time since his birth hours earlier, he was well established in his clear plastic bin, and drugged like I'd been. His nurses introduced us to our son, as they already knew him better than we did.

He lay on his back, very still, with his arms and legs spread wide. His brown eyes were closed. A clear, fat plastic tube protruded from his mouth, sealed with white surgical tape, and he was naked except for a diaper and round monitors stuck all over his perfect body like Band-Aids. Each limb served its own unique purpose, anchoring him to some device that tethered him to his high-tech, mechanized world.

Whoosh, the complex breathing machine said, exhaling for him. The room was hushed, the silence interrupted only periodically by what would soon become a familiar sucking sound, indicating that our baby's lungs were filling with oxygen before the subsequent whooshing sound exhaled for him again.

Whoosh, suck, whoosh, suck, replaced "Mommy loves you," as the lullaby of our son's life, and my own breathing rhythm soon harmonized with the machines. The nurses became our teachers around the clock while we learned the new language of this baby—oxygen saturation and surfactant and Fentanyl.

The nurse's voice reached through our initial shock as she explained, "We have to keep him drugged so he won't fight the ventilator."

Another terribly perfect patient, just like his big brothers before him.

Baby Kittel, his name tag read. "His name is Isaiah," I whispered.

"Surfactant is the substance of mature lungs," the kind Dr. P explained to Andy and me as we settled into the tiny universe revolving around our son. "It's what allows the alveoli in his lungs to inflate and deflate with elasticity instead of collapsing after each breath. Without elasticity, a baby has to reinflate his lungs with every breath and soon becomes exhausted. He is unable to expend the energy it takes to breathe. And he succumbs."

Dies, I translated to myself, even though they never use words like that. We nodded, holding hands and trying to comprehend the new reality of our son's condition, refusing to believe that terrible word could become part of his birth story, too. *That breathing thing again*, I thought, inhaling deeply and picturing the root system of the lungs with its bronchial tubes and over three hundred million alveoli. I still had a lot to learn about breathing. Later I'd research the topic and learn that what our son had affects only about 1 percent of newborn infants and is the single most common cause of death in the first month of life in the developed world. In spite of our best efforts, lightning had struck us again.

"Wasn't that what happened to Jackie O's babies?" I asked the new doctor, who replaced Dr. P when the calendar changed to December the next day.

"Yes, twenty years ago we couldn't save babies born early with immature lungs," he confirmed. "Artificial surfactant wasn't developed until the 1980s. I was in my residency in Boston when Jackie Kennedy delivered and lost her two boys there to RDS—Respiratory Distress Syndrome." It seemed more than coincidental that I'd learned her story while laboring with my own RDS baby.

Isaiah ultimately received two of the possible three doses of surfactant, artificially replacing what nature had not yet developed. On his third day of life, I ate my breakfast as quickly as I could, headed down the elevator, scrubbed in, and hurried into his bay, where I now spent every waking moment rocking in a chair by his feet. When I arrived, the nurse said, "We're going to extubate him now." I stepped back out of the way while a team of nurses and doctors bustled around my son in his plastic baby bin. I flinched as they pulled all the tape off his newborn skin, and my eyes widened as I watched them slowly turn the familiar rhythm of the ventilator off. *Whoosh, suck, whoo, suc, wh, su, wssss* . . . Silence filled our small space, and my own heart floundered without the rhythm of the machine to follow.

Nobody breathed.

Including Isaiah.

Breathe, Isaiah, breathe, breathe, damn it, please God, make him . . .

But before I could pray my final, *Breathe!* his team sprang into action, hooking him up and cranking the machine back up to *Whoo, su, whoosh, suck, WHOOSH, SUCK!* Seeing his chest rise and fall again, I exhaled my relief and expanded my own alveoli again. The trained professionals seemed unconcerned and nonchalant about my baby—these people who coolly walked the fine line between life and death every day, just doing their job while I'd nearly died watching them.

"He still has too much Fentanyl in his system," one of the nurses explained calmly to my horrified eyes when the crisis was over. They spent the next day or so weaning Isaiah off his drug addiction, Fentanyl being one hundred times stronger than morphine, ending my brief love affair with drugs right then and there. The second time they disconnected him was a success, and we all breathed easier.

Even though Isaiah was off the ventilator, he still had several more hoops to jump through and needed to stay in the hospital, while I was discharged a few days after his birth. "Call any time," they encouraged, and though I was by his side most of the day, I did call when I wasn't there, the phone suddenly becoming a lifeline.

"I'm calling to check on Isaiah Kittel," I whispered in the middle of the night when getting up to pump his milk, happy to relieve the pressure instead of packing and icing it down, praying it would go away. I pumped my breast milk the whole time he was in the NICU, storing enough Playtex plastic bags of the rich, yellow colostrum in the NICU freezer to feed several of his neighbors as well. I had more stored at home and every time I tucked a little bag in amongst my frozen vegetables, I prayed I'd never have to use it to nourish a tree.

They would patch me through to Isaiah's nurse who'd cheerfully update me on what he was doing, regardless of the hour. I got to know these nurses well. Before he even had a name, Isaiah's first nurse, Joe, had given him his first toy—a squishy yellow Pokémon Pikachu we noticed in his plexiglass bin the first time we visited him in the NICU. These nurses wasted no time; they knew there were no guarantees.

I stayed with Isaiah all day and most of the nights even after I was discharged, driving home from the hospital late at night to sleep but hurrying back in the morning while Andy got the kids off to school. I hated leaving my baby and worried constantly. Winter blew its icy breath, and I was terrified there'd be a power outage and the hospital generator would fail. Isaiah and all his fragile neighbors were totally dependent on their life-giving electricity, their new umbilical cords. I'd worked all those years in Oregon for an electric-power marketing agency and never fully appreciated it until now.

The NICU was comprised of four separate bays, each with a wide opening and about ten high-tech plexiglass incubators, or baby bins, arranged in a U around the perimeter of each bay, the bins separated by only three or four feet of space. Quick, easy viewing and access was imperative for the emergencies that popped up by the minute. Now and again, I watched the nurses set up portable curtains around one of their tiny patients but I soon learned not to covet a curtain. While privacy in other circumstances may be desirable, here it was reserved for surgeries and other hidden moments—like death. The cardinal rule of the NICU is that everyone minds their own business, respecting each other's invisible boundaries and never approaching any baby but their own unless specifically invited by the parents.

The world of the NICU fascinated me, with miracles and tragedies occurring all around me as I rocked in my chair, praying for my son while he learned to breathe. Slowly, I developed a level of comfort and stopped staring at Isaiah constantly, peripherally taking in the world of the room around us.

I watched big, beautiful babies transfer in from community hospitals on stretchers surrounded by protective circles of EMTs, all moving in unison in the choreographed rush I remembered from the day of Noah's death. Rocking alone in my padded chair, I witnessed the subsequent tragedy of their demise when the bustle of emergency dissipated and the privacy curtain was slowly drawn around them with finality.

I watched one new mother wheeled in, fresh from delivery, her family slowly encircling her wheelchair to meet their baby together and gaze through their tears at what might have been. All that possibility. Gone. My heart hugged those poor mothers, and I cried with them from across the room, one of the silent witnesses whom they could not see. Having been the blind object of such focus myself, now I wondered whom I had missed seeing.

Isaiah was the big man in his bay. All around him were impossibly teeny babies born months too soon. Looking at them, you could almost imagine reinserting them into the womb. Indeed, some were not much bigger than a super-plus tampon. His neighbor, Danielle, had entered the world at twenty-two weeks, the lower limit for saving these half-done babies who should have been swimming inside their watery homes where all the work was done for them. Danielle's card said she weighed in at a whopping 472 grams, less than a pound but much more than a soul. At least she had that in her favor. Isaiah's card read 2,845 grams.

"We call them big, weak white males," the nurse said, explaining that in the world of the preemie, white males fare the worst because their lungs are bigger and require more oxygen. "Black baby girls do the best, followed by all girls in general, and then black boys," she added.

Twice as many boys are born with RDS, like Isaiah, and it accounts for one-fifth of all infant deaths. At his gestational age and weight, he'd had only a 5 percent chance of RDS, lung tests or no. The odds had beaten us once again.

One of his neighbors was an adorable black boy with a head of soft dark chocolate curls. I never saw anybody visit him, not even once. He was so good and never complained or cried when they bathed or changed him, as if he already knew he had nobody to rely on but himself, and was well on his way to becoming self-sufficient when he hadn't even reached his projected birth date yet.

"He'll probably end up in foster care, like many of the babies that come through here," Joe the nurse said.

Prematurity, like abruption, often results from a lifestyle that includes poor prenatal care and drug abuse. The NICU is a very busy place these days due to all the multiple births from fertility treatment and because increasingly older mothers are giving birth and have more health issues. At thirty-eight, I was edging closer to that category myself.

The NICU is an amazing world, where the frailest of beings cling to life in the best medical approximation of the womb. The nurses who work there are the unsung heroes of the hospital as they routinely perform their duties, saving lives on every shift, then going home to make dinner. I could not imagine handling the delicate limbs and jellylike skin of their patients, and was fascinated by my intense introductory visit, even though I would have avoided it gladly.

Isaiah proceeded calmly and confidently through the milestones set for him. We celebrated as he progressed to breathing with a nasal cannula and then to room air. His artificial surfactant kept all those tiny alveoli open, and his oxygen sats stayed high. His lungs worked. He could breathe!

"He needs a bit of light therapy," the nurse explained when I arrived one day to find Isaiah bathed in yellow light with a soft mask over his eyes. He was jaundiced, and the light would help break up the bilirubin in his skin. Five days after his birth, I held my son for the first time since then and fed him my breast milk from a bottle while Andy watched over my shoulder. "It will probably take him some time to get the hang of nursing," the nurses warned. But the next day we skipped the bottle, and Isaiah nursed like a pro, belying the skeptics and his delayed start. This was a moment I had sought for over two years now. He was taken off the IV that same day and was moved to a regular bed on the next. On the seventh day, he rested.

Isaiah was to be ours through a miracle of modern medicine, and thanks to a research grant from the March of Dimes, an organization founded in the 1930s to combat polio and since expanded to promote the health of expectant mothers and babies in general. And also thanks to the perseverance of a doctor named Merritt, who developed artificial surfactant some fifty years later. Thanks to Dr. Merritt, on the tenth day, we happily brought Isaiah home.

I've saved a periodical from the day, month, and year in which each of my children were born to put in their baby books. On November 30, 1999, *The Providence Journal* headline read: "Report says thousands of deaths due to medical errors." The article disclosed that more people die erroneously in hospitals each year than from highway accidents, breast cancer, or AIDS, a statistic that is unacceptable from a medical system that promises to "first, do no harm."

Now, in addition to Dr. Carr's pronouncement, "Your baby should not have died," we had the lessons we'd learned from Isaiah to add to our understanding of what had happened to his brother, Jonah. Isaiah's birth and his first week of life taught us that you don't have to *guess* how the baby might be doing. Even though we'd lost the lottery on the lung-maturity test with Isaiah, we now knew it existed and wondered why we'd been limited to a midwife's hands to estimate Jonah's size and ability to function at delivery. We'd learned that there are better medications to control blood pressure in pregnancy. And we learned that we'd had no business delivering our premature baby in a community hospital where an emergency C-section took more than thirty minutes on a good day and the nearest NICU was an hour's drive instead of a short walk down a hallway.

Once Isaiah was safely on the road to recovery, his doctor told us that on the day he was born, by the time they had walked him down the short hall to the NICU, Isaiah was blue. When I'd first met him, I thought he looked like Noah; it turns out, though, that Isaiah had quickly developed a resemblance to his brother, Jonah, also. I thought of the babies I'd watched transfer into the NICU and shuddered to think how Isaiah might have fared with an hour's drive ahead of him.

"You're right, honey," I said to Andy. "Perhaps Jonah's death was the result of something more than 'There was nothing we could do.'"

Chapter Six

CHRISTMAS was a joyful occasion in our new home with our teddy bear–size baby nestled in his boppy, surrounded by decorative angels heralding the season and glad tidings of his birth. We resurrected some miscellaneous Baby's First Christmas things that had belonged to Noah, including the lovely and complicated stocking my mother had hand-stitched for Noah's only Christmas with his name embroidered at the top. I could still see Noah chewing on the felt tab as we hung it next to the other three again, but this year for his new brother, Isaiah.

"I can change the name to Isaiah," Mom said when she saw it. It was a bittersweet event, watching her seam ripper snip out the letters *N* and *O* stitch by stitch, with no ritual or ceremony to mark the cutting finality of it all. Certainly, I have never forgotten those two yellow letters she replaced. The needle holes marking their presence lie just underneath the letters *I*, *S*, *A*, and *I* that she embroidered over them. But like the diminished jingling of the silver bell in *The Polar Express*, I see them a little less clearly each holiday season. And I'm eternally grateful for those four new letters now hanging there with the *A* and the *H* that have added back some of the joy that had been missing for a few years.

Andy and I continued our morning beach walks throughout the winter and into spring with our son bundled like a warm, squishy smile underneath my grandfather's wool overcoat. Jonah's birthday in May coincided with the end of the two-year statute of limitations for filing a lawsuit, and Andy and I discussed it at great length. By giving birth to Isaiah, I had done what I could to heal myself and bring hope and joy back into our lives. Now we could begin to know the happiness of a baby again. The kids came home from school each day eager to see their brother and snuggle with him, and our home knew the sights and sounds of a baby once more. Isaiah had had a shaky start, but now that our family was set firmly in place, I could focus more earnestly on Andy's arguments for filing a lawsuit.

Hannah's birthday coincided with April vacation and she missed her West Coast friends, so I decided to have her eleventh birthday pool party at a Salem hotel. She and I flew to Oregon with Isaiah, where I relished introducing him around to my friends. Before I'd left Rhode Island, we'd obtained a referral to a Eugene-based attorney who handled medical malpractice suits, and I had scheduled an introductory meeting. I met him at a local park, where I could push Isaiah around while we talked at length. His name was Dan Holland, and he had silvery hair and intelligent blue eyes. I expressed my misgivings about suing Dr. Harmon, and he carefully countered them all. When I mentioned how kind she was to offer us the use of her beach house, he said, "Don't you think that's a bit strange? Maybe she's trying to compensate for something or win your favor." When he asked me to briefly relate what had happened the day Jonah died and I mentioned that the doctor was on vacation, he said, "Most of my cases happen when the doctor is on vacation." By the end of our meeting, he'd successfully sowed sufficient seeds of doubt, and I found myself signing the paperwork to hire him and see what grew out of it. Isaiah's birth had left me with a lot of unanswered questions about what had really happened to Jonah, and I was ready to find some answers.

In the following month, May 2000, when Jonah would have been turning two and Noah four, Dan filed a wrongful-death lawsuit in Multnomah County Circuit Court, and our education in the legal system began. "The task before us is to prove that the defendants violated the standard of care," Dan explained on the phone. We named as defendants Dr. Elizebeth Harmon, Salem Hospital, and Dr. Peter

Watson, the high-risk fetal and maternal medicine doctor. "Their defense will be that they did their best and followed normal procedures and that abruptions are difficult to predict, babies die, and they didn't do anything wrong. They will play the sympathy card that these 'poor doctors' are always getting sued. You need to be prepared for them to blame *you*, Kelly, for Jonah's death. They'll try to delay the trial, and they'll stall to keep their money in their pockets as long as possible. But hopefully it will be resolved within a year, with a trial next spring. The depositions will take place in the interim."

This seemed reasonable. We didn't want any fanfare and hoped to resolve the case quietly with as little outside attention as possible. We didn't plan on telling anyone and definitely didn't want Andy's family to know about it. Like any personal business or financial matter, we thought we could keep it discreet. We might as well have taken an ad out on public television for what that intention was worth.

Soon after this, we received an e-mail from our niece Cally, scolding us for filing the malpractice lawsuit. We were shocked. How had she found out about the trial? And why on earth was she, now a nineteen-year-old college student, writing to us? As usual, her bold diatribe was deeply disturbing. This was followed a few days later by a letter from Marcella, which concluded:

Andy and Kelly, I'm deeply saddened to hear of your suing Kelly's "Jonah" doctor. [Suzie] called last week to say someone at work asked her if the Kittel that was suing a doctor was related to her, so she called me, and I said yes. The rumor is all over Salem and now Eugene. Kelly, did you follow the doctor's explicit instructions? Did you go to this same doctor for Isaiah before you left in June '99? She was well liked in Salem, I heard. Enclosed find pictures, etc. etc. Love, Mother

Etc. etc., indeed, I thought. The word was out, and the tribe was warming up by flexing their muscles, exercising their usual lack of restraint by letting us know exactly what they thought. We'd told nobody and we knew Suzie was lying, which would be revealed in the months ahead. In spite of several attempts, we would never learn the truth about how they found out about our lawsuit. And though Andy's phone kept ringing with calls from them, which he tried to avoid, I felt happier than ever to be three thousand miles away from their opinions.

Like the Peace Corps, the lawsuit gave Andy and me a common goal to work toward and brought us together as a united front. In the fall, we learned that the plaintiffs had successfully petitioned to change the trial to Marion County, so it would be held in Salem instead of Portland. *Salem* derives from the word *shalom*, meaning peace, and I hoped this venue would live up to its name, even though it was also closer to our old neighbors.

Dan began the process of obtaining my medical records in their entirety from the various entities. This, too, was no easy feat. I'd already attempted to obtain my own records from my doctors and the hospital before we moved, but what they'd produced then was many inches thinner than what we ultimately received. One of the first lessons we were to learn about medical lawsuits was this: It's almost impossible to obtain your complete medical record without filing a lawsuit. Even then, it took at least three requests over several months for our attorney finally to obtain the complete record.

"It's like they take all the pages and throw them down the stairs, then gather them up and send them," Dan said. My chart was mixed up and backward, and putting the hundreds of pages in order was akin to repairing Humpty Dumpty.

Conversely, our duty was to produce all of our own private records, correspondence, calendars, journals, letters, and the like from the time period of my pregnancy leading up to Jonah's birth. I exhaled my great relief that Jonah's death had stolen my will to write in my personal journal, because if I'd written anything, I'd have had to produce that for the defense attorney's reading pleasure. It was bad enough having to lay bare as much of our personal lives as we did for their hostile examination without including my most private thoughts as well.

One day Dan sent us a copy of a letter from a Seattle law firm he'd petitioned for assistance. They declined with the following summary: "Given the limitations on damages and the fact that the case is at least a horse race, we are not interested in getting involved." And so began our adjustment to a world wherein our private lives and personal tragedies were examined by experts who calculated our odds like a day at the racetrack. We trained ourselves to endure people who viewed us as a cost/benefit ratio with billable hours. And we learned to judge ourselves in a whole new arena, checking our emotions at the door so we could someday find our way around the track and out through the exit. "People from Maine don't have heart, they have gizzard," Mom always said, and I sure hoped that I'd inherited one.

Chapter Seven

ISAIAH TURNED ONE, and the first year of the new millennium came to a close when I realized I was pregnant again. With a six-year gap between Micah and Isaiah, he seemed all alone at the end of the family, and I hoped to provide a sibling closer in age for him to grow up with. I didn't feel as obsessed with having another baby as I had after Jonah died, but I also didn't feel like I was done yet. Part of this may have been my need to replace what I'd lost—two babies. One down, one to go. Part may have been my stubborn Irish genes. Part was definitely my attempt at "family planning," my Game of Life dream of having an overflowing minivan, which clearly wasn't working out as I'd planned. All things considered, I was thrilled by my condition. Isaiah and this new baby would be almost two years apart, which sounded perfect.

But at my routine sixteen-week appointment in March, I was rendered a huge blow. The baby had no heartbeat. To see that miniature baby on the ultrasound screen with the spine and head and legs and feet and everything in place—but so still, so still—was heartbreaking. I'd already suffered through the nauseous first trimester and arrived in the "safe" zone, spreading the happy news of my pregnancy far and wide and engaging the hearts and minds of my children in anticipation of another bundle of joy. Again I wondered, when did this baby die? How could I carry a dead baby around and not know?

Being four months along, I had to have a D&E, a horrific dilation and evacuation. The doctor inserted seven small sticks of seaweed

(*Laminaria japonica*) in my cervix with a wet gauze pad and sent me home overnight while they expanded, slowly forcing open my cervix. I would never look at seaweed the same again as I kicked it along the beach. The pressure gave me cramps, and I felt awful.

The next day's weather matched my mood with torrential rains befitting of an evacuation. Before the procedure, I asked for another ultrasound, just in case. But whereas the day before the baby was all stretched out and we could see it's entire anatomy, now it lay all curled up in a ball at the bottom of my uterus—crumpled, like me. A normal male fetus, they'd tell us later. If The Book of Noah was a short story and The Book of Jonah was an essay, this little baby was more like a poem.

April rolled around, and friends from Oregon came for Easter weekend to run in the Boston Marathon. "Mommy, Mommy," Isaiah called to me all the time, excited to use his newfound vocabulary.

"That must drive you crazy," my friend remarked. I just smiled. Isaiah was now a month beyond the age Noah had reached, and there were a lot of things I'd missed out on Noah doing—calling me constantly being only one of them. Isaiah had more than his quota to fill. He was my opportunity to raise not one, but three little boys. This was one of so many things people either forgot or didn't understand in their blessed ignorance. To mark the occasion, Isaiah helped Andy dig a hole in our backyard, and they planted a flowering crab apple tree along with his placenta but, happily, no breast milk. As I watched them lovingly spread the tree roots in the soil, I thought of all the roots my children had nourished, either with their placentas or with their ashes. Trees are the lungs of our planet as they inhale carbon dioxide deeply into the earth and exhale oxygen into the air we all breathe, and I liked the idea that our children were helping us all to breathe a bit easier.

Chapter Eight

IN MAY, my parents stayed with the kids while Andy and I flew to Portland for the first round of depositions. We met up with Dan and reviewed our case to date.

"Dr. Carr completed his review of your records," he began, speaking of my high-risk doctor in Providence, "and he discovered that you had abnormally high protein in your urine, based on the twenty-four-hour collection they ordered when you were admitted on May 7, the weekend before Jonah died. Did you know about this?"

"No," I said.

"It means that you were exhibiting signs of toxemia, or preeclampsia, in addition to your high blood pressure, and nobody took note of it."

Not only had they apparently not reviewed my lab results before allowing me to go home, but they'd also never bothered to check me for symptoms again. This was both shocking and disturbing, of course, and of immense significance to the "mystery" of Jonah's death, since that sent my odds for having an abruption rocketing from 3 percent up to 22 percent.

In preparing for the depositions, Dan reminded us that the defendant's goal would be to pin the blame for Jonah's death on me. "They will try to push all your buttons," he warned, "so remember to answer only the question asked. Try not to let them get the best of you, and do not elaborate. Respond with 'yes,' 'no,' or 'I don't remember' unless you're pressed for more detail. Avoid narratives. They will call your baby a fetus to diminish its importance. Don't let them do this. You had a baby, and his name was Jonah."

The next day—D-day, deposition day—we met Dan and his partner, Tom, and together rode up, up, up in an elevator to an expansive office where high-priced lawyers wearing custom-tailored suits slithered down the halls in their fancy shoes. A well-coiffed secretary escorted us into a glass-walled conference room that overlooked the Portland skyline. I had lived with what they call the "fishbowl effect" for two years in the Peace Corps where, as the only white girl in town, everyone watched everything I did. So I knew instinctively that I would be performing for a crowd in this transparent room with its highly polished cherrywood table. Immediately, I had stage fright, and I removed myself to a different room where I would spend a lot of time that day—the law firm's elegant bathroom.

I returned to find the show ready to begin and the actors in their places—four lawyers, two doctors, and a stenographer—nails and pens all poised for action. We, in the audience, watched. We listened. And we waited for our dreaded cue calls.

Dr. Winkler, the partner of Dr. Watson and one of the high-risk pregnancy doctors I'd seen in Portland, was the first to be deposed. Dan began by asking him, "What are the main things you watch for as a high-risk caregiver?"

"Worsening hypertension that's associated with a nuance of protein in the urine," he confirmed. He spoke of the difficulty of diagnosing preeclampsia in a chronically hypertensive patient, like me, because it's normal for blood pressure to gradually increase with a pregnancy, and it can be difficult to determine if the patient has superimposed preeclampsia or if it's a worsening of her chronic hypertension. "So you have to monitor other things," he said. *Like protein in the urine*, I thought. Superimposed preeclampsia, especially in somebody who has chronic hypertension, increases the risk of maternal or fetal complications, he said. He confirmed that upper-right-quadrant uterine pain is actually indicative of preeclampsia, not a symptom of abruption. I could hear the echoing words of Kate, the midwife, telling me that I would recognize *abruption*, not preeclampsia, by a sharp, stabbing pain in the upper right quadrant of my uterus. After extensive questioning, Dr. Winkler was excused. Later, we dropped their office from the lawsuit entirely because their role in my care was already established in this deposition as well as by my medical records; nothing more would be gained by bringing them to trial.

For the next three hours we sat and listened with increasing frustration as Dr. Harmon was deposed and consistently misremembered what had transpired. First, Dan ascertained that my doctor had probably never even seen the results of the twenty-four-hour urine collection lab test that showed I had increased protein in my urine above the threshold for diagnosing preeclampsia. He asked her, "Just to make sure I've got the full record here: So, if I want to get all the lab records on Kelly Kittel and her pregnancy in May of '98, and if I had *your* chart, you're telling me I might not have everything?"

"There might be . . . some of her labs from the hospital might not be there. I didn't see her labs, but I was looking here at the time," she said, flipping through my chart, "and I might have missed one."

"Have you looked at the hospital chart to prepare for this deposition?"

"Yes."

"I just want to know if you can think of any reason why they would have a lab report that wouldn't be in your chart?"

"I can't think of any reason. I know that sometimes labs don't always get to us."

"Is it important when you order a lab on one of your patients that people get information to you that you want?"

"Yes," she said, which clearly begged the question as to why she hadn't bothered to find it.

Then we listened to her discount the textbook threshold for preeclampsia itself as being insignificant. And we listened as she misremembered significant facts, like my induction.

"And, now, a decision was made on the ninth of May to let Kelly Kittel go home when the induction was stopped. Do you remember that?" Dan asked.

"The induction didn't start."

"You say that you never started the induction?"

"Right."

"You don't consider putting a gel on the cervix two times the start of an induction?"

"Maybe I misunderstood. I thought we hadn't started it. I'd have to go back and review it again."

"Are you aware that gel or any other kind of substance or medicine was placed on the cervix?"

"I'd have to look in the chart now. I'm going totally on memory. Would it be easier if I just told you what happened?" she asked.

"That's fine."

"She had been in the hospital for two days. She was scheduled for induction on Saturday morning. And my midwife had gone in because Kelly had requested and come to our practice for midwifery care. And so the midwife had gone in and talked to her about, 'This is what we're going to do.' And then when I came to the hospital to be there when the induction was going to be started, she was dressed to leave. And I said, 'What is happening?' And she said, 'I've decided I don't want to be induced today.' And I said, 'Why don't you want to be induced today?' And she says, 'Well, I've discussed this with Lisa,' who was the midwife, 'and the baby's premature. My blood pressure is good when I'm lying down. I feel fine. I don't have any preeclampsia symptoms, and I'm concerned that my baby is small, and I'd like to have more time to let the baby grow.' And so we discussed, 'You understand that the reason we were going to induce you is because your blood pressure is up?' And she goes, 'Yes, but that's because I wasn't laying down before. Now I'm laying down, and I see the difference. When I lay down, my blood pressure is normal, and it stays down. So I think that if I can lay down at home that my blood pressure will be good, and I would rather wait.' I'm just kind of shortening the whole discussion."

None of this conversation she remembered had ever taken place, nor was I dressed to leave when I saw her. But I wished I could "lay" down, as she put it, even though I autocorrected it to "lie" in my head while she was speaking, right then and there—my blood pressure was rising just listening to her. This gave me my first inkling of how they would try to pin the blame on me: I was not "laying" down. She admitted she had never charted any of this but that Andy and Lisa

Litton, the midwife, were probably in the room when this mythical conversation occurred. Andy had not been in the room, and I'd never spoken any of these words Harmon swore under oath that she remembered.

She continued, "So this discussion goes back and forth. And at that point her blood pressure was normal; her baby was healthy. There were no signs of any fetal compromise. She felt fine, had no symptoms of preeclampsia. So we discussed what the symptoms of preeclampsia were and why we were doing the induction in the first place, and we reviewed all the symptoms to look for at home and why I wanted to do the induction, and we came to the conclusion that we would wait."

"What did you tell her to look for at home for preeclampsia?"

"I'll tell you what I tell everybody, because I can't remember that far back exactly what I said." I thought this was an interesting admission, considering how much she'd "remembered" so far. "But blurry vision, a headache that doesn't go away with Tylenol, swelling, side pain, nausea. And she was checking her blood pressure at home. And I told her if her blood pressure went up to call me. And then we discussed what bed rest meant. And if she went into labor or if she had bleeding or pain or anything at all that changed she was to call immediately."

"Did you talk to her about protein?"

"No. That wasn't something she'd be testing at home."

"Okay. Is that something that she should know about, from your perspective?"

"Well, we had done a protein test on her."

"Where? In the hospital?"

"Yes. And it was basically normal, and all her other blood tests had been normal."

"What did it show, the protein tests?"

"Let's just look," she said, flipping through my chart. "Three hundred sixty-four milligrams."

"Oh, I see. So you knew that at the time you discharged her?" Dan asked.

"Yes," she said.

"How did you know that if it wasn't reported back until the next morning?"

"I don't know. When was it reported? I don't know how to . . ."

"You're looking at the hospital chart, and you're looking at the twenty-four-hour urine collection report. Does it show you on that report date the time it was reported back?"

"I don't know. Here's May 10. Evidently I didn't know that. I'm sorry. I guess I didn't know that at that time," she admitted. This was the first of what would be five times that day that she'd admit she never saw the results of my lab report showing I was leaking protein in my urine, which was a signal that I was developing toxemia, as Dr. Winkler had just informed us in his deposition.

Dan continued, "Did you ever tell Kelly Kittel at any time that she had had protein in excess of 300 milligrams that was, by definition, proteinuria?"

"Proteinuria by definition is more than 300 milligrams, but proteinuria significant for preeclampsia would be much higher than that. And, no, I would not have."

This abnormally high amount of protein in my urine was one of several important details about my health Dr. Harmon had, indeed, failed to inform me about, details I was just learning about now because of this lawsuit. Details I should have known as part of my health history in subsequent pregnancies. When I'd read my medical chart to prepare for the trial, another startling discovery I'd made was that she'd consulted with Dr. Watson when I was admitted to the hospital on May 8 and that he'd recommended she induce and deliver me. But this deposition was the first time I'd hear Dr. Harmon say it. She'd failed to inform me of this salient fact at the time when I most needed to know it—when I was agonizing over whether to continue the induction to deliver Jonah or go home for Mother's Day. We were sailing in uncharted waters, and it was about to get even rougher.

Dan asked, "Independent of your attorney, has anyone ever said that Kelly Kittel was a noncompliant patient in any way?"

"Yes."

"Who's that?"

"Cody Martin."

And so, halfway through Dr. Harmon's testimony, came one of the greatest shocks of Andy's and my life together. Andy and I held hands and tried not to be thrown off our chairs by the two-word tidal wave that the doctor had just unleashed, filling our glass room while I held my breath. Cody. Martin. I looked around, half expecting her red head to swim into view at any moment. We clutched our seat cushions until the water drained and I could exhale. I took a deep breath as the doctor continued her tale.

"What did she say?" Dan asked.

"She said that Kelly was not at bed rest the whole time that I had asked her to be at bed rest."

"When did she tell you that?"

"I can't remember the day."

"Was it before the seventh?"

"No."

"When did Cody tell you that?"

"After the baby had died."

"When?"

"Maybe a couple of days after."

"And how do you know Cody Martin?"

"I think Cody is, I think she's Andrew's sister or sister-in-law. I know she lived across the street from them."

"Why were you seeing her a couple of days after the delivery?" he asked.

"Well, she was there with Kelly when she had the baby."

"Did she say anything else other than the words you've given to me, any details, any dates, any activity?"

"She told me that she had been up taking care of the kids and doing her normal things around the house, and I think Cody was the one that was checking her blood pressure for her. And then later she came to my office."

"When was that?"

"I can't remember the date she came to my office. It was after the lawsuit had been filed."

"And what did she tell you?"

"She told me that she was disappointed the lawsuit was filed, and that she wanted to talk to me about the case. And I told her I didn't feel comfortable discussing it with her, and I gave her the name of my lawyer. And I said, 'If you'd like to discuss what happened, you should talk to the lawyers and not to me.'"

"Do you know if she did?"

"Yes," she replied.

I felt like I'd just had all the breath sucked right out of me. Eventually it would sink in that Cody was perfectly willing to rush to the doctor's side, a person whom she barely knew, to volunteer her services as an expert witness. Indeed, we would learn throughout this process just how willing people were to misremember our story. But learning that our own "family is the most important thing" tribe members were equally willing was something we would never recover from. Now I was starting to understand where the doctor was getting her ideas about me not "laying" down. I stared out the window and pictured my own ancestors watching through the glass and shaking their heads in the blue, blue sky.

Dan asked, "Do you know of any other instance where anybody else or any document was revealed to you in any way that Kelly Kittel was in any way a noncompliant patient or conducted herself in any way that was possibly harmful to her pregnancy with Jonah?"

"I know that when she came to the hospital the day that the baby died that I had had her home on strict bed rest, which meant be in bed except to go to the bathroom or come to your office appointments, and she had come from her son's school program."

"And do you know any other details about that?"

"I know that she had been there for a couple of hours."

"Who told you that?"

"Kelly," she said.

"Did you write that down someplace?"

"Yes."

"Where did you write that?"

"I believe I wrote it . . . I'm not sure what I wrote, but . . . the fourteenth . . . I didn't write that she had been . . . but that she had been there . . . I guess I didn't write it down . . . but she had told me that," she said.

"So there's a clear record that you didn't write it down anyplace?"

"I did not write it down in the record, but I remember very clearly her telling me that."

"You have a very clear, very vivid memory that she told you what?"

"That she had come from her son's school program."

"And what else do you remember about that, if anything?"

"That she had been there for a couple of hours and that she had been bleeding and cramping the time that she was there. And when she started bleeding really heavy, she decided to come to the hospital." This was clearly not what had happened. Dan ascertained that, in fact, what the chart said was, "Today patient started cramping at 0700 or 0730 and came to the hospital at 1030 after bleeding. On arrival no heart tones." Nothing about an hours-long school program or spotting and bleeding and cramping for three hours.

Next, Dan asked a series of questions about the details of my hospital chart and the results of the twenty-four-hour urine test, concluding with, "And you don't know of any record that shows that you were ever aware of that lab test before the baby died—isn't that true?"

"There's no record that I know of that says that I had seen that test before that baby died." Harmon admitted for the fourth time that day.

He asked her a series of questions about her vacation, including, "Did you ever see Kelly Kittel after you talked to her on Saturday morning, the ninth, before she came in abrupting on the fourteenth?"

"No."

"No contact with her whatsoever?"

"I don't think so," she said, even though I saw her in her office waiting room on Monday, May 11, her cookie-baking day.

"Did you ever try to call her?"

"No."

"Did any midwife call you about anything during that period of time?"

"I called my office every day and checked on her to see if she came in," she said.

"I read through your chart, and I probably just missed that. But can you show me where your chart might help us reconstruct that you called in every day?"

"It's not in the chart. I was just calling because I liked Kelly and considered her a friend, and I wanted to make sure that she came in for her test every day. So I called the office every day to check that she came in." *A friend*? I thought. I was her patient.

"When you discharged her on May 9, what options did you give to her for staying in the hospital or going home? What alternatives did you explain that she had at the time?

"Those two options."

"And did you recommend one over the other?"

"I think I recall saying that my preference was that she would stay in the hospital and have her baby."

"And you told her that?"

"I'm pretty sure I did."

"Are you just guessing or…"

"I'm pretty sure I did, because I was really surprised when I walked in and she was dressed and going home." Except, of course, she hadn't told me that, and I wasn't dressed to go home.

"I see. So when you saw her like that, and you preferred she would stay, there must have been a reason why you wanted her to stay in the hospital to deliver the baby. What was that?" he asked.

"Call it gut instinct. It was just one of those things I had personally experienced, preeclampsia, in my own personal health, and I was worried that she might develop preeclampsia."

"You considered that she may have had or may not have had pre-eclampsia on May 9. Is that what you're telling me?"

"I had determined that she did not have preeclampsia. That's why I felt confident that she could go home." Though she was talking about me, I was having a lot of trouble wrapping my head around this logic.

"Why was the issue of preeclampsia important for you to consider at that time?"

"It can cause seizure in mothers, renal failure, strokes, abruption, stillbirths."

"And is that particularly true when it's superimposed on chronic hypertension or pregnancy-induced hypertension?"

"They're at a higher risk to develop those symptoms, and sometimes the symptoms are more severe."

"And that higher risk includes a risk of abruption?" he asked.

"Yes."

"And abruption leads to a risk of fetal demise?"

"Yes."

"Is that abruption like the kind of abruption that Kelly had on the fourteenth?"

"It could have been," she said.

"What's your thought process on the fourteenth as you're monitoring the induction of Kelly?"

"She didn't have the symptoms of preeclampsia when she came in."

"What was she missing?"

"Her blood pressure was not as high as you would expect for severe preeclampsia. She wasn't spilling protein," she said. Except that my blood pressure was low on the day Jonah died because I was hemorrhaging.

"How did you know that?"

"I dip it when they come in the door, the dipstick thing." In fact, she wasn't even there and nobody had bothered to check my urine when I came in with Joanne's towel between my legs.

"This is after the abruption?"

"And her lab tests were normal."

"I'm sorry?"

"Her lab tests that you would expect to be abnormal, they were not."

"In what way?"

"Her liver functions were normal. I'd have to go back and look to see what tests we had done."

"Okay. Please do. Let me know what labs you looked at on the fourteenth."

"When she came in here, hemoglobin was normal, her platelets were normal, and her liver functions were normal. Those were the labs that we ordered when she came in."

"What time?"

"11:29 and 10:21."

"This is after the abruption?"

"Yes."

"Do you have any labs before the abruption?"

"Those were done on the seventh."

"I'm sorry?"

"From the seventh."

"So we don't have any labs from the seventh until after the abruption—is that correct?" Which was one whole week.

"Yes."

"And based on that, it was your opinion at the time that she did not suffer from preeclampsia or had not suffered from preeclampsia, or did you consider something else to come to that conclusion?"

"She had been seen the day before and had a normal blood pressure. Her urine was negative the day before," she said, but in fact it was not. When Dan asked again why there was no record of the twenty-four-hour urine test, Harmon replied, "I don't know. It got lost in the mail or something." This, then, was the fifth time she admitted under oath that she had not seen the test results of the twenty-four-hour urine collection, although over a year later in the courtroom she would swear she had seen it and base her defense on that "fact."

Finally, Dr. Harmon's deposition concluded.

Chapter Nine

My DEPOSITION was next. I was so stressed by this time that though I'd eaten nothing, I had what Jamaicans call "running belly" and kept sprinting back and forth from the fish bowl to the marble bathroom. *You had a baby and his name was Jonah*, I repeated to myself like a mantra while inspecting my lips for erupting stress fractures. I was deposed by two attorneys, and the interrogation lasted almost six hours.

Dr. Harmon's attorney, John Harte, began by asking if I'd read anything to prepare for the deposition. I said I'd reviewed the medical records we'd received and that I was surprised to learn from reading it that Dr. Harmon had consulted with Dr. Watson regarding the induction, and to learn that I had proteinuria.

Harte asked me about the notes I'd taken during my pregnancy, about kick counts and blood pressure readings, and about bed rest, finally asking if anybody had told me I could go to a party on May 14, 1998.

"Did you go to a party on May 14, 1998?" Harte asked.

"No," I answered.

"Did you go to a school program on that date?"

"No."

I had not gone to a school program. I had gone to Micah's neighborhood music class program in my neighbor's basement for about a half hour. He asked me if I danced or if I stood to watch the program. He asked if I thought this was different from the bed rest instructions I was given at that time; if I wore shoes at home; if I asked Andy to drive me the three houses down because I thought there was a risk of abruption. We spent a lot of time talking about my knowledge of abruption, my definition of bed rest, my calendar and activities, my hospital and doctor visits.

"Did you provide child care during the last ten days before Jonah was born?"

"I don't consider caring for my own kids to be child care," I answered.

"Who were the top four people helping you while you were on bed rest besides Andy?" I told him the top three people helping me were Hannah, Christiana, and Micah, and the fourth was my friend Cindy, knowing full well there was another C-name he was hoping to hear.

He quizzed me about all the household things that needed doing and all of the kids' activities. We went through my Bob Marley calendar day by day and talked about who drove and who cooked and who did what. He quizzed me about Hannah's and Micah's birthdays and what we did to celebrate, and sorrow grabbed my vocal chords while I choked out that everything had been put on hold because I was on bed rest and we were waiting for the baby to be born to have our celebrations. I felt so badly for my kids who had sacrificed their birthday parties until they could share the fun with their brother, who was ultimately unable to attend after all.

We reviewed the weekend of the failed induction in excruciating detail. When it came to the Saturday morning part, when Cody had stopped by the hospital on her walk, he asked, "How's your relationship with her?"

Dan interjected: "Do you mean today?"

"Yes."

"I don't have much of a personal relationship with her today," I said.

Harte pressed on. "Do you like her?"

Dan objected and asked if it was really a fair question.

"It goes to bias, motives, and interest, I would think," Harte said.

So I had to answer the question. He repeated: "Do you like your sister-in-law?"

I stalled.

Dan objected to the form of the question, but he let me answer.

Did I like her? Did I have a choice? She was family, and I had honestly never considered the question in those terms before. There was so much more to it than that elementary-school sentiment and I remembered my surprise when Andy had told me his dad didn't like his brother, Buster, on the day Noah died. But could I honestly say, under oath, "I like Cody Martin?" I thought to myself.

Tell the truth, my ancestors encouraged.

"No," I said, finally, to the predatory gazes of the attorneys, whose hungry ears devoured my every word; to the court stenographer tap-tapping the permanent record of my words; to my husband; and, most of all, to my own troubled reflection staring back at me from the highly polished surface of that exquisite cherrywood table. No. I did not like my sister-in-law, Cody Martin.

But of course, Harte couldn't even let the echoes of that one-syllable word die in the air before nagging onward.

"And can you tell me, has that been your position for the last three-plus years, or has it changed in the last three years?"

"It has changed."

"And when, roughly?" This so he could establish my bias against my sister-in-law, his star witness.

"Over time," I said. "There's no specific date."

I waffled, wondering if I should divulge that it had clearly changed irreparably some hours ago in that very room when Harmon had sent her name swirling around the room.

He quizzed me about the days leading up to Jonah's death, the day itself, then about my visit afterward to Dr. Watson. "Did you ask him if Dr. Harmon performed appropriately or not?"

"No, I don't believe I asked him that."

He continued. "Were you suspicious at that time that she had not?"

"I can't answer that right now. I'd have to think about it."

"Let's do it."

"Let's think about it?"

"Yes."

I sighed, then took a few minutes to think about it while

everyone paused, waiting, pens and fingers poised. "Okay, I'll have to say yes."

"And why was that?"

"Because I believe that at that point in time, which is what you're asking me to remember, I was suspicious of everything. My baby had died. I wanted to know why my world was crushed. I needed a reason."

"Okay. So did Dr. Watson help you in any way in your legitimate wondering about whether Dr. Harmon had done a good job or not?"

I thought his word choice peculiar and wanted to hear him say "legitimate wondering" again. Did he really think it was legitimate for me to wonder if my doctor had done a good job? I told him Dr. Watson had helped me by providing additional information. Harte then went through a list of all the doctors I'd seen since then, asking if any of them had told me what caused the abruption or were critical of Dr. Harmon. My answers were all negative until we got to Dr. Carr, and I told him that Dr. Carr had said that Dr. O'Brien would never have let me walk out of his office with blood pressures like I had when I was seeing Dr. Harmon.

He quizzed me about my compliance as a patient, about my friends and Jonah's memorial service, and about any counseling we'd received. Then he asked, "And can you tell me whether . . . I mean, you've had some emotional issues in your lifetime. We all have. I think you've had more than your share. On the other hand, can you differentiate your emotional stressors arising from this fetal demise as opposed to, for example, the death of your other son?"

"Yes," I said, clenching my Irish fists at his insincere thought that perhaps I'd had more than my share of emotional stress while he simultaneously added to it. And then for him to use the term "fetal demise" again, along with the final insult of asking me this very question, even though he wasn't the first to do so.

"I mean, they're separate and distinct?" he went on.

"Yeah," I said again.

"And you can—how do you differentiate them?"

"How do I differentiate them?" I repeated. My Irish blood was boiling, but I managed to keep my fists in check and to rein-in my spinning brain. My tongue slapped back with, "Well, which of your arms would you miss the most, Mr. Harte, your right or your left? Or would you really be able to differentiate?"

"Unh-huh," he replied.

I took a deep breath and proceeded to commit the sin of elaborating, even though he hadn't asked me a question. "One is one event, and one is another event. They're two different people. They're two different children. They're completely different circumstances. Unfortunately, Jonah's death is my grief more than anyone else's. Noah's death caused a whole lot of people to grieve. It still does."

"How does this fetal demise affect you at present, emotionally, physically in your day-to-day life?"

"Jonah's death?" I asked, again unwilling to allow him to reduce my son to a "fetus," as Dan had warned me they'd do.

"The 'fetal demise' is what I said. How does it affect you in your day-to-day life?" he said.

"When you say the 'fetal demise,' do you mean Jonah's death?" I stubbornly insisted.

"Yes," he said.

"Okay," I said, feeling triumphant. "I'll never get over it. You don't ever recover from this. Your life is never, ever the same."

"Have you lost income because of the circumstances following this fetal death?" he asked.

"I have not functioned financially since Jonah died, yes."

"You haven't had a job?"

"I had a job. I don't have a job now, no. I was unable to deal with that."

"Is that exclusively because of the fetal demise?" he asked—again, that term, but I was too exhausted to correct him one more time.

"Yeah."

"And why?"

"Have you ever buried two children?"

"No, I haven't."

"In the space of nine months?"

"I have not."

"Then I can't explain it to you. If you had, I wouldn't have to. My heart has never been the same. The death of Jonah broke my heart, literally."

Of course I should never have said this, as he then chose to worry that statement to death by questioning me about each doctor I'd seen and what he or she had said about my heart's condition until I wanted to sprint down the hall to that other room I knew so well, screaming, "I had a baby! His name was Jonah!"

As Dan had warned, Harte's intent was to get me to divulge as much information as possible by probing and pushing all of my buttons—testing, testing—and I'd not only shown him where my buttons were, I'd practically pushed them all for him. I wondered at the level of robotic detachment required to be an attorney and what it ultimately did to your soul, your heart having clearly been checked along with your trench coat by your manicured secretary as the elevator doors slid behind you each day.

After several hours, Harte concluded his barrage, and the hospital's attorney, Keith Bauer, took his turn with me. Although Andy was scheduled to be deposed next, the clock glared 7:40 p.m. when my interrogation concluded, so we adjourned until the next day.

The elevator swallowed us up like an "Amen," and we descended to ground level, crossing the street with our attorneys to collapse into a soft chair and recap the day over a much-needed rum and tonic. I was exhausted, but the attorneys were filled with the pent-up energy and words that they'd swallowed all day. I squeezed lime into my rum and sipped the cool and bitter tonic, which slowly soothed my traumatized bloodstream, wondering, *If this was just the sideshow, how will I possibly make it through the main event?* Our brains still bulged from the shock of the doctor's testimony about her tea party with Cody. This was exactly the type of discovery these depositions were designed for.

"What kind of family do you come from?" Tom asked Andy, who couldn't answer. *The kind that eats its young for dinner*, I thought.

"I can't believe your sister will follow through with testifying against you," Dan said. "In my entire career, I've never seen a relative testify against another. Usually they are either in support of each other or they just don't get involved."

He had obviously never met Cody. But he would. We talked around our straws about what an unbelievable story this was and how truth is, indeed, stranger than fiction.

"Can I write your story some day?" Tom asked.

"I think I'll probably write it someday myself," I said.

"Nobody will ever believe it," he said.

"Well, if it wasn't my life, I wouldn't believe it either."

Chapter Ten

THE SHOW picked up again the next day in Salem, since most of the people being deposed were there. We arranged ourselves around a much duller table in a simpler law office with no skyline view, where we sat through Andy's deposition and those of four nurses, one of whom confirmed that it would take at least forty minutes at Salem Hospital to perform a C-section if a team was already assembled and ready to cut—forty minutes that Jonah didn't have to wait.

As a lover of stories, I found the deposition process to be fascinating; but it was also exhausting, since I was the protagonist. Some of the narrators remembered the story well, but many were living proof that nobody remembers your life as well as you do and that you never forget the way people make you feel. I will never forget some of these people for as long as I live. Yet three years after we'd met, they couldn't even remember my name, which would also prove to be a common problem in this case. We flew home to bake an angel food cake for Noah and Jonah, both of whose birthdays had fallen during the depositions.

In July, the judge moved our trial date to the following January due to delays in discovery—Dan had discovered that parts of my medical records were still missing. I flew back to Oregon in June and again in August for the depositions of more hospital personnel and midwives. As difficult as it was sometimes to see them all again and listen to what they had to say, they were telling the story of my life and Jonah's. I was still trying to figure out what had happened, and I didn't want to miss an episode. I had just learned that I was pregnant again and was due in April. The timing with the trial and all wasn't great, but still I was secretly thrilled.

In August, I also boarded a plane for Arizona for the deposition of Lisa Litton, the midwife whom I had seen on the Saturday I'd left the hospital undelivered. The midwife admitted that, like me, she didn't know that Dr. Watson had recommended induction and delivery. She reiterated how that one fateful Saturday had been our only interaction and that although she was concerned about my blood pressure at this critical juncture in my care, she barely knew me. Dan asked her what she talked to me about and she replied, "What I remember is she asked me how big did I think her baby was. So I felt her belly and told her what I thought. Her concerns about the baby being preterm. Her concerns about the whole induction process and how difficult it can sometimes be."

"Did you ever make any notes in the chart about this discussion?" he asked.

"No."

"Did you think that the discussion was important?"

"Yes."

"Why didn't you make any notes?"

"Because I didn't have an ongoing relationship with Kelly. She was more high risk. She knew Dr. Harmon, and I wasn't going to make the decision myself to discharge her. That was a decision that was going to be made between Dr. Harmon and Kelly. I didn't feel that I needed to chart our discussion because I knew Dr. Harmon was also going to have it with her."

"Do you recall that she was asking meaningful, intelligent questions?"

"Yes."

"Did you have any feeling at all that she would have done anything to harm the baby by making a choice to go home or stay?"

"No."

"Did you feel that she was trying to make an informed decision about what was best for the baby during your discussion?"

"Yes . . . I never met a patient like Kelly Kittel," she said, which caused at least four sets of eyebrows to raise. I looked at Dan, who looked down at his notes as we both wondered why on earth my care at this critical juncture in my pregnancy with Jonah had been in the hands of a midwife who'd never had a patient like me. And how had I not known that then?

After the deposition I told Dan that I was pregnant, and he said, "Well, then we'll have to move the trial date."

"Why?" I asked.

"Because there's no way I'd put you through that in your condition."

Soon after our conversation, the court moved our trial date ahead another six months anyway to June 17, 2002. But, as it turned out, they wouldn't need to move it for my sake.

The next month, on September 11, 2001, Isaiah's chubby toddler fingers toyed with my neck, reaching around now and again in a loving, choking hug as I strolled along Sachuest Beach with him riding along in his blue backpack. The September air suffused our skin with its final reminders of summer warmth, and the sky blanketed us in blue, the ocean reflecting its beauty with a peacefulness that would soon be shattered.

Later, I would recall this tranquility and remember another day twelve years earlier when, like today, an unusual stillness had permeated the air as I took my lunchtime walk along the San Francisco waterfront. The bay had glistened calmly, and the gulls were silent. The earth, as it turned out, had been holding its breath. But we modern men didn't remember how to discern its foreboding. And in a few short hours it had exhaled with a 7.1 Richter scale "OHM," blowing buildings off their foundations and buckling bridges, leaving cars and people dangling beneath them.

Today, too, would bring a bustling city to its knees, forcing folks to shed their coats of isolationism and embrace one another like small-town neighbors as they sought comfort and reassurance. But this day was not to be defined by Mother Nature. This day would be remembered for Human Nature. And on this day, I was preoccupied with my own struggle with life and death.

I pried Isaiah's fingers from my neck, kissing them, as the gentle Atlantic reached out to caress her own babies, the grains of sand surrounding my bare toes. The comforting weight of my chattering bundle was an antidote for the loss of his brother, who'd been due to arrive on that auspicious day but had been evacuated so painfully by the D&E in March. I'd headed to the beach on this morning to commemorate the short life I'd held for a few months within the depths of my body and which remained in my soul, still, like a tiny shard of glass not yet tumbled smooth by the sea of time. I kicked at some seaweed and sighed, but smiled at the glimmer of hope now starting to make itself known to me by its flutter kicks as it swam in circles around my womb. I exhaled my own short, silent prayer, *Please, God, please, let everything go well this time.* I thought, *Baby in April, just like Hannah,* who'd been one and a half for that Loma Prieta earthquake, *and a trial in June.* The gulls screamed overhead, sensing no earthly need for silence.

Isaiah and I finished our walk, turning our backs on the sea and folding ourselves back in the car, and headed off to my doctor's appointment with the radio tuned to its usual station, NPR. Within minutes my meditation was interrupted with breaking news; something was happening a hundred miles away in Manhattan. I listened, stunned, as the familiar voice narrated the unfolding story—a plane had crashed into the World Trade Center, a fire burned, thousands were engulfed in a jet-fueled hell. I called Andy, who turned on the TV just as a second plane struck the second tower.

"What is . . . people," he said. "Oh my God, people are jumping out of the windows."

The beautiful blue day shone all around us as I continued driving to my appointment, life marching on for the rest of us as we kept our eyes and ears tuned. When I arrived home later, ready to settle into the couch for the next few days to watch the twenty-four-hour broadcasts, the phone rang. I cringed when I recognized Cody's voice.

"Are you all okay?" she blurted out with no perfunctory greeting, as usual.

I hesitated while my rational mind tried to comprehend what my ears translated. Was she really calling us? I hadn't spoken to her since

June when I'd asked her why she was testifying against us. "I just wanted to know what you guys were doing," she'd replied, but she'd had no answer when I asked why she hadn't just asked us instead. Were we *OKAY*? I had no intention of ever speaking to her again, but found my voice long enough to say, "I find it very interesting but not very believable that you are concerned about our well-being." Then I handed the phone over to Andy, who grimaced when her voice hit his ear.

On this same unforgettable day, we received a letter from Dan with a copy of the notes from Karen, the counselor Andy and I had seen in Oregon before moving. I took a break from CNN to read our personal history through Karen's eyes. She wrote about our initial interview in March of 1999, soon after the kitchen-table meeting when Bud recommended that Andy and I get a divorce. After reading some background information about the length of our marriage and our children, I read the CliffsNotes version of our loss of Noah and Jonah:

> Noah was run over by Andy's sixteen-year-old niece in driveway at coast. Kelly and Andy live across from niece and family in Salem. They are renting a house from them. Many incidents were reported by couple of grave insensitivity to their loss by many family members, particularly by the niece and her parents. A pregnancy followed the loss of Noah. A son Jonah, born May 14, 1998, died at birth. Kelly reported this was a high-risk pregnancy due to high blood pressure. Her placenta detached, killing the baby. Key issues: Grief compounded by seemingly abusive family (Andy's). Lack of support from Andy's family. Family wants them "to get over it." Andy experiencing split loyalty. Different grief styles also a problem. Too much exposure to Andy's family given there's no comfort . . . Living location, too close to niece and her family. Devastating losses. Buried two babies in nine months.

At our second meeting a week later she'd noted:

Stories pouring out about insensitivity of family concerning losses. Kelly particularly seems the target. Andy's family is blaming Kelly for the loss of both babies. Some members seem more vocal than others do, although there seems to be no real support anywhere. Kelly touched on concerns about the doctor's choices in letting her labor, and lack of nursing attention when the crisis hit, which ended in Jonah's death.

Again, on March 16, she wrote:

So much hurt and raw pain. They are coping day by day. They both are surprisingly lucid and are taking care of their family. Recommendation to move made. The location to the most abusive family is taking too much energy.

On March 22:

Both are trying to cope with grief and abuse from Andy's family. They are split at times and at odds with each other. Talked again about moving. Where? Kelly prefers near her family on the East Coast, Andy wants to stay in Oregon.

April 5:

Offered support for grief. Talked about setting limits and ending contact with abusive family. This is very hard for Andy. He seems to experience confusion at knowing who to be loyal to. Kelly really wants these people to love and support her. She doesn't want to give up on them.

This, I recalled, was the day Andy had stormed out and Karen had told me to go and save myself.

April 13:

Talked about all the children today, those alive and those

dead. They are very sad and traumatized parents. Strong feelings of not being able to keep children safe. There is such raw vulnerability.

April 21:

They are getting closer to a moving decision. We talked about securing an unencumbered place to grieve.

May 5:

There are new waves of pain and grief for both. There is such sadness and sense of disbelief and the preponderance of death and loss. Moving plans are in process.

And finally, on May 11:

Moving plans are underway. I have encouraged both to get counseling at their new location. They promised to keep in touch.

I read her notes with great interest. I felt validated, reading the turmoil of that emotional time as summarized and recorded so rationally by her.

Two weeks later, I went for an ultrasound as part of an experimental new study called Faster, to screen for birth defects earlier than usual. I'd done the same with the last baby, and all had looked good with him at the time. I was chatting away with the technician this time, certainly not expecting any new disaster so soon after 9/11, when I should have known better. She scanned my belly and became very quiet. Hadn't I been through this sudden deathly silence before, too many times? My heart knew first and alerted my brain to tell my mouth to shut up while my soul began to mourn the loss of yet another little Kittel. The baby was twelve weeks old and just at the point when all should have been cleared for me to shout its presence to the world. But there was no heartbeat. The baby was no longer swimming inside me; it, too, had drowned.

I had to wait a week to see if the pregnancy would resolve itself. A week of walking around with a dead little baby crumpled on the bottom of my womb while New Yorkers walked around clutching photos of their missing babies. A week of checking constantly for any signs that my body was rejecting it while folks in Manhattan searched through mountains of rubble for any sign of their loved ones. But it remained buried within me, so I reluctantly agreed to be scheduled for a D&C, dilation and curettage.

I didn't want to undergo the withdrawals from anesthesia I'd experienced with the last surgery, so I elected to have an epidural instead. This turned out to be a bad decision, since I remained lucid during the procedure when I would have preferred to be anywhere but in that room at the time. I closed my eyes and imagined I could hear the echoes of funeral bells filling the void in the New York skyline, while screaming gulls filled the void in my belly where a heart used to beat. And I saw people stepping out of windows and flying off to meet my baby.

It was Columbus Day weekend, and we'd planned to go to Maine with the kids to celebrate our thirteenth wedding anniversary. I had a terrible headache when we left but thought it would get better. I was wrong. Andy took me out for our anniversary dinner to a quaint country restaurant where I proceeded to cry through the whole meal. The waiter probably thought we were getting divorced. We were under an increasing amount of pressure from the lawsuit, and this second late miscarriage plus my massive headache had really put me over the edge. Instead of the joys we'd had in our thirteen years together, I felt overwhelmed with sadness for all that we'd been through. I felt like I'd failed even Andy. No champagne was called for. No Lucky 13 this year.

I suffered through the whole weekend underneath the pain, only to call the doctor when I got home and learn that I had what is called a "spinal headache" from the epidural. And to learn that we'd lost another normal, male fetus. Another little poem was added to our anthology.

A month later, Andy went to Oregon for his birthday to go elk hunting, and while he was there, he called Cody and asked if she'd meet him for lunch.

"I want to hear what on earth she's thinking from her own lips," he said when he told me about his plan. Later that day, he called to tell me about it.

He started by saying to his sister, "I have three questions I need to ask, and depending on your answers, this could be a very short lunch. How did you find out about the lawsuit?"

"I read about it in the paper," Cody said.

"Did you go to the doctor on your own?"

"Yes, I did," she said.

"Why are you doing this?" he asked.

"Because I am Salem!" she said.

"Then lunch is over. I have nothing more to say to you." Andy then got up and left, walking out on his sister, who had saved him from drowning once but seemed to be pushing him off the inner tube herself this time.

"I am Salem?" I asked. "What the heck is that supposed to mean?"

"I have no idea," he said. "I guess it has something to do with how she sees herself as a vital part of the medical community in Salem." Which was clearly more important to her than her family—or than we were, anyway. Whatever she meant by it would remain a mystery.

Chapter Eleven

W<small>E WENT</small> to Florida in November to celebrate our fortieth birthdays and Isaiah's second, eating our Thanksgiving turkey with my parents and, again, spending time on Captiva. I fed my children beach snacks while we watched the ospreys feed their babies, and we all lined up in a row along the water's edge, burying our legs with tiny shells while watching the coquinas bury themselves with every wave. I was thankful for the three years that had passed and that I no longer felt like burying myself along with them. We returned to Rhode Island to hang Isaiah's stocking for the third year. He was such a lovely boy, with a head of blond hair and a sweet disposition. He loved to swim, play ball, and read books. And he loved boats. "My love boats," he'd said often while zooming around my parents' pool in Florida.

At the end of January, Andy flew to Oregon and returned with Marcella and a big surprise for Christiana's tenth birthday—the puppy he'd promised almost three years ago when we'd left Dude behind. Dude had become a faithful companion to Marcella since Bud's death, and I was now happy that she had him. "Happy Birthday, Christiana," Andy said when we picked the three of them up at the airport, handing her the wagging bundle of caramel-colored fur and tying up that loose end. "We need an east coast name for him," I said, and we settled on Dunkin after the donuts for sale on every New England corner and, yes, my first word.

June loomed large on the calendar, and I packed for the trial trip to Oregon, resurrecting my business wardrobe from the depths of my closet and trying on clothes I hadn't worn in the five years since Jonah died, choosing all of my conservative outfits in advance so I'd have one less thing to think about each day of the trial. I ripped off dry-cleaning bags that had traveled the Oregon Trail in reverse to Rhode Island, examined my detested pantyhose collection for signs of aging, and dusted off high heels that had sat patiently on my shelf, toes pointed inward, ready to be called to active duty. I could hear my kids outside playing and wished I could join their ball game. The phone rang. It was Andy's sister Phoebe.

"Now, when are you guys coming?" she asked.

I gave her our itinerary and told her we'd be stopping by her house to get our car seat.

"I won't be home," she said, "but you know how to get in."

We chatted a bit and then, buoyed by the trial wardrobe scattered across my bed, I tried to talk to her about Cody, her sister, star witness for the defense.

"I don't want to hear about it"—she sighed—"It's just too stressful for me."

"Well then, imagine how your brother feels," I said. "Do you have any idea how stressful this is for him? He's the one who has to keep answering when people ask him what kind of family he comes from."

The voice of Scarlett O'Hara chimed along in my brain: "I just *cain't* think about it tuhday. Ah'll go *crayzee*." And then my brother's favorite line: "I'll think about it too-marrah."

"Is this the kind of family you want to be in?" I asked. But she didn't answer and changed the subject.

We had attempted to enlist other members of the family to reason with Cody. But suddenly the tribe had nothing to say to her—no advice, no admonishment, nothing. Since when had they become people who minded their own business? Why was everyone so afraid of Cody? Was it the free dental care? We received no answers and were left to conclude that they agreed with her and, indeed, were on her side. Our fan section remained silent and rather empty.

When we'd tried to talk to Marcella about it when she'd visited, she'd cried and said, "You can't tell me not to like Cody," as if we had, and all she would say by way of defense is, "Oh, that Cody, she's so nosy." Now that had to be the understatement of the century.

Andy called his brother Joe. "Well, I don't believe in lawsuits," he said. "What do you expect?" As far as he was concerned, we'd asked for it by filing and got what we deserved. "I don't know what you're trying to prove," he said.

So it fell to Andy to explain over and over to a whole host of people we encountered just what kind of family he had—no easy task because we were still trying to define it for ourselves. It was tiresome once again to watch everyone line up against us or cop a plea.

The extended Kittel family had become de facto parts of the lawsuit. Ever since Cody had swum into our deposition, we had to guard our interactions with the whole tribe, as our attorney cautioned us that anything and everything we said, or even didn't say, could be misconstrued and used against us in a court of law. So this added yet another unpleasant and unforeseen dimension to the whole difficult business.

We flew to Oregon and headed to the coast to drop off our kids with Diane, who'd graciously agreed to watch them for us. On our way there, we stopped in to see Marcella, and while we were talking, her phone rang. Marcella answered and then handed the phone to Christiana.

"Who's that?" Andy asked.

"Cally," she said.

Andy grabbed the phone away from her and told Cally that if she wanted to speak to the kids, she'd have to do it in our presence. Until the trial concluded, Dan had advised us not to let any family members speak with our kids alone, and not to let them have any interaction whatsoever with their aunt.

"You're so weird," Cally told Andy. "I practically raised those kids. I'll see you in court. I wouldn't miss it!" She hung up.

Diane understood the necessity of our rules; Marcella did not. "Oh, why do the kids have to be involved?" she lamented. When we were leaving, she added, "Well, I just feel so sorry for these doctors, and it's just terrible that there are these lawsuits."

We drove back to Salem and met with our attorneys on that Sunday night, which was Father's Day. They'd been holed up at the Comfort Inn all weekend preparing for Monday and looked anything but comfortable. We discussed the case and the schedule for the week. Dan told us in no uncertain terms that our case had problems and that Cody was 90 percent of them. We had already amassed a bill of $25,000, and the costs were mounting. This was the very real price tag for finding out what happened to Jonah and trying to prevent it from happening to others. Now we truly couldn't afford to lose.

We stayed at a friend's house in Portland for the week, where we tried to sleep but instead lay awake most nights with our private nightmares washing over us as we treaded water and tried not to sink. The sun rose each morning as usual, giving us an excuse to get up, shower, dress, and drive an hour south each day, buying a coffee at Starbucks on the way. Hurrying into the white marble building where the scales of justice weighed our truth, we'd rush through our daily metal detection test, barely making it to the courthouse bathroom before our customized mochas came rushing back out again.

On Monday we entered the room of our trial for the first time. Judge Norblatt faced us diagonally at the left front side of the room behind his elevated, expansive wooden desk, which stretched across the corner. The court reporter was seated to his right and the soon-to-be-filled jury box to his left. Attached to the left end of the judge's desk, facing the jury, was the witness stand. I noted with relief that on the ledge of the hot seat were a silver pitcher sweating water and a stack of plastic cups. A friend had once told me that you can't cry when you're drinking water, and I knew I would need that liquid courage and more when I was called to testify.

Several rows of wooden benches stretched along the back of the courtroom, the gallery for the eager rubberneckers, with a waist-high wooden divider creating the illusion of separation between the audience and the stage. In front of the divider facing the judge, two long tables sat ready to hold the laptops and books and tapping pens of the attorneys and their assistants, one for each side. Dr. Harmon would be given a seat at her table next to her attorney, John Harte, and the attorney representing Salem Hospital, Keith Bauer. But Andy and I sat crossing and recrossing our legs in two padded chairs behind Dan and Tom, our legal duo. There was no clicking stenotype; our trial was videotaped—a recent innovation.

"I always tell people that the best thing you can do if you need a divorce is to get it in my courtroom so you can go home and watch it forever," Judge Norblatt joked.

Jury selection took most of the morning. Judge Norblatt introduced himself to the thirty or forty potential jurors. "I recently had throat surgery," he rasped in his Darth Vader voice, pressing against the hole in his throat to talk. Throughout the trial he would make lots of loud, throat-clearing noises that added yet another medical element—and sometimes levity—to the otherwise solemn proceedings.

"The trial is expected to last six days," the judge explained on that first Monday. "We'll be selecting fourteen jurors, two of whom will be alternates in case of sickness. If all goes well, those two will be dropped off at the end before deliberations begin. The case is entitled ANDREW KITTEL, Personal Representative of the Estate of JONAH EMMANUEL MOORE KITTEL; and KELLY KITTEL, individually, Plaintiffs, v. ELIZEBETH HARMON, MD, SALEM WOMEN'S CLINIC, INC, an Oregon corporation; and SALEM HOSPITAL, INC, an Oregon corporation, Defendants." He pronounced Jonah as "Jonnah" and introduced me as "Ketty." In the seven days of the trial he would refer to me randomly as Ketty, Kitty, or Kelly, followed by Kettle or Kittel.

He explained that we were suing for noneconomic damages for the loss of society and companionship of Jonah in the amount of $2.5 million and an additional pecuniary loss to his estate of $750,000. We were also suing for noneconomic damages on my behalf of $1 million and another $25,000 for future medical expenditures. There were other detailed expenditures and some of these categories would be automatically capped by the state below these amounts, but this was roughly the starting point.

For Dr. Harmon's side, Harte asserted that I failed to remain on complete bed rest or to call in if there was a change in my condition, and they asked that no money be awarded.

Harte began jury selection by saying, "Dr. Harmon says that 'No matter what you allege, I gave Kerry Kittel reasonable care.'" He, too, would consistently misremember my name.

After the lawyers delivered their speeches, the potential jurors asked them any questions they had, and then the attorneys recessed to the judge's chambers, returning in less than an hour to read the numbers representing the twelve jurors plus two alternates selected. Edith, Paulette, Joel, Florence, Jennifer, Christian, Jessica, Martha, Carol Ann, Marya, Robert, Larry, Priscilla, and Deborah took their new assigned seats, straightening their shoulders and beginning their complete education about the world of Kelly Kittel, or whatever her name was. These fourteen strangers would hold my past in their heads, my present in their eyes, and my future in their hands, and I prayed that they would cradle it all with wisdom and grace. Or at least pay attention.

The courtroom door swung open, and the relieved potential jurors filed out. While the benches cleared, my nieces—Chane, who was now sixteen, and Cally, who was twenty-one—filed in as promised and sat down in the gallery behind the doctor, smirking in our direction. The judge gave the jury instructions, and we broke for lunch.

"Hungry?" Andy asked.

"Umm, no," I said, my standard reply for the week, during which I lost ten pounds.

We were instructed to avoid the jury and other members of our courtroom. In our efforts to do so, we ended up buying something to drink and spending our lunch hours slinking around the gardens of the capitol building behind the courthouse or kneeling at the altar of our old church, which was located right across the street— ironically, on the corner of Church and State Streets. There we found sanctuary in the sacred space where we had worshiped God and buried our son. I eyeballed the grand piano, wishing again that I could crawl in and shut the lid until the trial concluded. After we prayed, we wandered outside in the garden and stood in the shade of Noah's tupelo or Jonah's Stewartia tree. We ran our hands over their rough bark and stared up at the sky through the green filter of their leaves, as each tree reached its roots into the ground, nurtured by the minerals from our sons' ashes, and surrounded us with the breath of life.

After lunch, my nieces again filed in, but this time they sat right behind us, so close I could hear them breathing. The attorneys took their turns addressing the jury with their opening statements. "This was an important pregnancy for the Kittels," Dan said, reminding the jury that there were two patients here, me and Jonah, and therefore two sets of damages. He said I'd had blood transfusions, a severe blood pressure drop, and that my damages include the memory of the trauma, severe anxiety, and a loss of income. "On May 14, 1998, Jonah died at thirty-seven weeks, two days gestation. Mrs. Kittel had to be induced and deliver knowing that he was dead."

Dan said this was a medical negligence case, and the elements of the case would describe what the doctors should have done and then show if they'd done it. "The first element is the standard of care, and I will show you that they failed to achieve that. The second element is informed consent. The doctor should tell the patient about risks and procedures, and the midwives, nurses, and doctor should have delivered the baby on May 9, but they convinced Mrs. Kittel to go home. The third and fourth elements are causation and damages. Dr. Harmon comanaged Mrs. Kittel's care with the midwives, even though she was a high-risk patient.

"The defense will blame Kelly Kittel for the death of her child," he said, "but Kelly Kittel was a very compliant patient." He told the jurors that I went to the hospital four times, started the induction, and then the midwives debated the baby's potential problems with prematurity. "The baby was ready, he should have been induced, the perinatologist told Dr. Harmon to induce the baby, the midwives failed to do their jobs, they told her to go home, and the baby died."

Harte's opening statement went on for hours while it seemed like he tried his case right then and there. He said that Dr. Harmon and her midwives cared very deeply for me and fought "in a fun way" over who would meet with me because "she was a very good patient to have." He said that I was "basically seen every day" in my pregnancy after I chose Salem Women's Clinic and that Dr. Harmon, who "liked me a great deal," arrived on May 9, to be greeted by her nurse-midwife with, "Kelly wants to go home." He gave a scripted account of that day like he was there and said my blood pressures were "totally normal" for me and were "doing the same thing they were doing all along," and he said that I had no signs or symptoms of preeclampsia.

Harte then announced, "I will introduce her relatives!" I half expected the announcer from the game show of my youth to burst in then and there, singing, "Kelly Kittel, This is Your Life!"

"Cody Martin," Harte continued, "her sister-in-law, went to several appointments with her. Kelly, in her sworn testimony, says she only heard about abruption once. Evidence will show that she heard about it from thirty different sources in this plus her prior pregnancies." Then he hit them with what must have been his favorite line to say in the whole trial: "Her own relatives will tell you that!" *Relatives*, I thought, *plural?*

Harte said that at 8:00 a.m. on May 14, my abdomen became hard, and that I knew there was no movement of the baby. He said that at eight thirty I had breakfast and there was still no movement. He said that I'd told Cody Martin there had been no movement since 4:00 a.m. and that I told Terri Wright there had been none since the night before. Then he said I had "participated in a lively dance" called the "Jump Song" and that "Kerry Kittel understands the management of chronic hypertension well because of her experience." He told them I was "very bright, highly intelligent, and highly experienced with this, her third afflicted childbirth with hypertension of a chronic nature" and that I "seemed and acted like a very compliant patient." I knew better than to be flattered by any of his false compliments and found some of what he said to be interesting, wondering just who he was talking about anyway.

Afterward, each attorney read their lists of witnesses and that's when we learned that Pat, Cody's sister-in-law and NICU nurse, would also be testifying on behalf of the defense. Our family was, indeed, on trial.

Chapter Twelve

W E SPENT SIX more long days in the Marion County courthouse receiving our slap shot final lessons in the judicial system. Three doctors, one nurse-midwife, one economist, our family counselor, and four of our friends testified on our behalf, and to them we are eternally grateful.

On Tuesday, the second day of the trial, our friend told the jury, "I can't think of anything more devastating than the loss of this child that I have ever seen. Noah's death was a horrible blow to everyone, and we were all expecting something very joyous to happen with the birth of this child. After that [Jonah's death] Andy and Kelly were so very brave, but every bit of hope and energy had gone out of them. They looked like ghosts walking around."

Karen, our family counselor, took the stand next and explained to the jury that Andy and I both suffered from Post Traumatic Stress Disorder. "That means you are reliving something over and over, something so shocking and horrifying the mind can't forget about it—it can't say 'it's a new day' and move on."

"Denial," she said, "is like an insulating blanket that we wrap around us, and we say, yes, I know it happened, but I'll deal with it later." We knew all about the land of denial since so many of our family members had moved there.

"The Kittel family was not supportive," Karen continued. "Kelly's family was. Andy's was not, and unfortunately that makes it harder for the person to adjust."

"Did that include Cody Martin?" Dan asked.

"Yes, she and the young niece were particularly cruel, I would say. People do a lot of different things with grief. Sometimes it literally splits and divides the family. Sometimes forever." My nieces were not there that day to hear this.

Economics is not a subject of great interest to me, but I sat riveted by the testimony given to explain the damages we were requesting. "First," the economist said, "I assessed the pecuniary loss to the estate of Jonah Emmanuel Moore Kittel. It is a little bit different since there is no earnings history, etc., to look at for determining projections into the future, so we look at the strong relationship between parents and children." In our case, he said, we were both college graduates, so there was a high probability that our children would be also. "We have projections for the average earnings of college graduates. Then we calculate the work life expectancy, allow for inflation…We reduce the loss of total earnings and calculate the present value minus the money Jonah would have spent on his personal needs. All this leads to our determination that the pecuniary loss to Jonah's estate would be $1,446,881."

He went on to explain his use of government data for the average earnings of male college graduates for each decade and said, "We assume Jonah would be one person in a household of four," meaning Jonah would have had a wife and two children. "We calculated the present value of his future earnings to be $2,096,926 before deducting the 31 percent on his household spending."

All of this was news to me.

It was more than a little disconcerting to sit and listen to the potential future life of our son—attending college, getting married, fathering two children, hopefully burying neither of them, and retiring at age sixty-two after a lucrative career—when he never even took his first breath.

They say when you lose your child you lose your future.

So here was that future spelled out in cold, hard econometrics for our intellectual edification and our emotional devastation. This was exactly the future that we had lost. Our perfect Little Boy Blue could have been all of these things. He could have had all of these markings of success. He should have been the lover of a woman and the father of her children and the apple of our eye and so much more. This was what had been stilled.

And this is all we could hope to gain—a set of government statistics and mathematical calculations. Luckily, we had unwittingly jumped through some of the correct hoops by graduating from college, getting married, and being gainfully employed when Jonah died. But maybe there were some factors we were lacking, some multiples of zero we'll never know about? Maybe there should be other multiples, like for the number of surviving siblings who have lost their brother and who will mourn his absence while they play without him for the rest of their lives? Because even with all of this in our favor, we still felt like the biggest losers.

Harte stood and began his cross-examination of our economist by bragging that *he* had a son who was graduating from college that year, and that both of *his* son's parents are college graduates. "So, I want to know if you are saying that anyone in my son's position would earn the amount you have calculated for Jonah?"

"I am not saying 'anyone,' but based on statistics, that would be the most likely outcome."

"And further," Harte asked, "have you calculated paying for the cost of college?"

"No, because that does not figure into the pecuniary loss to the estate."

"Going back to *my* son," he said, "your assumption is that as he works, for every $1,000 earned he will save $690, is that true?"

"Yes, but it is more accurate to say that the estate will accumulate $690 for every $1,000 earned."

"Are you saying that some of that wouldn't go to the government for taxes?"

"We make no allowance for taxes because if we reduced it off the top it would essentially be a double deduction, since any dollar amount rewarded in the lawsuit and subsequently invested would also be taxed on interest earned, and taxing them twice seems unfair to the family." *Like so many other unfair things,* I thought.

"Can you assure *my* son that he will not pay 20 percent taxes over the life of his earnings?"

"Actually, I cannot assure anything regarding taxes since congress changes tax laws with some regularity, so you cannot make any assumptions about what congress will do in the future."

"So," Harte continued, "this calculation is based on no taxes and college not being paid for, and yet to reduce it to the present value you earn interest on the money. Again, can you assure *my* son that for every $1,000 he earns he will save $690?"

"I cannot assure your son of anything; I have not met your son."

"And how much time have you spent with Mr. and Mrs. Kittel to derive this information about their son?"

"I have not spent any time with them, but I have reviewed their records and could glean the fact that they are both very successful in college and in their careers and have provided a stable home life, all of which are powerful indicators."

"But all of my children," Harte continued, "college educated or not, may not do what you've projected, and that is true for Mr. and Mrs. Kittel's children also."

"That's true," agreed the economist. "It could be that a child would do much better than this—he might earn a graduate degree or become an attorney like you!"

That bit of levity we all enjoyed at Harte's expense. Especially because sitting there listening to Harte introduce his son—his living, breathing son, the new college-graduate-to-be—during this medical malpractice trial for *my* son's death infuriated me. College debt or no, lucrative professional career or no, saving $690 for every $1,000 earned or no, his son was having the opportunity of a lifetime that our son was not. For Jonah, the odds were actually 100 percent certain that he would never go to college, or kindergarten, or anywhere. He would make love to no woman and welcome no slippery son of his own to his world. He would neither earn nor save one single penny nor owe anything to the other guarantee in life—taxes—having already met its guaranteed partner—death. That was the reason we were all sitting there.

On Wednesday, one of our expert witnesses, Dr. Murphy, an ob-gyn from Bend, Oregon, testified that no midwife should care for or comanage high-risk patients, adding, "Someone needs to take full responsibility for the patient, as when you have multiple care providers the ball gets dropped."

"Who should look up the twenty-four-hour urine results?" Dan asked him.

"The person who ordered it. When you have one person follow through and take all responsibility, it works better. In fact, on May 13, [the day before Jonah died] in her prenatal chart it said, 'Mrs. Kittel came to see nurse at clinic, NST 157, reported increased painful contractions X 24 hours'!"

"If that was what Mrs. Kittel had reported to the clinic," Dan said, "was she being a compliant patient by reporting that she was having increased painful contractions over the last twenty-four hours?"

"Yes."

"Does it say what the doctor said about that or if she was told about it?"

"No."

"In fact," Dan said, "Mrs. Kittel reported that she was having increased painful contractions for the past twenty-four hours, and she was told to come back *tomorrow* and we'll check your cervix, right?"

"Yes."

I closed my eyes and returned to the morning of May 14, 1998. I remembered Andy kissing me awake, and I remembered realizing that my contractions were getting more uncomfortable. I heard myself say, "I hope these contractions are working," and, "that nurse better check my dilation today, or you'll have to," and I saw Andy grin and reply, "Gladly." And I wished I could take myself straight to the hospital and deliver my baby.

Andy had his turn on the stand on Wednesday as well. Watching my spouse and my friends sitting in the witness chair was as nerve-racking for me as sitting in it myself. Dan asked Andy to tell the jury how the death had affected him, and he said, "It is something you don't like to describe. You don't like to talk about it because it makes you very sad." His eyes filled with tears, and his voice caught in his throat, so Dan mercifully withdrew the question. "Did it affect you?" he asked instead. "More than you can imagine," Andy replied.

I drank from the sweaty water pitcher as the last witness of the day on both Tuesday and Wednesday and would be called a total of four times on four different days. On Thursday, the fourth day of the trial, the hospital offered to settle with us, and their place at the defense table was cleared, leaving Dr. Harmon and Harte alone. We agreed to the settlement for several reasons, the mounting legal bills we owed being one of them. That same day, my nieces were back in the gallery, sitting directly behind us, again so close I could hear them breathing.

I was the first witness called that Thursday morning, my third time in the hot seat. I poured myself a glass of water as Dan began, "Now, we've heard comments from counsel and learned about the witness lists: Who is Cody Martin?"

"Cody Martin is my sister-in-law; she's my husband's sister."

He turned to the gallery where my nieces were sitting behind Andy and asked, "Who are these two people out here in the courtroom?"

"They are my nieces," I said quietly, indicating with my hand to the jury. "My niece on the right is Cally, who was unfortunately responsible for running over Noah; my niece on the left is her sister, Chane, who was also present and in the car that day."

"And they came here the first day of court?"

"Yes, they did."

Dan showed a video clip from Monday of Cally and Chane, reminding me that I, too, was being filmed, and asked, "Are these Cody Martin's daughters sitting right here behind you?"

"Yes."

"When this lawsuit was filed, did Cody Martin call Dr. Harmon and her attorney?"

"That's what we learned at Dr. Harmon's deposition on May 18 of last year, 2001, yes." *On Noah's birthday*, I thought.

"Do you know why she sent her daughters here?"

And while Harte was objecting that the question assumed facts not in evidence, Cally had the audacity to shout out in the courtroom, "She didn't send us here!"

Everyone paused. My ancestors and I were equally shocked, though we probably should not have been by now. Dan withdrew the question. He went on to extract my testimony about our renting a house from Cody and trying to buy it, and the saga of the rent increase and our subsequent eviction. The jury heard me recount Andy saying, "And how long will I owe you that money, Cody?" and her reply, "Until you can forget about your son!" They heard all about Noah and the hated Tahoe and Cody's role in the drama unfolding before us.

"Did she tell you why she wanted to prove you a bad mother?" Dan asked.

"I have no idea. After Noah was killed we asked them to come to counseling with us, and she always said it was our problem. 'This is your "guyses" problem, it has nothing to do with us,' she'd say. It seems all along that she has wanted to blame me for the death of Noah and absolve her daughter and herself of any responsibility."

Then he broached the subject I was dreading most. If the court recording had a soundtrack, this moment would have been preceded by a drumroll. "Next I want to talk about the events at the hospital on May 14. I'm sorry, but I have to take you there just a little bit. When you arrived you were bleeding, correct?"

"Yes."

"What did Terri Wright do?"

"I remember she took us to a room and had me go in the bathroom to change"—I paused—"and I remember being in the bathroom and thinking, *What am I doing in here?*"

"Were you all there; were you mentally functioning properly?"

"No, I remember some things about it, but I was in shock or whatever, and I was panicking. I had never bled before in a pregnancy, but you know it's not good, and I remember thinking *you need to do something*, and Terri Wright was on my bed and saying, 'How long has your tummy been hard like this,' and I was saying, 'I don't know, I don't know.'" My voice cracked when I began to feel the frustration of that moment again.

"When you have a contraction, does your stomach get hard?" Dan began, approaching the stand to hand me a box of Kleenex.

Harte objected to the leading question and said, "If this is an emotional time, we should take a break."

I thought, *If we're going to wait until there's a less emotional time, it might be a really long wait.*

"Yes," I said, "they squeeze and you have to catch your breath."

"Did you know there was no heartbeat?"

"No, not right away, and they were asking me all these questions and bringing in all these machines and nothing was happening, and I was thinking, *You have to do something for this baby*, and then she was searching and searching my belly with the ultrasound and there was no heartbeat, and I was thinking, *There is no way this can be happening to me*." I started to cry again, thinking, *so much for not crying when you drink*, as I gulped away, rapidly disproving my friend's advice.

"Do you want to take a break?" Dan asked.

"No, let's just get through it. I'm sorry," I said to the faces of the jurors, who sat almost close enough to wipe at my tears.

"Did they tell you they were going to induce you?"

"Dr. Harmon said she would not do a C-section and wanted to move to induction and deliver the baby as soon as possible, and I checked out after that. I was in shock, and I was thinking there was no way this could be happening." And then, water or no, I couldn't stop crying.

"We'll take a break," Dan said.

"Should I leave now?" I turned to ask the judge, unsure of what to do.

"Yes, you can," he said.

I stepped down and rushed across the room where I collapsed against Andy, who had stood up to catch me. We went out into the hall, stopping just outside the door, where we hugged each other desperately under the combined weight of all our sadness, crying on each other's dry-clean-only shoulders. The courtroom door banged open, startling me, and I looked up to see Cally march out of the courtroom. As she sauntered past us, her eyes hooked onto mine and she threw me a satisfied smirk—this from my niece whom I had forgiven on a moonlit night for running over my son. I thought of

Karen's words from the witness stand two days ago—"particularly cruel."

Andy and I were still holding each other when an elfish woman entered the hallway from a side door. Without catching our eyes, she appeared at our sides, pressing something cool and round into our palms. "You two just hold on to these," she whispered, disappearing before we could say a word. We disentangled ourselves, wiping our eyes and fortifying ourselves with a few deep breaths. Unclenching our fists we each stared in wonder at our palms to find the fresh imprints of two angels whose images were held in relief on two silver medallions.

Once again, our life had telescoped so that only the courtroom held our attention. Like the NICU moms mourning their babies, we had no concept of the rest of the bay or the world or what was going on in it. But once again, though we were oblivious to our surroundings, others in our vicinity were bearing witness, acutely aware of us. And watching.

We re-entered the courtroom armed with angels in our palms. I reclaimed my seat in the witness stand, poured myself a fresh glass of cool water, faced the kindness of strangers, and told them the story of my son's birth.

Harte's cross-examination was an endurance test for me. One line of questioning went like this:

"Is it your testimony that Dr. Harmon stuck her head in the door and said, 'I hear you're going home.' Is that your sworn testimony?" he asked.

"Yes, sir."

"Is it possible in this emotional time, and no one envies your situation before May 14, 1998, is it possible Dr. Harmon came in and sat on your bed but because of all the tragedies in your life you don't remember?" he asked.

"No, I remember that very clearly," I said, annoyed at his statement about no one envying me.

"As clearly as your not dancing?"

"I don't know how to answer that," I said.

Later on he asked, "Did you know to do kick counts during this pregnancy?"

"Yes, usually a doctor gives you a chart and you record the baby's movements on your own. I've never had a doctor even ask me for the results or how it's going."

"Were you doing them in spite of this awful care? Them not asking you?" he said.

"I'm sorry, could you repeat that?" I asked. I couldn't believe my ears and wanted to hear him to say "awful care" again.

"Yes, you just said no one ever asked you. Did you know to do them even if you had no doctor?"

"I'm sorry, but if I had not had a doctor I would not have done them, no," I said.

As for the plan for Jonah's delivery, Harte continued, "You said yesterday there was no plan when you left the hospital on May 9, correct?"

"Plan for what?"

"Plan for your pregnancy."

"The plan was to come in every day for a NST, there was no plan for delivery, no, I don't know what the plan was."

"Is it possible someone said to you, perhaps the nurse-midwife or Dr. Harmon more specifically, that we're going to do this surveillance for a specific period of time and deliver the baby before thirty-eight weeks?"

"I don't recall that, no, sir."

"And again, I know I'm being a little pushy here, but does that mean it didn't happen or you just don't know?"

"I don't believe that happened, no. I don't ever remember anyone saying the plan was to deliver at thirty-eight weeks. There was a plan for thirty-nine weeks, thirty-seven weeks, and induction at thirty-six-plus weeks. I don't ever recall anyone mentioning a plan to deliver at thirty-eight weeks, no."

"And so what was the end point of this surveillance if there was no plan? Was it just going to continue on until forty-one weeks or forty weeks?"

This was a very good question that I wished I had the answer to. I said, "I'm sorry, sir, but I'm not the one who was making the plan and determining what my care would be. I don't know. It's frustrating to me to this day, believe me. I don't know what the plan was. Obviously I'm hoping nobody planned for what actually occurred."

"So you didn't know what the end point would be? You were just going to remain on bed rest and go in daily?"

"Yes, it seemed what everyone was waiting for was me to go into labor naturally."

"Is that what you wanted?"

"What I wanted . . . what I wanted was to have a healthy baby, however that was going to take place, sir."

"Yes, the reason I've said a number of questions to try to be sensitive in a million-dollar lawsuit is because I've tried to frame it on 'as of May 13,' so that we're talking about knowledge and information and memories before the awful events of May 14. Now, as of May 13, are you telling the jury that you don't remember or that there was no plan about what the end point would be?"

"There was no plan that was communicated to me as to what the end point would be."

"And so, if we were having this discussion on the thirteenth in your living room and you were in the lounger, you would say 'I don't know how long this is going to go on,' correct?" he asked.

"Correct, yes," I said, recalling having said those exact words to my friends.

Chapter Thirteen

THE DEFENSE began calling their witnesses on Thursday afternoon, starting with our family lineup. Cody's sister-in-law Pat began our family trial by swearing that she'd mailed me documents about abruption before Jonah died, when actually she'd sent them after he had died, when I was trying to fathom what had happened. "This is what you *had*," (emphasis mine) she'd handwritten on the bottom of the technical papers, which I'd saved, in permanently inked contradiction of her testimony. Dan produced them but the judge disallowed the documents as evidence because we had not produced them sooner. We were only required to produce documentation up to the day of Jonah's death. These were from afterward. And we had not known that our relatives would be lining up to testify. At the same time, he'd also produced the few photos of Jonah that we had, including the first photo that Andy had taken of him lying so serenely on the hospital scale. The judge had flipped through them all, choosing a few, but ruling Jonah's first photo unacceptable for the jurors to see. I wished somebody would have had the same consideration for me, flipping through all the possible photos my life could engender, and protecting me from the more difficult ones.

After Pat was dismissed and it was time for his star witness, Harte left the courtroom, returning to announce, "Your honor, we've got technical difficulties. I know that they've been in the hall for most of the day, but they're not there right now. I don't know if they're out in the sun—"

The judge interrupted. "It's my experience that anybody we're ready to call goes downstairs to the bathroom."

Cally shot out of the courtroom to find her mother, always eager to take charge. A few minutes later the door banged open, and she rocketed back in with her mother on her heels. True to form, Cody appeared only when she was good and ready. She stepped through the magic divider that turned her from spectator to player with her red nails swinging, marching past me so close I could have easily stuck my foot out and tripped her in her favorite Clark's sandals. Same old sandals. Same old sister-in-law. Even though we had known she would testify against us, it still seemed unbelievable that it would really happen.

"Your Honor, I call Cody Martin," Harte said, as if we were picking sides for a kickball game.

She was sworn in for the opposing team.

"My name is Cody Martin." I waited, but she refrained from saying, "And I am Salem!"

I tried to focus but could barely hear her words over the sound of hammers pounding the final nails into the coffin of our relationship. Harte began his examination, saying, "I'm gonna ask you a few questions. Are you Andy Kittel's sister?"

"Yes, I am."

"And your daughters have been at the trial or some moments of some periods of the trial?"

"Yes, they have been."

"And then we've heard a lot about the unfortunate events about nine months before this delivery that's brought us here today, um, involving your son, Noah?" The banging in my head stopped and my Irish blood rose; I heard him clearly now. *Did he really just say "her son"?* I wondered. *Did he know she always called my kids hers, or was he just nervous?*

"My nephew Noah?" she asked.

"Yes sir, yes ma'am," he stumbled. *Okay, nervous,* I thought.

"Oh, yes," she laughed.

"And that caused some consternation, to put it mildly, among some family members?" *Consternation? Really?*

"It has . . . It was a tragedy."

"And please, instead of me telling you everything, why don't you tell the jurors what role you played in this pregnancy as far as advisor and escort, you know, for Kelly Kittel."

"I was her sister-in-law, who was concerned about her health care and her health because of her previous history of high blood pressure with pregnancy . . . and the trauma and tragedy that occurred in our families, um . . ."

Um, I thought, *speaks volumes in this instance.*

"Therefore," she continued, "I was very concerned about her health and the health of the kids and the health of the whole family, and mine. I participated in her taking her blood pressure at various times and actually documenting and calling the hospital later on in the pregnancy because of an elevated blood pressure . . . and other than that I was the sister-in-law and sister to my brother who helped with the kids and helped with the house, family, just, having the kids over for dinner and going over there for dinner . . ."

I wondered if the jury would consider it *helpful*, her showing up at our house for dinner. She continued listing things she'd already said above, adding, "and talking about . . . the potential extreme death to Kelly for having high blood pressures because of an experience I had had in my navy career seeing a young mother, and so to me blood pressure's extremely important." *Extreme death?*

Harte didn't ask for clarification though, saying, "Okay, uh, Ms. Martin, will you tell the jurors if you talked about the subject of abruption with your sister-in-law before . . . the week before the baby died?"

Cody gave a dramatic sigh, and then went on to give a whole diatribe on Pregnancy-Induced Hypertension, PIH, which can lead to toxemia or preeclampsia, which I'd had but which went undiagnosed and which was the reason we were sitting there. I wondered if he'd instructed her to answer only the question asked as she rattled on about it.

"Did the subject of abruption come up?" he asked again.

"Yes, the subject of having the placenta just tear off from the uterus did come up."

"Okay, there were, just to expedite it, there are signs and symptoms of high blood pressure, and I know you've never seen this before," Harte said as he held up a chart. "Did you talk about these various things in your discussions before the unfortunate death of the fetus?"

"Fortunately I talked about several of them . . . for sure the headaches, visual changes because these again were my . . . my . . . I'm experienced with hypertension and pregnancy because of my patients," she said, sounding like she had a hospital full of pregnant patients waiting for her return. Then she read the symptoms from the chart, concluding, ". . . and everything was normal," like she'd been hired as a medical expert instead of a helpful sister-in-law who worked as the office manager of her husband's dental practice.

"And, was this casual family discussion, I mean you weren't lecturing, I mean you were just having a discussion with your sister-in-law?"

"In the Kittel families they're all lectures, no, I mean . . ." she said, laughing at her own joke.

"Are you the lecturer?" he asked.

She laughed, saying, "That's a joke, sir, it's discussions, it's talking, walking or just sitting around, just what's happening, what's going on here, and it's, it's for Kelly being very inquisitive and she loves to do, she loves, I mean, she asks questions, she's good at asking questions, and so we went out to find answers, and if we couldn't, we found people who would give her answers."

He asked her about the weekend of May 7, saying, "And did you think she was gonna have an induction?"

"I was told she was having an induction by the doctor; if she didn't go into labor that night they would do her at Saturday morning."

"And did you learn the next day that she, uh, left the hospital?"

"I learned the next day that she was leaving the hospital; I walked in on her, to see her."

"Did, uh, did you ask her if she polled, or did she say or did you ask, did she poll the nurses at . . . ?"

Is he asking her if I'd taken a poll of the nurses, as if I'd walked around in my Johnnie with a clipboard and pen? I wondered.

"At that morning I did not discuss any of it with her, I had a, uh, frustrating time and had to leave, um, and this was just my seeing she was going home, so it wasn't until later on that I tried to find out why she was leaving."

"Did she tell you?"

"She, it was in a vague response, that, that she had asked some of the nurses about whether it would be better to keep the baby longer and a couple of them said yes, and a couple of them said, you know, no, and, uh, that's kind of what was the talk after."

Ahh, so now I see where he got the idea that I'd taken a survey of the nurses.

"Did she want to go home, from what she told you?"

"When I walked in on her, my sister-in-law was laying in the bed back like this," Cody stretched back on the witness stand and folded her arms behind her head, "all dressed up ready to go, and my response was, 'What are you doing?' And she said, 'I'm going home,' and I just was, 'cause I came down expecting to see her in a hospital gown with an IV on ready to be pitted out . . . and to see her dressed and ready to go home I was speechless. I literally stayed less than three minutes, turned around, and walked out of there."

"Did she tell you that, um, she had initiated a conversation with Dr. Harmon about leaving the hospital?"

"No."

"Okay, what else did she tell you about the decision to leave the hospital, if anything?"

"At that time nothing . . . at that time . . . at that time she told me nothing and I didn't stay around to quiz her anymore because of my frustration that she was going home. It was like hold on, we were gonna induce this baby, and so I'm like okay, something changed, I'm outta here!" she said. I'd had no idea she'd been this upset about the decision and wondered why she hadn't said so then or when she'd returned to pick me up in her Tahoe.

Harte asked her some questions about my preference for natural birth and midwifery care, and then the conversation shifted when he asked, "Did you have further discussion at that point about what she had done on the fourteenth, the day of the stillbirth?"

"The day, that day, the, uh, the trauma of the day is trying to find out what happened because I entered into the delivery just as little

Jonah was being born." I frowned, not remembering her at Jonah's birth but clearly remembering her arriving later with the kids. She continued, "And so my questioning was what happened because I had left Kelly at ten thirty the night before and, um, she was sitting up at the counter and waiting, you know, just . . . and maybe we had just talked about how she had done for the day, about the stress test for the doctors and, um, things had been going fine, everything was normal, um, and I left her . . ." This, too, differed from my own memory. I wasn't sitting at my counter and didn't even remember her being there that night, for starters. But she continued, "And so next I get a call at quarter to one in the afternoon and it's, 'Come quick to the hospital,' and so, um, in describing what had happened is, Kelly had . . . or Andy or Kelly had said that they had gone to . . . that she thought she may have been in labor in the morning, but, um, they went to the little program, and then she thought her water burst, she started bleeding, and they went immediately to the hospital."

"Did she say she had danced or been physically active at the music program?" he asked.

"What she said is she had gone down and she had sat there and she got up and did the little, did the little music program with Michael," she said. I couldn't believe that among other things, she'd forgotten that her nephew's name is Micah as it had been for five years now, but then she went on to misremember this: "and then she felt something and felt she had to go sit down."

"Did she say that she felt fetal movement?"

"I can't remember that."

"Did she say—"

"Oh, excuse me," Cody interrupted. "Go ahead, repeat that question," she said, waiting expectantly, as if they'd rehearsed this and she'd forgotten her lines.

"Did she say, 'I hadn't felt fetal movement for a period of time?'"

"Yes, she did comment to me that the last time she felt the baby had moved was about four o'clock in the morning, on the morning of the fourteenth."

"Had you talked about strict bed rest with her before the thirteenth, the day before the unfortunate death?"

"I was not her management care," she said. *Thank you for reminding us*, I thought. *Even I was starting to get confused.* "I followed whatever or concurred with whatever the doctor was doing. I was just there in the sense of monitoring the blood pressures and if she was up, whatever. Kelly was her own person, and we knew that she knew the importance of bed rest and she spent it, she was in bed or she was in her lounger chair and sitting up in the house and, um, walking around the outside a little bit." When she said this last part, it reminded me of her insistence that I go sit outside in my yard to test my blood pressure.

"Okay, would that have been in the last week before the delivery?

"Yes."

"You saw her in your yard?"

"Yes, yes, yes, I saw her in her yard." *She practically put me in my yard*, I thought.

"Okay, and uh, stopping at, uh, Starbucks?"

"I didn't see her stopping at Starbucks because that's, no, I did see her driving in the car away from my house, so I don't know if she was on her way to doctor appointments or anything like that. I, we, I'm just in the way and my kitchen window looks out on the street."

"Okay, and had it been difficult for her because of the children and other responsibilities to comply with bed rest before the last week of the pregnancy?"

"In all fairness, it's extremely hard to comply with bed rest. Twenty-four-hour bed rest in anything with three children around, it's probably very trying, um, that's why they hospitalize people a lot of times because they won't do it." I appreciated her attempt at sympathy, but I hadn't minded the bed rest all that much and resented her, *um*, implication that I hadn't complied, which, of course, was her role here.

"Did she, uh, did Kelly Kittel speak highly of Dr. Harmon both before and after the stillbirth?"

"Kelly spoke very highly of Dr. Harmon and the nurse-midwives who did her care."

Harte asked her about our neighbor, Joanne Ellis, alluding to some "more information" Cody supposedly had but not saying what it was and then said, "There was some earlier testimony that was given, and I want to ask you this about it: Did you in effect raise their rent, refuse to let them buy the house, and evict them in July of 2000 or so?"

"That's three questions, I . . ."

"Okay, I'll do 'em—" Harte started to say when Cody interrupted, taking charge.

"First one," she said, "they were given a written notice, hand-delivered to their house for a rent increase." *Hand-delivered to our counter while we were in Florida*, I translated.

"Okay, from what to what?"

"From $550 to $925."

"Okay, was that in an effort to have them move out?"

"No, it was not in an effort to move out," she said correctly, since her *eviction*, not the rent increase, was her effort to have *us* move out; she wasn't moving anywhere.

"Do you still rent the place?" he asked, skipping over questions two and three.

"I still rent the place."

"And, uh, how much do you get now?"

"$1,125."

"Um, did you, um, did they encourage you to have counseling?"

"Me? No," she said. Another thing I remembered very differently.

"Did you say to anyone that you wanted people to think that Kelly Kittel was a bad mother?"

"No, I did not."

"And did you at one point contact, when you heard about the lawsuit, Dr. Harmon?"

"Yes, I did."

"And would you tell the jurors why you did that?" We all leaned in to hear her answer.

"I had been given the information that my brother and sister-in-law were suing Dr. Harmon by an acquaintance of both Kelly's and mine, and it shocked me, and since my brother and sister-in-law had chosen not to correspond with me, I felt that the only straight answer I could get would be maybe Dr. Harmon would be able to tell me what it was, so I did go to her office and her staff made me, you know, had me sit out for a while, and she finally did see me, and she said she could not talk about the confidential nature, and I asked, well, I asked you know what was, what could they be suing you for, and she said that she really couldn't say, and she said if I wanted to know I could call her attorney or her attorney would get a hold of me, and so I did pursue that."

"And did myself and Connie McKelvey, who's seated behind me, talk to you as lawyers for Dr. Harmon?"

"Yes, they did," she said.

"Have—are you motivated to say things that are not true in any way to harm their chances in the lawsuit?"

"No, I'm not," she said. Which begged the question, *then why was she here?*

"Is everything you've told us truthful and accurate?" he asked. *A good question*, I thought.

"Yes it is."

"That's all I have, Mrs. Martin."

Wow, I thought, *that was interesting*. Andy and I stretched our legs and recrossed them, held hands, and waited for the second act to begin. I pressed my back against the chair and straightened my neck to take a look at Cody. She took a sip of water and gave an abbreviated Cheshire Cat smile toward the jury. She seemed fairly uncomfortable; I noticed that her face and neck were red and blotchy. *Well, you wanted a straight answer*, I thought.

Dan rose from his chair to begin his cross-examination of Cody. "You've never had any contact with the hospital in any relationship; you or your husband have never had any relationship with the hospital—"

But Cody cut him right off at the jugular, saying, "Excuse me, and who are you?"

He looked up from his notes and fixed his blue eyes on her while I thought, *Meet Cody Martin*. He put on his best lawyer voice, but I knew he had her number as he replied, "Who am I? I'm the guy you wouldn't talk to. My name is Dan Holland."

"Okay," she said.

"Okay?" he asked.

"Thank you," she said.

"Okay," he said. "I tried to call and talk to you. You wouldn't do it, would you?"

"I told you you could subpoena me."

"That I could subpoena you?"

"Yes."

"And you gave a statement to Mr. Harte, and I asked you, 'Could we have a copy of that?'"

"I didn't give a statement to Mr. Harte," she said.

"Did you talk to Mr. Harte?"

"No, I didn't."

"Did you talk to his associate?"

"I did talk to Connie."

"Connie McKelvey back there, did you give her a statement?"

"I talked to Connie."

"Did we ask you if we could see that?"

"I don't know if anything was written down."

"Why wouldn't you talk to me?" he asked.

"Because by this time my friends had told me that if I'm to talk to any more attorneys, to please have them subpoena me."

"Well, you knew I represented your brother, right?"

"Hmm?" she asked.

"You knew I represented your brother, Andy, and his wife, Kelly?"

"I didn't know anything at the time."

"I told you that, didn't I?"

"You did tell me that."

"And you said you wouldn't talk to me, right?"

"I said you could subpoena me," she said.

"Umm, don't you think it's a little unusual that when you found out they were filing a lawsuit against Dr. Harmon that you went to Dr. Harmon's office? Is that maybe just a little bit out of the norm?"

"It would not be out of the normal for me," she said.

"For you it's not out of the normal?"

"No."

"And when you went to her office, wasn't it so you could hurt Andy and Kelly and testify against them because you think Kelly Kittel's a bad mother and this is a way to prove that?"

"No, that's not why I went."

"You don't have any motive at all to hurt Kelly Kittel?"

"No."

"Or Andrew?"

"No, I have no motive to hurt Kelly or my brother Andy."

"And you haven't done that in this courtroom?"

"I have no control over what happens, to what my words say to them," she said, her self-righteous tone and words as familiar to me as her sandals.

"You haven't voluntarily come to this courtroom to tell what your version is of the events and voluntarily submit yourself to these attorneys for Dr. Harmon so you could come to this courtroom and tell us your version of the events? You didn't do that all on your own?"

"I was subpoenaed."

"Did you tell your daughter to come sit right between, ah, right behind Mr. and Mrs. Kittel," he said, gesturing back toward us. "Right there from day one in this court?"

"No, I did not."

"Was she gonna report back to you as a witness everything that was gonna go on in this court so you'd know what happened before you testified?"

"I have absolutely—" she began.

"She didn't send us!" Cally yelled from behind us, startling me once again.

Harte interrupted. "Your Honor, that would be pretty hard to do if she," meaning Cally, "isn't here all the time. It's an improper question."

"I'm gonna allow it," the judge said. I could have kissed him.

"Could you repeat the question?" Cody asked.

"Was that your purpose, to have your daughters sit here so they could report back to you everything that was going on in the courtroom?" Dan repeated.

"I did not ask my daughters to attend this session," Cody said.

"She didn't send us!" Cally called out from the peanut gallery. I couldn't believe the judge was allowing these outbursts.

Dan pressed on in spite of the interruptions. "And did you and your family try to come here and sit right behind the Kittels to make them feel uncomfortable in this lawsuit?"

"I have no control over how my brother and sister-in-law can feel," she said. Her face was fully flushed to the color of her hair and nails now, and she was becoming visibly uncomfortable.

"Do you think that's a little unusual that you send your daughters here in the courtroom to sit right here behind Andrew and—"

Harte interrupted again, "That's an improper question. She said she didn't—"

Judge Norblatt interrupted him, sustaining the objection.

"So," Dan continued, "you said you found out there was a lawsuit. How'd you find out?"

"As I told you, a mutual friend of Kelly's and I's informed me."

"A mutual friend, who was that?" he asked as we all leaned in again to hear.

"Uh, Marena."

"Marena?" Dan asked. *Marena?* I exchanged raised eyebrows with Andy.

"Pereyra," she added.

"Pereyra," Dan mused. "And didn't you, you said you didn't tell them that you saw it in the newspaper?"

"No, I didn't," she said, even though that was exactly what she'd told Andy at their "I am Salem" lunch. *And if Suzie had taken the stand, she probably would have denied "hearing it at work" also,* I thought.

"And when this happened and you found out that there was a lawsuit, you're the one who went to Dr. Harmon and mentioned the music program?"

"No, I didn't go to Dr. Harmon and mention the music program."

"How did they find out about that?"

"I think they told Dr. Harmon where they were coming from when they came in to the hospital."

"So it wasn't that big of a deal because they were talking to Dr. Harmon about it and they told her about it right there at that time, is that right?"

"Excuse me, could you repeat the question?" she asked.

"Yeah, it was a bad question," he said.

"Right," she said with a smirk.

"They're not hiding that she went by the music program," Dan said.

Cody mumbled something, and Judge Norblatt interrupted, saying, "Ma'am, you're gonna have to speak up. They can't hear you."

"Oh, excuse me, what was the question?" she asked.

"I don't remember; it just went right out of my head," Dan said, toying with her like she truly was a Cheshire Cat. Cody smirked again, and I enjoyed watching their little playdate.

Dan sat back down, looked at his notes, and moved on. "You talked to them and you were trying to list all the ways that you thought that Kelly Kittel was a bad mother, is that right?" he asked.

"No, I did not."

"And you were gonna tell them how Kelly Kittel was not compliant, and did you say she was driving?"

"I did say that she was driving."

"Do you have a witness to that or do you have a photograph of that or do you have a note of that?"

"No, I don't."

"Are you the only person in the world who has seen that?"

"I don't know!" she said.

"I see," Dan said. "And you said she's out sitting in her yard, is that something that you have a picture of or that you participated in or that you . . . how did you see that?"

"Can I show, stand up and show, kind of, relationships?" she turned and asked Judge Norblatt.

"No," said the judge, clearing his stoma, "just answer the question." I wondered what she was going to demonstrate by standing up anyway.

"Oh, um, my kitchen window or my living room window looks out onto the, I mean, my living room window looks out onto their yard, so I have . . . in my whole front of my house I have windows," she said, gesturing grandly, "so if I'm walking by in that area or if I'm out doing yard work I can see the neighborhood, half of my neighborhood, my sister-in-law's, my neighbors . . . I'm one of the few that has my kitchen window out on the street."

"So, you're driveway's kind of right across from them?"

"No, we're kitty-corner."

"Kitty-corner," Dan mused, "Kittel corner . . ."

"No, it's kitty-corner," she said, smirking at him again. Seeing his opening here, Dan drove right on in.

"And when you're right across from them, did you keep your car that was involved in Noah's death in that driveway?" he asked, backing her right into her own driveway.

"I keep my car in the garage," she said.

"The car that was involved in Noah's death, did you keep that car in the driveway there?"

"I keep my car in the garage," she repeated, a little more adamantly.

"Did you keep ownership of that car for the whole time, a year after his death?"

"I kept ownership of *my* car, yes," she said.

"And did you leave it in the driveway across the street from the Kittels' sometimes?"

"It's—it could potentially be there, I don't know," she finally admitted, and I could have kissed Dan then and there for making Cody talk about her Tahoe, demonstrating for all just how sanctimonious she was about her beloved vehicle.

"And do you think that by telling us here in the courtroom that you saw her once over in her yard that that might make her a bad mother, a noncompliant patient?"

"I never said she was a bad mother," she said.

"And do you think talking about her laying back like this"—Dan leaned back in his chair with his arms folded behind his head in perfect imitation of how she'd described me—"in the hospital bed, that that might make her look like sort of a jerk?"

"I have no idea what it will make her look like," she said, although he had a point, I thought. I did usually lay with my right arm folded behind my head, but not with both of them.

"Is that what you wanted to convey to this jury, that your sister-in-law is just a carefree, ahh, no-care kind of person that just hangs out and doesn't really care about her baby? Is that your intent here in this courtroom?"

"That is not my intent to do in the courtroom."

"Well, why did you lean back like this," he leaned back again, stretching, "and say, 'Well she's just laying in bed like this,' like she didn't care at the hospital, why'd you do that?"

"Because my gift for words are limited, instead of attorneys, and sometimes I found that that physical or form or whatever we're doing create a different picture than words!" Her twisted tongue betrayed her discomfort, perfectly illustrating her confessed limitations as she tripped over this sentence.

"You didn't want to hurt Kelly when you did that, did you?" he asked.

"I have no control over what happens to Kelly." *Except perhaps if she eats tomatoes or trips over my trampoline or drives to the coast to help my mother or raises her own children or lives in my house,* I thought as I counted off on my fingers a quick handful of things in my life she'd exercised quite a bit of control over.

"And all of your effort, all of your contact with the doctor and the doctors of the attorney, or, the attorneys of the doctor, none of that, all of your reluctance and refusal to talk to us, that doesn't have anything to do with your desire to come to this courtroom and hurt Kelly Kittel, does it?"

"I did not . . . I am not . . . my intention is never to hurt my sister-in-law," she said. I exhaled a long, yogic Ujjayi breath—the ocean-sounding breath—at that one, keeping my lips sealed so that only Andy could hear me.

"You know, counsel was asking you questions, and he was asking you questions like it was right down a script, about talking about proteinuria and cramping and about lectures and about induction. Did you come up with all those ideas, or did you talk to somebody about those things—like have you mentioned all those things to Mrs. McKelvey, or have you discussed those things with people before coming into the courtroom?"

"In what, in the last four years?" she asked.

"Yes," he clarified and continued, "and when you were, and when she was all dressed up and ready to go from the hospital and you were speechless, at that time did you go to Dr. Harmon like you did after you found out that there was a lawsuit?"

"I walked out the door," she said with the same disgust she had supposedly felt that day, which she had kept to herself until now.

"You said that you have learned information about the music program, that you have talked to Joanne Ellis and done those other things. Are you out investigating this case?" he asked. "Do you think that your role and your purpose in this case is to go out and find witnesses for people and to investigate this case?"

"What's the question you're asking me?" she said.

"Do you think it's your role in this case to go out and to find witnesses?"

"No."

"And to investigate things that are going on?"

"No, sir."

"Inject yourself into this case?"

"No, sir."

"That's all I have," Dan said, having successfully shone the light on so many things and, I dare say, blinded Cody in the process. It was worth all the agony of the trial to have a front-row seat as he put her under a microscope for the entire courtroom to see. I could have almost felt sorry for her, if it weren't my life she was messing with. I was glad that she'd shown up today and introduced her true self to Dan and the jury.

But before I could exhale a sigh of relief, Harte resumed with his star witness, saying, "I just have a couple of questions. Was your sister-in-law very self-directed and made her own decisions?"

"Would you please repeat that?" Cody asked.

"Yes, was your sister-in-law, before May and including May of 1998, self-directed? She made her own decisions?"

"I would say Kelly is very in control of herself and makes her own decisions."

"And among the conversations that my partner Connie and I have had with you, um, have we told you that we would like you to testify because she said she had only heard the word *abruption* once from the nurse during her pregnancy?"

"You had asked me about the discussion of *placentus abruptus* in our conversation, in our nine months of pregnancy and to discuss that, yes," she said, attempting to sound professional but wrongly naming the *placentia abruptio* that I had in "our" pregnancy.

"And did we discuss the importance of bed rest and whether you talked about that?"

"You did talk about that."

"Thank you, that's all I have," Harte concluded, permitting the real Cody Martin to march past us and on out the door, her entourage following in her wake. Andy and I both glanced at each other, stretching our legs out straight as the door shut behind us. Dan and Tom both stood up and looked briefly back at us, eyebrows raised. With the jury still in the room, none of us could say or do much, and we still had more witnesses to hear from. But getting that one over with was a relief for us all.

That night we would learn that earlier that day, while Andy and I were at the church during our lunch break, Cally had rushed home to tell Cody and Pat, who were waiting their turns to testify, that I had stood up in the courtroom, pointed my finger at her, and shouted, "She killed my son!" They say a lie travels halfway around the world while the truth is still putting its boots on and so it was with her story. By dinnertime, the tribe digested these words with their meat and potatoes. In spite of the horror Andy and I had felt at the prospect of suing our family when Noah died, going through this trial made us feel like we had anyway. And made us wish that we had, too. Not because of what we might have gained—we had already lost our sons and most of this extended family—but because it would have forced everyone to take the stand, sit up straight, and tell the truth, the whole truth, and nothing but the truth, so help me God. And to be on record.

Chapter Fourteen

ONCE AGAIN, we were at our wits' end—where God supposedly lives. We prayed He was home and that He would answer the door if we knocked. In her book, *Breath, Eyes, Memory,* Edwidge Danticat writes that there's a group of people who carry the sky on their heads. They are the people of Creation. Strong, tall, and mighty people who can bear anything. Their Maker gives them the sky to carry because they are so strong. These people do not know who they are, but if you see a lot of trouble in your life, it is because you were chosen to carry part of the sky on your head. We understood this burden, but frankly, my chunk of sky was giving me a headache.

All told, the defense called four doctors, including Harmon, five nurse-midwives, three nurses, two members of our family, and one friend, Joanne Ellis from Micah's music program, to testify against us. We all sat for seven days and heard more about Kelly Kittel than any of us cared to know—including Kelly, or Kerry, or Kitty, or whatever her name was, herself. One of their doctors had coauthored a best-selling guide to help parents whose child dies before, during, or after birth, claiming to help prepare parents for the days ahead. I'd read it, and I could picture it on my bookshelf. But it had certainly fallen short in preparing me for the time when I'd sit there and listen to its author testify against me in his fine British accent. I cringed as he concluded, " . . . the baby is clearly totally dependant on effective placental function, and if the placenta is separated from the uterine wall completely . . . then the baby is going to survive for no more than ten or fifteen minutes after that complete separation. It is, probably the most, for a complete abruption, it is the most acute obstetric emergency that we face."

Also on Thursday, Dr. Harmon contradicted her sworn deposition when Dan cross-examined her and asked, "And when I took your deposition, you said Mrs. Kittel was already dressed and ready to go. Is that your testimony?"

"Right, and I was in error. But I was surprised; I was expecting her to be on the monitor and ready for induction. That had been the plan the night before, so when I walked in I was stunned," she said, even though she also testified that in the hall she'd already met the nurse-midwife Lisa Litton, who told her I was going home. So how stunned could she have been?

"Just a second," Dan said. "I came to your attorney's office in a very formal way, you were sworn to tell the truth, right, before an official court reporter, your attorney Mr. Harte sat right next to you, and I asked you questions just like I am now, and you were free to answer each question under oath, and I told you that testimony was just like on the stand in front of Judge Norblatt and this jury, correct?"

"Yes."

"And in that deposition when you told me she was dressed and ready to go, you made an error in your testimony?"

"Yes, I was going based on a memory of something three years prior, and at that time I recalled that she was dressed."

"And weren't you telling me in the deposition when I was first meeting you, 'Hey, the decision was already made that she was dressed and ready to go.' Weren't you trying to give me that impression?"

"No," she said.

Dan asked, "Do you understand, as the doctor, the patients are looking to you to make the best possible decision they can for the health of their baby?"

"Oh, yes."

"And do you understand that it's a very emotional time for patients?"

"Oh, yes, I have four children."

"And do you understand then from having your own children and in your role as an OB that the patient is looking to you to help guide them in making decisions?"

"Oh, yes."

"Wasn't this really your medical decision whether to continue the induction?"

"It was a joint decision with Kelly and I," she said.

"So, she was making the decision, or you were making the decision?"

"I made the decision with her involvement."

"So, did you try to persuade her either way?"

And in spite of the fact that she couldn't remember what I was wearing, she proceeded to rattle off another lengthy discussion she swore that we had had in my bed that day, giving even more details than in her deposition. "I was very concerned about her leaving the hospital, and I remember sitting on the bed and saying, 'Do you understand what we're doing here?' I says, 'The reason why we brought you in, this was what was happening,' and Kelly was very intelligent, she's a very bright, fun . . . we all loved her . . . and so every decision, every piece of information that we shared we would sit down, and we were helping her process this information because it was very important to her to process, so every little thing we sat down and said, you know your labs are normal, we don't think you have preeclampsia, and her concern was the size of the baby. She says, 'But I know if the baby stays in it's going to grow about one half pound a week,' this was knowledge she gleaned and we've helped her and she obviously was motivated and retaining lots of information and that was her assessment. That, you know, if I wait two more weeks, the baby will be a pound bigger than now, so if the baby continues to grow, we had every evidence the baby was healthy, we'd have a healthier baby and more likely the baby could go home right when mama went home and of all the normal newborn things and that was important and it's always important."

I was doing my best to follow along and I wondered how the jurors were doing. I'm acutely aware of my personal space, given my Puritan background, and I would have remembered her sitting on my bed because I probably would have had some degree of discomfort.

Hospital beds aren't exactly queen-size, after all. But if she'd actually said all this on May 9, I thought, it probably would have encouraged me to go home, given my normal labs and all, which had clearly been the wrong decision.

And though the doctor and her minions all swore under oath that I knew all about abruption, because they had all told me about it time and again, when Dan asked her, "Now, were you trained and did you know that labile blood pressure itself is associated with abruptions?" the court heard the following testimony from Dr. Harmon.

"Yes."

"And did you tell Mrs. Kittel that labile blood pressures like hers are associated with abruption?"

"I don't know if I used those terms, but I know I rarely use medical terms because it isn't going to register in their minds, so when I'm teaching patients, I always sit down and say about preeclampsia, you know, your blood pressure can go really high, and when that happens it can create a lot of pressure on your placenta, and when that happens your placenta can come completely detached and loose from the uterus, and as you can imagine, no connection, that's your baby's connection to the blood supply and oxygen, so of course your baby can die instantly…So those are the kind of words I use to describe this is what preeclampsia is, and I know that with all my patients I tell them about my own experience, and I almost died, so I tell them it's so important because you don't feel sick and there aren't warning signs, and that's why it's so important they understand how important it is to come in, so, yes, I had a conversation like that." I wished with all my heart that she'd said all this prior to May 14, 1998, instead of dreaming it up four years later. Because even though she was admitting to not using terms like "abruption," even now, when it was too late, the words "your baby can die instantly" raised alarm bells I wouldn't soon forget.

Dan continued, "Now here's the thing I need help understanding. You had a gut instinct she should stay, you're worried she might develop preeclampsia with chronic hypertension, you're having this preference she should stay in the hospital, and yet you're giving her options and telling her, 'I'm not concerned, you can go home.' Now, which was it, was it, 'I'm not concerned,' or 'I'm really having a gut instinct you should stay,' which were you really trying to persuade her to do, Dr. Harmon, on May 9?"

"I was trying to help her make the decision . . . that she felt part of the decision-making process, balancing the risks and benefits of all the things that could happen to her and saying here's the risks, we've talked about this, you understand that these things can happen, but the benefits are your baby's going to grow more if you wait, and my preference was I'm going on vacation. I'd have preferred that she deliver that day so I didn't have to be sitting on vacation worrying every single day and calling and worrying that there's something going to happen, so . . . and she knew I was going on vacation . . . that's why I went in there and said I'm not going to be here, and so I'm going to change my plans so I can accommodate and be available for you because I'm worried about you, and I really, really wanted to be there for her."

I didn't want to make that decision! I wanted to stand up and scream. I could still feel its ugly weight on my shoulders and would have gladly shrugged it off. *And if she was so worried about me,* I wondered then, *why had she breezed right on past me on her way to bake cookies?*

"So when I took your deposition in this lawsuit, you said you had a gut instinct and, 'I really preferred she stay. I thought she should stay.' I suppose that's what you're trying to tell us; that's what you told Mrs. Kittel—she should stay, you had a gut instinct she should stay, you'd talked to Dr. Watson, and all these things, yet and she was saying, 'I don't care what you say, Doctor, I'm going to go,' is that what you're telling us?" Dan asked.

Harmon replied, "She didn't quite say it that way, but she was *very, very* adamant. I mean Kelly, you know, when you walk in the room she's sitting there saying my blood pressures are normal, my labs are normal, I have no symptoms of preeclampsia, she's very . . . what's the word . . . medically savvy—we've talked about this so much that she can rattle this talk off as well as I can. I don't have swelling, I don't have side pain, I don't have headaches, nausea, my blood pressure is good, my labs are normal, and I think it would be better for me not to have my baby today because I want my baby to be bigger. So, you know, gut feeling or not, I'm sitting there going okay, she's presenting a *very valid* argument to not deliver a baby prematurely, not have a long, difficult induction, and give it some more time, knowing that there's an end point as soon as I come back from vacation. So, you know, gut instinct or not, Kelly presented a very legitimate medical argument to not continue with her induction!"

I didn't want a "bigger" baby; I wanted a healthy, breathing baby! What mother wants to push even one more ounce out of her body, never mind a whole pound or two? *Beware of being smart,* I thought, although she was giving me much more credit than was due. Adamant? My brain had been rattling with indecision, not lists of preeclampsia symptoms. But this was to be one of the theme songs of the defense.

"Well, Kelly is a very intelligent woman. She's probably just as smart, if not smarter than me," Dr. Harmon sang at one point. And Kate, the nurse-midwife, chortled, "And she was very smart! I have a very distinct memory of Kelly . . . Kelly was a fun patient, we enjoyed having her, she was intelligent and she challenged us; she was a scientist!" Harte even added his baritone to the mix, intoning, "She's an *extremely* smart woman who is a *scientist* and asked the right questions."

And here is how Harmon tried to explain to Dan the abnormal test result for the protein in my urine—a test she suddenly remembered seeing, in spite of admitting five times in her deposition that she had not seen it:

"Did you ever talk to Mrs. Kittel about the proteinuria of over 300 milligrams?" he asked.

"I don't know. I know when I talked to her on Saturday I was aware of it because that was the thing that we were waiting for to find out. I mean, when we started the induction, we didn't have that information, and that would be the information that would help us determine to *not* continue the induction."

"Wait a minute, you lost me there."

"Sorry." She giggled.

"You're telling me that you started the induction Friday morning and you went all day, I mean you started the ripening and you were waiting for the twenty-four-hour urine to decide whether to continue, and when it came back abnormal, you decided it was okay to discontinue it? Is that what you just said?"

"When it came back it was so *minimally abnormal* that it was not elevated enough to cause concern," she said.

"Before you even *knew* the information, you started the process, and when you got the abnormal result you said that was good enough to stop it, or that was the *reason* you were going to stop it?" he asked.

"No, it was multiple, nothing is made from some one piece of information. You have to take everything and put it together or else you don't *need* a doctor! That's *my* job, is to put all the pieces together and help make the best decision, and I can't base it based on one little piece of information, and it's like what does the patient look like, what is her blood pressure, what is her other symptoms, what are her other lab work, what is going on with her at this point in time? And since she had the chronic hypertension and we thought she might be developing preeclampsia, you don't want to wait another twenty-four hours to say, 'Let's start now, she's really sick.' You want to get things started just in case that helps you make that decision when she's really sick. Does that explain that?"

"I don't think you want me to answer that," Dan replied.

"All right." Harmon giggled again. I couldn't believe my ears. I hoped for her sake that she was one of those people who laugh when they're nervous. But I found it interesting that she'd just said it was *her* job to make decisions. If she and I had been building a puzzle together, I realized now, then she'd been hiding some of the pieces from me. Or she'd lost them.

Dan said, "I think what I want to establish here is that it's really true, when it really comes down to it, is that you guys just missed that lab, didn't you?"

"Oh, no, absolutely not . . . why would I order a test that takes twenty-four hours to collect, which is the basis for what we're waiting for, and not look at it?"

"Well, that's the question," Dan said.

"Yeah, I wouldn't have!"

"When you breeze through there Saturday morning at ten thirty, why wouldn't you take a look back over a test ordered a day before when the midwives were really doing her care?"

"My midwives weren't doing her care. It's very clear, and we even at one point—we even wrote in the chart, 'DH making the decisions for management of her hypertension.'" *Exactly*, I agreed, and felt like shouting, "The Emperor has no clothes!" It *was* written in my chart, yet I'd been given midwife after midwife to try on and was even sporting a simple nurse when Jonah died!

"Well, this is the thing," Dan concluded. "If this was the thing that really made you decide not to do the induction, why didn't you put that in the record, 'Looked at twenty-four-hour urine labs?'"

"I guess because it was so close to normal it just didn't impact me. I mean"—she tittered again—"a twenty-four-hour urine protein of 364 in somebody that has chronic hypertension is . . . is totally acceptable and almost, I mean, I wouldn't call it normal because it *is* proteinuria but it is not a concerning proteinuria . . . " Well, it sure sounded to me like the "nuance" that Dr. Winkler had described in his deposition.

Earlier in the day, when Harte had questioned Harmon about the twenty-four-hour lab result, Harmon had explained that she might have missed it because perhaps coffee had been spilled on the initial lab report on Saturday. Now, in his cross-examination, Dan attempted to clean this up by asking, "You were talking about somebody spilling some coffee on the lab report and that's why it's not in the record?"

"I didn't say that," she said.

"Did you . . . is . . ."

"But it happens often, yeah," she interrupted.

"It does . . . in your practice it's often you lose medical records?"

"No, it's not medical records. The copies of the lab reports at labor and delivery are left on the desk for us, and many times people are sitting and working and charting, and they've got their cup of coffee and"—she paused and blew a loud raspberry—"there goes the cup of coffee, and many times we just pitch 'em . . ." I think everyone in the room, except maybe her, found this to be shocking and one of the male jurors chose that moment to stick his pen in his shirt pocket with finality, looking right at Dan as he did so.

When Harte re-examined Dr. Harmon, he tried to exonerate her from saying in her deposition that she'd never seen my lab result, with or without coffee stains, by asking, "Okay, I want to turn to the subject of proteinuria and your testimony. In your deposition on page thirty-three, you said, 'I guess I didn't have the 364.'"

"Right," Harmon said.

"Can you explain what happened, what occurred at your deposition when you said that?"

"Well, the whole deposition with Mr. Holland was focusing on this proteinuria, and I, you know, not knowing what his thoughts were, it just seemed kind of strange to me because it was such a low number and, you know, you're sitting there and you're nervous and it just goes on and on, and you knew it and you knew it, and finally he throws in front of me this test, this test that's dated the tenth and you're not realizing that he had that up his sleeve, and I was shocked, and I was like, well, maybe I didn't know, but I know that I could not have made that decision without that information." Dan interrupted, objecting to her characterization of him as being sneaky.

"Yeah, just answer the question," Judge Norblatt said.

"Let's start over," said Harte. "What happened at the deposition when you said words to the effect, 'I guess I didn't know about the 364'?"

"Right," Harmon said. "[Dan] basically showed me a lab that was dated the next day, and it took me off guard that it would be dated that day, and of course you're nervous and you don't know all the details and your mind is going, 'Wow, how did this happen,' and so at that point I says, 'Well, maybe I didn't know,' but I knew to discharge Kelly. I could not have discharged her without that information; so I knew I had to know."

"Did you poke your head in her room and nothing more on the ninth?" Harte asked.

"Absolutely not," she said, again causing me to mentally shake my head. She went on to give him yet another lengthy account of that Saturday morning, beginning with pulling into the hospital parking lot and seeing Andy leaving, and ending with her calling me "medically savvy" and saying I presented a good medical argument. But this time she ended the account with her telling me, "Now, you understand that you're still a high-risk pregnancy?"

To which I supposedly said, "Oh, yes," as she sat on my bed.

Then she'd purportedly said, "And you understand that you know my druthers is that if you wanna wait that we wait in the hospital." Hearing her say this now made my blood boil; I wished like hell she'd said it then and ached with sorrow that she hadn't.

Even though this option was never given to me, she claimed I replied, "Well, what good does it do me to wait in the hospital? I can do the same thing at home." *I wish my hospital room had been videotaped like this courtroom*, I thought.

To which she'd said, "Okay, so we've got three options here. Our first option is let's just get going, go gangbusters, and let's get this baby out and continue the induction 'cause then that's a sure thing, then we have a baby." I listened to her, clenched my fists, and thought, *Why would I have turned down a "sure thing"?*

Harmon continued, "And the other option—and you know I agreed with her, her labs were normal and she had no symptoms, there's no evidence of preeclampsia, which was our fear—so the other option is, you can stay in the hospital and we'll watch you really closely, you're here and we can do everything."

She told the court that I'd then replied, "Well that's gonna stress me 'cause I'm here and I'd rather be at home resting because it's my own bed and my own things." *That sounds nothing like me*, I thought, because it wasn't something I'd ever said.

To which she'd said, flipping her unruly hair over her shoulder, "The third option is to go home knowing that your gonna come in at least every single day and if you turn a hair—and that's how I always say this, 'if you just turn a hair'—you come back. If you feel a headache, you know, any of the symptoms we've talked about, and those are the things that we're gonna be watching very closely."

And I supposedly replied, "I can do that, I can do this, I'm totally . . . I've got everybody arranged, everybody's gonna help me, I can do this."

Harmon claimed this conversation went on for probably ten to twelve minutes while she and I jointly weighed the pros and cons until, as she said, "We made that joint decision that going home would be the best for her." It made me so angry to listen to the options and support I suddenly had from her when I no longer needed them. She also swore more than once that she'd given me three options instead of two on that fateful day when I left the hospital, but that I'd "insisted" on leaving and then had gone home and violated my bed rest orders. I was raised in the era of "new math," but even I was amazed by how she managed to turn the two options I'd had into three.

And all this from a doctor who said she was my "friend" and that everyone in her office loved me, as if that explained why I saw her midwives instead of her, my primary caregiver. Harte asked, "Did you, in a kidding fashion, argue with the folks that worked with you over who would see Kelly for prenatal visits?"

Harmon replied, "Many times. It was kind of this fun kidding in the hall, whose turn it was to get to see Kelly, even though I almost always saw her, and if I didn't see her as a patient, I usually patted her tummy on the way by my desk—my desk was in the hallway; we had this little teeny office with just six exam rooms and so it was very close proximity, so if I wasn't physically going to see her as a patient many times it was patting her on the tummy on the way in and out."

Harte asked Harmon, "Mrs. Kittel said that you told her long after or sometime after the delivery that you had a gut feeling that the baby should have been delivered on Monday. Would you tell the jurors if you said something like that and why?"

"Um, when she was, um, being observed daily, coming into the office every day, I had just dreamed about her and just, you know, you wake up from a bad dream like, oh, and I just kind of had that feeling that, you know, because you dream about somebody you're thinking about 'em a lot, and I had mentioned that to her. I had had those feelings, but it was a dream, and you can't run a medical practice based on dreams . . . " I wished again that she had told me all this four years ago.

"Okay, were you trying to comfort her when you were telling her about the dream?" Harte asked.

"I was just trying to comfort her with—I know that we made a really, we made a really difficult decision, you know, in hindsight it became more difficult than it was at the time, that all of us, me included, was looking back and saying, What if? What if? What if? And I know that in my heart, I know Kelly had to be having those same thoughts magnified a thousand million times more even than I did of, 'What if I would have stayed?' 'What if I would have done this?' 'What if I wouldn't have done that?' And I was just trying my very, very, very hardest to assure her that the decisions she made with the information that she had on the ninth was the best decision on the ninth and of course it wasn't the best decision on the fourteenth 'cause we all know what happened, but we didn't have that information on the ninth or nobody would have made that decision."

I wanted to scream, because we actually did have more information on the ninth, after all. But nobody had bothered to look at it until three years later.

Unlike the other doctors who testified, Dr. Harmon took the stand wearing clothes you might wear to meet your friends for coffee instead of to attend a trial about your professional conduct. When Dan was concluding his examination of her, he said, "Last question, Dr. Harmon: How do you explain your testimony that she wasn't dressed as far as your memory?"

"Well, of course I'm dressed up every day here," she said, rolling her eyes toward the jury, "but I'm like the least fashion-conscious physicians you'll ever know and it's just something that I just remember, her being ready to leave and I overstated it and I was wrong when I said she was dressed."

We'd filed this lawsuit to get some answers as to why Jonah had died, and while we did get some answers, much of her testimony raised even more questions. She gave long and winding responses to most of the questions she was asked, and I wondered, again, if her lawyer had not instructed her to take a shorter, more direct path, or if she, like Cody, simply thought she knew best. Instead of blaming myself even more for Jonah's death, most of what I heard caused me to think, *No wonder.*

In addition to Dr. Harmon, we listened to her peers dispute the significance of my abnormal proteinuria lab value and discount the truth and relevance of the abnormal definitions and thresholds stated in their own professional medical journals, the guidebooks by which they practiced their medicine. We saw the confusion that resulted from too many care providers playing telephone with my baby and my life—"too many cooks in the kitchen," as Dan would conclude— too many nurses and midwives comanaging my high-risk care and making decisions and assumptions independent of the doctor. Even on the witness stand, the nurses and midwives had a difficult time finding their own notes while they flipped, flipped, flipped through my inches-thick chart.

Another witness for the defense, Dr. Catherine Carr (no rela- tion to our Dr. Carr), testified that I had labile blood pressures that weren't being controlled by Aldomet, my medication. She said, "Well, by *labile*, we mean her blood pressures were all over the place. They were normal some of the time and they were abnormal some of the time, and I don't know if she may have more insight into what was related to her blood pressure elevations. Uh, as far as activity level, I think that she was a *very stressed person*, you know, I mean this is a woman who just lost a baby, a child that got run over by a car. This is a woman that had a very busy lifestyle, I mean, when I read her deposition and that talked about her calendar, I thought, how could you keep up with all of this, you know, this is a pretty intense, you know, this is not easy for somebody to go on bed rest, and I have to believe that she did her very, very best, you know, to do whatever she could do, because every mother cares about their baby and wants the best for them, but on the other hand, you know, what really made her blood pressure labile I don't know . . . and she certainly didn't have long-term high blood pressure throughout the whole pregnancy because then we know that her baby would have been really small for gestational age or have IUGR, and it didn't have that, and her pla- centa also was normal and her amniotic fluid level also was normal, and the baby's activity level was normal, so all those, all those, you know, there was no sign of fetal compromise . . ."

All in all, we heard enough about placentas and PIH and bio- physical profiles and blood pressure to last a lifetime. And we heard the one true thing that Dr. Catherine Carr and all seventeen medical professionals who testified for or against us agreed upon: Jonah Kittel was healthy and ready to live, right up until the moment he died.

Chapter Fifteen

Oɴ THE LAST day of the trial, Andy and I packed our bags and left a thank-you note for our hostess on the dining room table. The combination of anticipation and dread was slowly pulling us apart at the seams. We would take a deep breath and start to speak to each other, but it took too much effort to get the words out. It had been one of the top three most all-encompassing and overwhelming weeks of our lives, the other two being losing Noah and Jonah. Like grief, it was hitting us hard emotionally, physically, mentally, and spiritually.

As it was, we had answered our questions and spoken our minds and hearts the best we could, and we told our story and had it told to us by twenty-five friends and enemies and strangers, some more accurately than others. We had listened to the truth while our hearts broke anew and listened to fabrications while restraining ourselves from yelling out in court. It was a lot to take in, to hold, and to store in increasingly unavailable space where the body stashes stress and inner screams. Our verdict lay fifty miles south down I–5 from Portland in the Marion County Courthouse in the hands of twelve strangers. We followed the yellow-lined blacktop, which was preheating to baking temperature in the rising sun, passed between fields of wilted irises and daffodils left in the fields for the bulbs to strengthen, and braced ourselves for what lay ahead on this hot and fateful day.

Back in court, the morning was consumed by each attorney presenting his closing arguments. Dan reminded the jurors, "If a witness is false in part, if the person has intentionally given false testimony, then you can distrust the rest of that person's testimony." I wondered if that included Dr. Harmon's insistence that I was dressed or that she hadn't seen my lab tests. And then, on that seventh day, the attorneys finally rested. The jurors were given their instructions, and we broke at lunchtime so they could begin their deliberations. We were told to stay within ten minutes of the courthouse and to listen for the cell phone call that would summon us back.

Diane had driven over with the kids, and she and Cindy had taken them to a nearby pool, so we met them there, watching as they played and laughed in the water while our minds swam in turmoil. I thought about Noah, who should have been a boisterous six-year-old paddling alongside of them all. I thought about Jonah, and I wished I were sitting in the shallow kiddie pool splashing in my bathing suit instead of sitting in the shade, sweating in my business suit and nylons while waiting for the verdict of his life. I watched Hannah holding Isaiah and bouncing him around in the big kid's pool, and I gave thanks for him.

"Cally called me yesterday," Diane said. "She said she happened to be at the coast and wanted to come by and see your kids."

"What?" I asked with alarm, remembering my relief that she hadn't been in the courtroom that day.

"I know," she said, "but don't worry. I told her, 'I know Uncle Andy and Aunt Kelly told you that you can't see them unless they're there,' and she quickly changed her tone, called me some names, and hung up on me."

"That's just crazy," I said. "I'm so sorry to have put you in that position."

"Oh, it's fine," she said, "don't worry about it." But I did. I was glad the trial was almost over; I was tired of worrying that my kids were being stalked and tired of dragging others through my drama. In a few hours, while Diane and Cindy were loading the kids into the car, Cody herself would come pealing into the pool parking lot looking for them—but they'd escape before she parked. Then she'd leave the pool and try to stop by Cindy's house to see the kids, again unsuccessfully. She was relentless.

Three long hours after the adjournment, our cell phone buzzed. We kissed our kids and hurried back to take our seats in the courtroom for the last blessed time. The jury filed in. I bowed my head, closed my eyes, and listened.

"May I have the verdict, please?" Judge Norblatt asked without preamble.

The head juror handed it to him.

"Is this verdict by at least nine of you?"

"Yes, Your Honor."

"And all nine agreed on each and every question?"

"Yes, Your Honor."

"Okay." He began to read our fate in his raspy, stomatic voice, but the proclamation I heard rang clearly, as if God, Himself, had handed it to him on a carved stone tablet.

"Were the defendants, Elizebeth Harmon and SWC, negligent? Yes."

"Did Elizebeth Harmon fail to obtain informed consent? Yes."

"Was plaintiff Kitty Kettle negligent in any way? No." And I hoped he meant me, as I shouted my joy with my raised eyebrows and squeezed Andy's hand even harder. "What are the damages?"

He read the economic and noneconomic damages for both Jonah and me and declared that the maximum amounts allowable were being awarded in all categories.

With each answer I found it more and more difficult to hear the next one as the crowd inside of me roared—Noah, Jonah, my ancestors. An incredible surge of overwhelming relief rolled right through me, and I exhaled, feeling instantly lighter, like I'd just given birth. Although now I understood completely why Dan had said he'd never put me through the trial if I were pregnant.

My entire being filled with eternal gratitude for those twelve strangers who had listened to all the complex medical jargon and who'd believed me when I told them what had happened, exonerating me from purported negligence. Twelve strangers saw through the web the defense had tried to spin to trap me in their silky threads of blame. They saw through the deceit and the truth-stretching perpetrated by witnesses who'd been sworn to tell the truth but paid to enshroud it.

Unadulterated joy permeated all my formerly stress-filled cells. We won.

All twelve jurors individually attested that they had agreed on the verdict. They all agreed that Jonah had died because of the negligence of Dr. Harmon and the Salem Women's Clinic. They all agreed that Dr. Harmon had failed to obtain my informed consent. And they all sang together the sweetest music to my ears: "No, Kelly Kittel was not negligent in any way."

"Thank you, thank you, thank you!" I wanted to jump up and cry out loud, but my Mayflower decorum prevailed.

The judge said he understood that the jurors wanted to ask some questions and talk about the verdict, and the attorneys agreed. He said the attorneys also wanted to talk with the jurors and maybe ask some questions. He asked the lawyers to return for a confidential discussion after their clients had left the room.

So we had to leave the party and couldn't listen in. We hugged and cried and said our farewells to Dan and Tom and tried not to make eye contact with the defendants. We had children to collect and a plane to catch.

Later that day, Dan told us the jurors wanted to know more about why the case against the hospital was dropped and why they couldn't award us more money than the statutory limits. Both of the alternate jurors were so interested in the trial that they'd stayed the whole week and sat in on the verdict.

Later that week, a Statesman Journal article would call it "another one of those screwy jury verdicts." And Cody would tell everyone that the jury had found the doctor innocent but decided to award us some money because they felt sorry for me. I spoke with our friend Marena, who unequivocally denied telling Cody about the lawsuit. And as usual, people chose to believe whatever fit into their view of truth.

We had won. Something. And try as they would, nobody could take that away from us.

I now better understood my own body, which I'd blamed for

killing my baby, when all along it had been trying to warn us as best it could that all was not well. The people trained to listen to it had not heeded its warnings. It was not about me deciding to leave the hospital or attend Micah's music program. It was not my fault because I was a bad patient or a bad mother or ate too many ortaniques. It was not my fault in spite of all the things they tried to prove that I knew but that I did not. In spite of how smart they said I was—implying that I was smart enough to save my own baby.

Andy and I were given a huge vote of confidence by the jurors and could perhaps start to rebuild the confidence we had lost in ourselves. Some smattering of our self-esteem had been returned to us. We were given some relief from financial worries and were able to pay our large debt to the attorneys. We had survived the ordeal. I felt the long fingers of God Himself reach down into my spine, releasing the heavy burden that had hunched me over and forcing me to sit up straight—like a sky-carrying winner.

Once we had thought that family was the most important thing in life, but it was twelve strangers we'd never seen before nor would ever see again who had given us all this—even when our own family had lined up to try to take it away. We passed the metal detector one final time and stepped out of the courtroom into a warm June day. The clang from the golden scales of justice could be heard ringing behind us, registering our final verdict, balancing in our favor.

We had won this particular round in our Game of Life, triumphing over medical malpractice and deceit. But there is no victory over the grave. I had the shape of an angel imprinted in one palm but no toddler fist clenched firmly in the other. No four-year-old boy named Jonah tugged on my arm, saying, "Stop, Mommy, stop here, let's smell these pretty flowers."

Silence filled my head in the void.

The blood-red rose petals bloomed in sharp relief against the white marble portals of justice. I inhaled deeply and let their perfume fill my lungs. Andy took my hand, and our skin stuck together with sweat and happiness. We paused, east and west, to breathe, breathe, breathe, exhaling the sigh of a lifetime in unison. Then we headed off through the garden to collect our children and begin the rest of our lives together.

Epilogue:
The Book of Bella

I AM NOT a numbers person. I like words. But if I had to pick the number that is the most likely candidate for my lucky one, the number that seems to recur in my life is thirteen. I was born on November 13, and before I retired my uterus from active duty, it held thirteen babies in various stages of development, trying desperately to nurture them to life, tucking them gently into its folds, and clinging to them with its warm embrace. Some of these little poems stayed for only a matter of days; some are epic tales that have been around for more than twenty years now.

We long had the goal of living abroad with our children, and when high school was on the horizon for Hannah, we determined that the upcoming school year would be the best time for an adventure. Andy took leave from work, and after scouting around the planet a bit, we decided to move to Portugal. As the summer of 2003 progressed and we made our arrangements to leave North America, the last little Kittel implanted in my womb and refused to let go.

When the summer heat faded into photo books, we flew east against the sun and settled into Casa Mocho—House of the Owls—in the coastal Algarve region, where the kids were all four enrolled in a British school near the beach in Almancil. Our tongues reshaped themselves around Iberian words, and we hiked daily along the beach beneath ochre cliffs that guarded us just as they had stood sentry for their own people against marauding Moors over the centuries. I worried incessantly as I rubbed my growing belly and rested more and more as it expanded. Our friends from Jamaica had moved there, and Peter did ultrasounds on the baby often. Before I'd left the States, I'd had an elevated Alpha-Fetoprotein reading, a blood test that can detect genetic abnormalities and indicated there was a risk for Down syndrome; but Peter found no evidence of this as the baby grew on the screen before our watchful eyes.

The doctors advised traveling to the States for delivery, so in January I flew to Rhode Island with Isaiah, who'd just turned four and was only in school two or three days a week, leaving Andy behind with the other kids. Their school break was coming up, and Andy was taking them snowboarding in Spain and then later to

Egypt—neither trip would have been possible with Isaiah in tow. I think it was of some relief for Andy not to have to go through yet another potentially stressful birth and I wouldn't have to try to wake him up this time. I was thirty weeks along, and Peter advised that if any problems were to occur, they would probably begin by the thirty-two-week mark.

And they did.

I was not home more than a week before my blood pressure destabilized like it had with Jonah, and Dr. O'Brien admitted me to the hospital on bed rest for the remaining weeks. I settled into my Johnnie and checked off the calendar days, caught up on American TV shows, and watched the winter snows fall outside my window. Thanks to the trial, we now knew my true medical history with toxemia and were on the lookout when proteinuria reared its ugly head once again. The condition progressed, but this time I was properly monitored for almost a month, with the doctors keeping a careful eye on my daily lab test results before the late-term amnio needle was inserted into my swollen belly one afternoon. Once again, I held my breath, the L/S ratio was positive, and given my worsening labs, Dr. O'Brien decided they'd induce labor in the morning. The baby was thirty-four weeks along.

I called Erin, who planned to be there for the delivery, along with my friend Deanna. In the morning the nurse wheeled me down to the labor and delivery floor and into a room near the one Isaiah had been born in. Right away I realized this was going to be a completely different birthing experience as she began strapping bulky blue pads to the metal bed rails around me.

"What are those for?" I asked.

"Oh, in case you have convulsions," the nurse said, leaving me to understand that this might not go well.

The pitocin began dripping into my veins, and I settled in for the long haul with those pads ever in my peripheral vision, feeling like I was surrounded by a waterproof sea of blue. My contractions were beginning to develop with some regularity and that familiar pain had worsened when Erin and Deanna arrived, so they decided they'd better eat breakfast before things progressed. I felt a bit relieved when they left as I didn't necessarily want them to bear witness to my pain, and I also wanted to protect their innocence from the drama I knew could lie ahead. They'd only known happy endings.

While they were gone, I got an epidural, but then for some reason, the monitor showed that my contractions were decreasing instead of progressing. The nurse rang for Dr. Klein, who was on duty, then rolled me onto my side and tried to readjust the baby's heart monitor, but suddenly, in addition to the slighter contractions, she couldn't find any *bah-bum, bah-bum* beating. Dr. Klein arrived and took over, searching and searching all over my lower belly with the monitors while the room grew deafeningly quiet in a frightening and familiar way. I stopped breathing and started praying. *Please, God, help her find that heartbeat . . .*

"That's odd," the nurse remarked casually, breaking our code of silence as I gripped the blue pads and willed myself not to scream.

"Let me check her cervix," Dr. Klein said, leaving the monitors and stepping between my legs, which were numb from the epidural so the nurse had to help her open them for me. She reached inside of me while I held my breath and prayed, *Please, God, please, please, please . . .* I stared at the clock on the wall and desperately watched the second hand marching around, silently calculating how much of my guaranteed five-minute C-section time was elapsing.

Suddenly, she broke the silence. "Is that a foot?"

"A foot?" the nurse echoed, resuming her search with the heart monitor on the upper side of my belly now. *Bah-bum, bah-bum,* the machine replied as I exhaled a giant sigh of relief and harmonized my breathing to match, extracting my fingernails from their death grip on the pads.

"Bring in the ultrasound machine," Dr. Klein ordered while we all settled into the rhythmic relief of her discovery. Sure enough, the image on the screen confirmed that the baby had flipped in labor. *Thank God*, I thought.

By the time Erin and Deanna returned from breakfast, the emergency was over and the doctor was in the midst of a version. They entered in time to watch the ultrasound image as she attempted with considerable force to turn the baby back to its former and proper

head-down position. She tried three times to no avail before informing me that a C-section would be the only option. I eyeballed the
perfect impressions of my fingertips in the blue pads and agreed,
silently thanking my wise baby for deciding that labor was not going
to go well for either one of us.

"And while I'm in there, I can tie your tubes," Dr. Klein said. "I
know we talked about birth control before. Do you want me to do it?"

"Give me a minute to think about it," I said, flip turning my swimming mind around from no heartbeat and my imminent surgical
future to take a lap down my long history of pregnancy. "Actually, I
don't need a minute," I said. "Do it." Erin and Deanna both looked at
me with surprise, but I knew, for the first time in my life, that regardless of how today turned out, I was done having babies.

Very soon I found my belly blocked from my view by a blue
cloth barrier but exposed to everyone else by the bright lights of the
surgery as my abdomen was sliced open for the first time and my
thirteenth and final baby was pulled from inside of me. The nurse
gave me a brief viewing as she whisked "It's a Girl" around to my side
of the curtain and into the warmth of her waiting incubator, located
kitty-corner behind me. Then off my baby went, whisked to the
NICU before I could even turn to Deanna and exclaim, "She doesn't
have Down syndrome!"

But I scarcely had time to contemplate my miracle as the surgeon
continued her work down there by my ying-yang. I could feel a painful tugging and pulling on the side of my body that lay out of view
behind the blue privacy curtain. "Ouch," I gasped.

"You can feel that?" the anesthesiologist said behind my head, elic-
iting a flurry of discussion and activity as he adjusted the dials on his
machine. I could still feel the pulling sensations of what I imagined
were them sewing me up and Deanna stroked comforting circles on
my forehead while they finished up down there.

After they lifted the curtain and covered me up, they wheeled me
down the hallway to where Erin was waiting, and I met my daughter
in the NICU, one bay over from where her brother had learned to
breathe. At six weeks early, she weighed only five pounds, but she was
breathing on her own and ready to go. As they squeezed me in my

giant bed past the rows of familiar-looking tiny babies and parked me next to her, the NICU phone rang. It was Andy in Portugal.

"Well, it's not an Owen," I told his waiting ear.

"It's a Bella," he cried, letting out a whoop so loud I could almost hear his cheer carried across the Atlantic.

"Yep, tell the kids that their Bella Grace has arrived," I said with all the joy that the name they'd all chosen could bring, adding, "Tuesday's child is full of Grace!"

"Second time's the charm," he said. "And give that Isaiah a great big brother hug from his dad."

So we both met Bella Grace together for the first time, me from my bed next to her and he from three thousand miles away. Photos were snapped on cell phones and sent through cyberspace for immediate viewing and sharing with Bella's siblings, who were eating dinner—technology that hadn't existed for any of our other births. The church bulletin words of Pastor Jane came into my head, delivered to my ears from six bygone years like a promise from God himself: "That's amazing! That's Grace!"

The next day, Dr. Klein informed me that my tubes were still intact. "Because the anesthesia was insufficient," she explained, "your muscles were clenched, and I was unable to exteriorize your uterus to access the fallopian tubes."

I translated her medical terms in my head to understand for the first time that in order to tie my tubes, she needed to pull my uterus out of my body, to get it out of the way. "Yikes," I said, unsure how to feel about either that or her news.

"Okay, honey, you can finally reschedule that appointment," I said to Andy later that year when we returned to the States. He agreed and we kept our family planning between the two of us. This time I drove him to get the Big V and back home again, stopping to buy him a bag of frozen niblets myself. And this time, he really needed them.

Bella Grace Kittel was embroidered on Grandma's Crew sweatshirt and became the exclamation point at the end of our family. Finally, finally, finally I was finished having babies, and that long chapter in the book of my life slammed shut with my thirteenth baby's cry, her blue eyes squinting back at me. At long last, our family was complete. And it was, and remains, the most important thing to us.

At the time of this writing:

Hannah, twenty-four, graduated from Georgetown University with a major in physics, a minor in Portuguese, and a concentration in premed. She works in Washington, DC, for a non-profit organization on a project to increase patient safety at teaching hospitals while doing post-graduate studies in the medical field; her goal is to help people.

Christiana, twenty-one, is at Oregon State University studying forestry operations management with a minor in business. She works as a wildland firefighter in the summers where her nickname is Bubbles; her goal is to work internationally.

Micah, twenty, is at Trinity University in San Antonio, Texas, studying engineering with a passion for both fishing and climbing trees. He still loves anything with an engine that makes noise.

Noah, at seventeen, would be a senior in high school.

Jonah, at fifteen, would be a sophomore in high school.

Isaiah, fourteen, is in eighth grade. He plays soccer, basketball, hockey, and the French horn, and he still loves boats.

Bella Grace, nine, is in fourth grade and loves to dance.

Andy and I celebrated our twenty-fifth wedding anniversary.

Andy's mom, Marcella, is ninety-nine years old.

Dr. Harmon went on to sue both her attorney for mishandling her case and Salem Hospital for suspending her privileges in 2007, after which she retired from obstetrics.

We have little to no contact with most of the members of Andy's family except Buster.

Acknowledgments

BECAUSE THIS is my first book and because it took me seven years to write, I have at least one hundred people to thank, some of whom are deceased but who remain alive on my ever-growing list (My shaman, Mary B., my fellow word-lover, Dr. Taverner, and lovely Janet, who recently reminded me, once again, that life is uncertain and death can come calling to collect us at any time, or, as Sam would say, "It's later than you think."). Without lapsing into an abundance of adverbs or exclamation points, I will attempt to corral my effusiveness in expressing my eternal gratitude for all of you, as follows, as well as for the many coffee beans that were sacrificed on my behalf and the Glen Ridge Farm Huacaya alpacas who grew the wool from which my glittens were knit. I owe you all the literary equivalent of a fruit basket.

For everyone who helped me begin this book in any way, whether by believing in my writing skills for so many, many years and asking, repeatedly, when I was going to write a book (Dolly, Joyce, Uncle Bernie) or who, like my Mom, said other encouraging things like, "it's such a shame that you're wasting your talent."

For those who accompanied me while I puzzled out the theme, structure, and plot of this story during countless beach walks in Rhode Island, Oregon, Portugal, and Costa Rica (Christiana, Margaret, Rachel, Duncan, Eileen, The Ladies of Tamarindo), ocean swims

(Hannah, Micah, Rachel, Liz, Paul, and all SOS'ers), pool laps (in both Newports—RI and OR), lake swims (Sue, Sarah, and my many spotters) and hikes along Canal Creek looking for salmon (Andy, Buster, Isaiah, and Bella with her salmon whistle) or by breathing alongside of me through yoga classes or building elaborate drippy sandcastles (Erin). And for all of the waters in these many places, sweet and salty, which held my pain, absorbed my sorrow, and bid me enter.

For the legions who taught me about the craft of writing from the Guatemalan shores of Lake Atitlan (Joyce, Ann, Craig, and my first writing friends, including Yoga Matt) to Writers on the Sound near Seattle to the monthly meetings of the Willamette Writers Coastal Chapter in Newport, OR with my co-hag, Determined Dorothy, to Wordstock and the annual Willamette Writers Conferences in Portland to the many, many authors and books who have informed my journey.

For my many editors, including the indomitable Phyllis Hatfield who added a large dose of brevity by helping me eliminate over 200 pages of my formerly epic tale, concrete evidence of my innate motto, "Why say less when you can say more?", the master of ratcheting tension-building, Eric Witchey, the brave Barrett Briske who dared go where angels fear to tread, and Chicago Manual of Style expert Carissa Bluestone, who rescued me when my modifiers were, um, dangling.

For all of my early readers (Claire, Amy, Supah Wendy, Teri, Kim, Tracey, Susan) from the sun-kissed members of Tuesdays with Amy and our panini-eating poolside lounge meetings courtesy of our Francophile hosts at Langosta Beach Club in Tamarindo (home of the best papas frites on the playa) to the Providence Writers Guild whose tabard-cloaked members can be found skillfully wielding their red pens in the many eclectic establishments along Wickenden Street (Nick, Susan, Jen, Geoff, Julie, Kell, Val). And for every single one of you who ever reads this story, know that I am beholden to you for taking this closer walk with me.

For the doulas who helped me to finally birth this book—my patient publisher, Brooke Warner, her ex-tiger-trainer-turned-author-handler, Caitlyn Levin, and the brave, new world that is She Writes Press where "women don't let women write alone" and where my story found a place to rest its weary feet after more than, gulp, 120 rejections. And for my Sisterhood of the Spring Authors!

For every one of you who have helped me in any way, however small or large, to live through this story (Cindy, Sally, Linda, Mary Kay, Diane, JJ, Julie, Karen, Stephanie, Salem United Methodist Church, Queen of Peace, Wayne Community Church, Portsmouth United Methodist Church, The Compassionate Friends, The Jamaican Posse!, Women and Infants Hospital), I thank you all from the bottom of my heart, where your names are permanently inscribed. (Along with everyone else I forgot to name.) And for those of you who loved my sons while they lived, believed in their stories after they died (Dan, Tom, Becki, Robin, The Bean), and carry them with you, still, my gratitude for each and every one of you is eternal.

And last, but not least, I have to thank my family, first, foremost, and forevermore, who not only lived this story, but then had to put up with me, hunched over my laptop and ruining my posture, while typing away from the shores of Rhode Island to the playas of Costa Rica to our yurts in Oregon, and who waited patiently when I said so many, many times, "just a minute," while we solidified our reputation as a family who is late for everything. And who hung the clothes for me. And took them in. And folded them. And put them away. And ate Uncrustables for lunch and Top Ramen for dinner. You are, to me, the most precious and important thing in my life and I love you all from the bottom of my gizzard.

Muchísimas gracias por todo.

About the Author

KELLY KITTEL is a fish biologist by trade but a writer at heart. She is married with five living children, her best work beyond compare. She lives with her husband and their two youngest children in Rhode Island but her favorite writing space is in their yurts on the coast of Oregon. She has been published in magazines and anthologies and has written many notes to teachers, but this is her first book.

SELECTED TITLES FROM SHE WRITES PRESS

She Writes Press is an independent publishing company
founded to serve women writers everywhere.
Visit us at www.shewritespress.com.

Think Better. Live Better. 5 Steps to Your Best Life by Francine Huss
$16.95, 978-1-938314-66-7
With the help of this guide, readers will learn to cultivate more creative thoughts, realign their mindset, and gain a new perspective on life.

Letting Go into Perfect Love: Discovering the Extraordinary After Abuse by Gwendolyn M. Plano. $16.95, 978-1-938314-74-2
After staying in an abusive marriage for twenty-five years, Gwen Plano finally broke free—and started down the long road toward healing.

Don't Call Me Mother: A Daughter's Journey from Abandonment to Forgiveness by Linda Joy Myers $16.95, 978-1-938314-02-5
Linda Joy Myers's story of how she transcended the prisons of her childhood by seeking—and offering—forgiveness for her family's sins.

Seeing Red: A Woman's Quest for Truth, Power, and the Sacred by Lone Morch $16.95, 978-1-938314-12-4
One woman's journey over inner and outer mountains—a quest that takes her to the holy Mt. Kailas in Tibet, through a seven-year marriage, and into the arms of the fierce goddess Kali, where she discovers her powerful, feminine self.

The Complete Enneagram: 27 Paths to Greater Self-Knowledge by Beatrice Chestnut, PhD. $24.95, 978-1-938314-54-4
A comprehensive handbook on using the Enneagram to do the self-work required to reach a higher stage of personal development.

Loveyoubye: Hanging On, Letting Go, And Then There's The Dog by Rossandra White $16.95, 978-1-938314-50-6
A soul-searching memoir detailing the painful, but ultimately liberating, disintegration of a twenty-five-year marriage.